THE PERVERTED CONSCIOUSNESS

The Perverted Consciousness

Sexuality and Sartre

Andrew N. Leak
Lecturer in French
University College, London

MACMILLAN

© Andrew N. Leak 1989

All rights reserved. No reproduction, copy or transmission of this publication may be made without written permission.

No paragraph of this publication may be reproduced, copied or transmitted save with written permission or in accordance with the provisions of the Copyright Act 1956 (as amended), or under the terms of any licence permitting limited copying issued by the Copyright Licensing Agency, 33–4 Alfred Place, London WC1E 7DP.

Any person who does any unauthorised act in relation to this publication may be liable to criminal prosecution and civil claims for damages.

First published 1989

Published by
THE MACMILLAN PRESS LTD
Houndmills, Basingstoke, Hampshire RG21 2XS
and London
Companies and representatives
throughout the world

Typeset by Wessex Typesetters
(Division of The Eastern Press Ltd)
Frome, Somerset.

Printed in Hong Kong

British Library Cataloguing in Publication Data
Leak, Andrew N., *1956–*
The perverted consciousness: sexuality and Sartre.
1. French literature. Sartre, Jean-Paul—
1905–1980—Critical Studies
I. Title
848'.91209
ISBN 0–333–46432–X

Contents

Acknowledgements vi

List of Abbreviations vii

Prefatory Remarks ix

1 Theorising the Difference 1

    Gender differentiation 1
    The difference in theory 12

2 Representations 23

    Swamp and mirage 24
    The Genitor 35
    From thematic to phantasmatic 43

3 Theorising Desire 56

4 The Staging of Desire 79

5 The Perverted Consciousness 103

    The original possession 103
    The repossession 109

Concluding Remarks 129

Notes 135

Bibliography 147

Glossary 153

Index 159

Acknowledgements

Thanks to Professor Malcolm Bowie, who gave generously of his time and advice when this book was still only a vague project. Thanks to Professor Mike Kelly and the French Department at Southampton University for providing financial assistance in the very early stages of production. Especial thanks to Professor Annette Lavers, who supervised my doctoral thesis, and without whom this book would not have materialised. Despite the assistance from the above-mentioned, I alone am responsible for whatever faults the present volume may have.

I should also like to thank Editions Gallimard for kind permission to quote from the works of Jean-Paul Sartre.

List of Abbreviations

Baud	Baudelaire
Cah	*Cahiers pour une morale*
Car	*Les Carnets de la drôle de guerre*
CRD	*Critique de la raison dialectique*
DBD	*Le Diable et le bon Dieu*
EN	*L'Etre et le néant*
Esq	*Esquisse d'une théorie phénoménologique des émotions*
Ext	*L'Existentialisme est un humanisme*
HC	*Huis clos*
IF	*L'Idiot de la famille*
Imag	*L'Imaginaire*
LAC	*Lettres au Castor*
Mots	*Les Mots*
Mou	*Les Mouches*
MS	*Les Mains sales*
OR	*Oeuvres romanesques* (Pléiade)
Séq	*Les Séquestrés d'Altona*
SF	*Le Scénario Freud*
SG	*Saint Genet, comédien et martyr*
Sit	*Situations* (vols I–X)
TE	*La Transcendance de l'Ego, esquisse d'une description phénoménologique*

The above abbreviations are used only in references. The editions to which they relate are given in the Bibliography. Where more than one edition is listed, reference is to the most recent.

Prefatory Remarks

'The literary text, the work of art',[1] writes one critic, 'is a form of persuasion whereby bodies are speaking to bodies, not merely minds speaking to minds.' I should like to reformulate this by saying that a literary text involves both an appeal from one conscious intellect to another, and a call for recognition from one unconscious to another. And it is this formulation that goes a long way towards explaining the existence of this book. The appeal to – not to say the demands on – the intellect constituted by Sartre's works, both theory and fiction, has been the subject of countless works of criticism. But all too often it is assumed that the only 'form of persuasion' passing from body to body in the Sartrean *corpus* is one that invites the reader to retch!

The present book originated some ten years ago as a doctoral thesis, and the starting-point for that thesis was an almost physical sense of unease; a certain uncanniness that was not primarily of the mind. First, a series of questions: why were Sartre's representations of women, bourgeois notables, men of action, and so on, so prone to stereotyping when Sartre denounced the stereotype as a bourgeois device, and theorised 'character' as an empty form? Why the repeated patterns of failure in the work of a thinker who preached freedom and change, and the positive value of the explosive project, as opposed to the reactionary stagnation of repetition? Why this feeling that successive biographies were not quite 'about' their putative subjects (except in the sense of approximation), but that their centre lay in some indefinable 'elsewhere'? Why the repeated images, the obsessive metaphors, the recurrent phantasies, especially when these textual elements occurred in contexts with no apparent thematic connection? The unease grew in direct proportion to my successive rereadings of the texts: the unsettling networks spread outwards and continued to link up; the resonances became more and more frequent, less and less easy to overlook. It eventually became evident that the common factor in these networks was sexuality. All of this is to say that a 'transferential' relationship had been established between reader and text: one 'body' was speaking to another, and my own unease, or puzzlement, was the first sign of a transference already operated at the unconscious level. It should be understood that a transference is not established on the basis of nothing: it is not sufficient to argue that the reader simply 'projects' his own conscious or unconscious preoccupations onto the innocent text. Any reading of any text, if it carries at least a minimal interpretative force, could be said to be 'elicited' by visible features of that text; it is not a question of 'reading something into' the text, or simply finding what one has already put there oneself.

The present book is situated, then, within a psychoanalytic framework. There is clearly not the space, at this point, to engage in a discussion of psychoanalytic literary criticism: many excellent studies, moreover, already exist on this subject.[2] In this respect, the text that follows could be regarded as a contribution to this discussion. None the less, it is necessary to say a few words about the use of psychoanalysis in this book.

There is no such thing as an 'innocent' discourse – I take this as axiomatic – and to claim allegiance with, or inspiration from, psychoanalysis is simply to lay my cards on the table. Some Sartrean critics have argued that *because* Sartre's work is invested with such a strong authorial *vouloir-dire*, psychoanalysis should leave it well alone: whatever the critic might 'discover', Sartre had got there first and his own theory of consciousness is more than adequate to account for the apparent manifestations of some hypothetical unconscious. Whilst one might sympathise with its motivation, this objection, in itself, is patently absurd: texts are made of language, and language is the medium in which psychoanalysis has always operated, both at a theoretical and clinical level. It follows that psychoanalysis *must* have something to say about the processes whereby texts are produced. And this holds true as much for texts that appear under the banner of 'theory' as for those that call themselves 'fiction'. Indeed, the very distinction between 'theory' and 'fiction' becomes blurred in psychoanalytic readings: if one can no longer rely on the author's intentions to validate a particular discourse, the distinction between discourses is seen increasingly to derive from the 'pact' between reader and text which comes into play as soon as the words 'philosophical essay' or 'novel' appear on the front cover.

A second objection which can be levelled at psychoanalysis is somewhat less easy to brush aside: reductivity. In place of the intentional fallacy which sees meaning ultimately as the function of authorial design, there is the risk of substituting an 'unintentional fallacy' which dismisses the surface meanings of a text by claiming that, *vis-à-vis* unconscious desire, they stand in the same symbolic relationship as do the manifest images of a dream with regard to the latent dream-thoughts. In this way, one psychoanalytic critic writing on Sartre has felt it necessary to describe the latter's theoretical objections to psychoanalysis as 'rationalisations' or mere 'quibbling'; his active involvement in political struggle as a 'formation réactionnelle', and his championing of the oppressed as 'd'origine narcissique'.[3] From a certain psychoanalytic point of view, this could well be argued with some force, but it is a point of view which also implies that psychoanalysis need not concern itself with concrete oppression or with strategies worked out to end the oppression. This is surely wrong. The Chilean woman whose whole family has 'disappeared' is hardly likely to be comforted by being told that the generals who perpetrated the act suffered from the lingering effects of a badly resolved Oedipus complex; any more than she would reject the help of the revolutionary who brings down that regime on the grounds that he is driven by obscure narcissistic impulses. But the real affront of psychoanalytic reductivism is not just to the 'author'; it is to the conduct of interpretation itself: if Freud showed anything, it was not just that the unconscious existed, or even that it was an unfathomable and poetic mystery; his work is wholly concerned with the *interplay* of conscious and unconscious determinants, whether it be in dreams, parapraxes, jokes, neurotic symptoms or works of art. So, although any hermeneutic procedure – my own included – will involve a necessarily reductive first movement, I try in the following pages to concentrate on the creative intersection between conscious and unconscious in the Sartrean *oeuvre*.

Text: intellect speaking to intellect, body to body. But these two 'discourses' are not independent of each other, either at the level of creation, or at that of reception. They feed off each other, strike sparks off each other.

I do not attempt a psychoanalysis of 'characters': it would be absurd to suggest, for example, that Roquentin himself suffers from castration anxiety; he suffers from nothing because 'he' is not. Neither do I share the confidence of a critic such as Josette Pacaly, who would clearly have liked to have got Sartre himself on the couch, but who will make do with his texts in the place of his free associations.[4] I do not believe that a text provides *direct* access to the unconscious of its author any more than a dream provides direct access to the unconscious of the dreamer. Quite apart from the qualitative difference between these two kinds of 'text' (the literary text is interpersonal, the dream endopsychic), in neither case do we meet with anything more *real* than representations. It was Freud who insisted that we only ever meet with the representations or representatives of unconscious desire, and never with that desire itself. This is not to say that some impersonal 'desire' has lodged itself in some authorless 'text'. Desire does not arise in a textual or intertextual limbo, waiting to be discovered. Neither do texts magically create themselves *ex nihilo*. The desire that invests Sartre's texts *is* the desire of Sartre, and that of the reader. But this is a conviction destined to remain at the level of hypothesis: the lived experience of the author will never be accessible to the reader except in the form in which it presents itself (to the author as much as to the reader): as *fiction*. This is one reason why I also believe it is futile to seek corroboration for a reading of fiction in the biographical 'facts' of the author's life: the 'facts' are themselves known only as texts.

I use the term 'phantasmatic' throughout this book. The phantasmatic stands in the same relation to the phantasy (*phantasme* in French), as does a 'thematic' to a theme. I take this term to refer to a set of related phantasies inasmuch as they are invested with a structuring force. In this way it is possible to examine how textual structures, scenes or scenarios repeat themselves, and draw in new material throughout the whole *oeuvre*. The attraction of the 'phantasy' as an object of investigation lies in the fact that it embraces both quite conscious products – such as daydreams – and deeply unconscious ones, such as the so-called primal phantasy. From this perspective it is possible to see how an exchange is set up in Sartre's texts between the phantasmatic structures of the texts, and the conscious thematic ordering, an exchange which functions *in both directions*.

I shall look at various aspects of Sartre's work, including his theorisation of sexuality, his representational strategies and schemas, his imagery and use of figurative language, in an attempt to trace the interplay of conscious and unconscious, thematic and phantasmatic. As is quite possibly the case with any labour of interpretation, the reading that emerges can claim only the relative status of any other reading; its only validity will lie in its power of conviction.

A.L.

1
Theorising the Difference

In this chapter I shall look first at the way in which Sartre theorises sexuality from *L'Etre et le néant* through to *L'Idiot de la famille*. It will be seen that one of Sartre's most abiding *bêtes noires* in this enterprise is the psychoanalytic theory of Freud. Sartre's own theorisation of the sexual difference can be read in many ways, but at one level certainly it is an attempt to define his own position over and against that of Freud to keep the latter at a safe distance. *L'Idiot de la famille* is particularly interesting in this respect since it marks the closest point in Sartre's *rapprochement* with Freud, whilst still being underpinned by a desire to sidestep many crucial Freudian concepts, not least the dynamic unconscious.

In the second part of this chapter I shall examine areas of *L'Etre et le néant* that do not ostensibly deal with the problem of sexual differentiation: holes, the Viscous, *glissement* and so on. The fascination of these passages resides, for me, in their overdetermination. On the one hand, they put flesh on the bones of Sartre's own theory of sexuality; on the other, they are shot through with images that are profoundly redolent of the very Freudian problematic that Sartre is, consciously, at pains to discredit. At that point it will be possible to start to speculate as to whether the text bears the marks of a phantasmatic organisation functioning in opposition to, if not autonomously of, the authorial *vouloir-dire*.

GENDER DIFFERENTIATION

If sexuality were considered to fall into the domain of the purely physiological, it would have no place in a phenomenological ontology. So the very fact that Sartre grants sexuality a place in such a study is already instructive. The distinction to bear in mind is that between 'sexual difference' and 'sexual differentiation': 'Que la différence sexuelle soit du domaine de la facticité, nous l'accepterons à la rigueur' (*EN* 433). The contingent fact of being born with a male or female sexual organ and secondary sexual characteristics is entirely contingent. Sartre accepts this fact 'at a push'. What he will not accept however is that masculinity and femininity – as human attitudes – can be reduced to the status of simple psychological correlates of biological matters of fact. To admit to the primacy of the physiological over the psychical is to open the door to determinism. Either sexuality falls outside the realm of consciousness and into the realm of the somatic – in which case large areas of human experience must be quite opaque to consciousness, and consciousness itself ceases to be defined by its free project – or sexuality is fundamentally independent of any physiological determination: a necessary structure of human reality. The latter is Sartre's position in *L'Etre et le néant*. By this move he seeks to rescue sexuality from the obscure recesses of the body, and re-establish it in the bright light of day. However, this extreme and somewhat suspect divorce of sexuality from its somatic roots causes Sartre to fall into a dualism from which he is quite unable to extricate himself.

The term 'sexuality' undergoes a shift in meaning away from the biological when Sartre writes, 'Ainsi pourrons-nous dire que le Pour-soi est sexuel dans son surgissement même en face d'Autrui et que, par lui, la sexualité vient au monde' (*EN* 457). What precisely is meant by 'sexuel' in this passage? To clarify the position it would be useful to establish what it cannot mean. Sexuality is an 'original conduct' (*EN* 457) and Sartre rejects the subordination of this conduct to any physiological and empirical constitution. Above all, it cannot mean 'relative to a sexual instinct'. The very term 'instinct' smacks, for Sartre, of a quite unacceptable physiologism, inasmuch as it qualifies contingent structures of psychical life (*EN* 433). There is little doubt that Sartre at this stage is anxious to discredit the very basis of Freud's theorisation of gender development.

This is probably as good a place as any to recall the broad outlines of that theory, since I shall be referring to it in subsequent pages. This will also be necessary for a grasp of the theory of *L'Idiot de la famille*, wherein some kind of *rapprochement* with Freudian theory is effected.

Freud establishes three basic developmental stages: the oral, anal and phallic stages. In the oral stage, the mouth is the dominant erotogenic – that is to say, pleasure-giving – zone; then the anus, and finally the penis or clitoris, takes over this role. It should also be remembered that the sexual instinct attaches itself 'anaclitically'

Theorising the Difference

to what is, in the first instance, an asexual need for nourishment. The suckling infant experiences pleasure at the nipple and seeks to repeat this experience of pleasure subsequently, above and beyond the simple need for nourishment. Freud, of course, ascribes far greater importance to biological factors than would be acceptable to Sartre; the succession of these pre-Oedipal stages is regulated, in theory, by the progressive maturation of the infant and the growing organic sensitivity of the erotogenic zones, as well as by the attention accorded to the child's body in feeding and potty-training and so on, by its entourage. It is important to note that, at this stage, we are not yet able to talk of sexuality proper: '[In the sadistic–anal organisation] the opposition between two currents, which runs through all sexual life, is already developed: they cannot yet, however, be described as "masculine" and "feminine" but only as "active" and "passive".'[1] There is, as yet, no match between biological maleness and femaleness and masculinity and femininity. The sexuality of the infant at this stage is labelled 'polymorphously perverse' to emphasise the extreme plasticity of the sexual drive, its aims and its objects. The fundamental antithesis is that between activity and passivity.

The next, and crucial, stage is the Oedipal phase. This is considered by Freud – although not necessarily by all post-Freudians – to be the crux of gender development. Masculinity only results in the boy if he successfully surmounts the danger of imagined castration by the father; while in the girl the castration complex ushers in the Oedipus complex. The development of 'femininity' precedes the Oedipal conflict and is the prerequisite of its occurrence. It is only when the girl becomes 'feminine' that she gives up her attachment to her mother and turns her attention to her father.

One could, indeed should, note the notorious phallocentricity of this account. In reality, femaleness and femininity are missing from this account: 'Maleness exists but not femaleness. The antithesis is here between having a male genital and being castrated.'[2] The female is regarded as a castrated male. The phallus is, to use a Lacanian term, the prime signifier, and the development of masculinity and femininity is determined by the attitude adopted towards this 'fact'. The account relies, at least in part, on Freud's assertion that the vagina is not known by the girl at this stage, and thus signifies nothing, whereas the clitoris is merely a penis 'en moins bien'.

In brief, the Oedipus complex/castration complex explains the accession to gender roles in terms of positionality. In adopting a masculine gender identity, for example, the child is identifying with a position in the Oedipal triangle: in relinquishing the desire for the mother and identifying with the position of the father, the child merely puts off until later the consummation of this desire. In the negative outcome of the Oedipus complex, the child is unable to effect this identification and may instead come to occupy the place of the mother in the triangle, thus placing himself in the (imaginary) position of passive submission to the desire of the father.[3]

In between the Oedipus complex and puberty there intervenes the latency period. The Oedipal crisis does not *determine*, once and for all, the sexual orientation of the subject. We have to wait until after puberty for the final disposition to be achieved. It is the somatic maturation which makes possible actual reproduction that causes the sexual aim to change: the erotogenic zones become subordinated to the primacy of the genital zone.[4] It is here that Freud's biologistic leanings come to the fore. The subject is recuperated by a wider biological determination, a drive towards the continuation of the species which is ultimately seen as part of a phylogenetic inheritance. As for the girl, she must relinquish her attachment to the clitoris (as pseudo-penis) and establish the vagina as the primary genital zone – thus recognising once again that she is castrated.

This is, of course, a much abridged and simplified account, but even from this it is evident that for psychoanalysis the acquisition of a stable gender identity involves a complex play of somatic and psychological factors. Other somatic factors, such as biological bisexuality and libido theory itself, play an important part, as do sociological factors such as the nature of the power structure within any given family, the prevailing cultural norms regarding sexual practices and infant education, and so on. Even contingent circumstances such as seduction, rape and forced abstinence have a variable role to play. Having said all of this, it remains true that the Oedipus complex was utterly central to Freud's account in that it demonstrated how the unconditional desire of the infant was given lasting orientation within a pre-existing structure.[5]

This diversion into Freudian theory has brought us no closer to grasping what Sartre does understand by 'sexual'. I believe that it is necessary to distinguish between two usages of the term in *L'Etre et le néant*. The first approximates to what we normally understand by 'sexual' in ordinary language: human relations in which the procurement of genital pleasure is a principal aim. The second is a fundamental sexuality that could appear, at times, to bear little relationship to what occurs between the sheets. It is to this that Sartre refers when he writes that '[La sexualité] comporte toutes ses déterminations dès le surgissement du Pour-soi dans le monde ou "il y a" des Autres' (*EN* 458). The birth of sexuality is coincident with the eruption of the *pour-soi* into the world. Indeed, sexuality is so fundamental as to be considered a descriptive determinant of consciousness itself. The logical conclusion of this extreme ontologising of sexuality would be to posit masculine and feminine consciousnesses.

Biological constitution cannot, of course, be invoked at this level of analysis, and one is forced to suppose that masculinity and femininity are originally ways which the *pour-soi* has of erupting towards its objects. So a masculine *pour-soi*, as it were, could manifest itself in the conduct of a biological female, and a feminine *pour-soi* in the behaviour of a biological male. At this point it would appear that the very terms 'masculine' and 'feminine' are fairly redundant, or at least devoid of genital–sexual content. In order to provide this content, it is necessary to look at the kinds of relations in which the sexual attitude manifests itself in its 'explicit purity'.

Sartre enumerates a handful of these fundamental attitudes: love, desire, masochism, sadism and hatred, but in each case the underpinning is provided by the dialectic of the look: the choice between 'regarder' and 'être regardé'. This dialectic is by now well known and amply commented, so there is no need to enter into a lengthy discussion. Suffice it to say that the look is the means by which the subject can bring about the 'objectivisation' of the Other: when I am looked at, I am forced into complicity with my pseudo-objective being-for-others; into complicity, therefore, with my corporeal being. This objectivisation can be avoided by returning the gaze and objectifying the Other. When two looks meet they do not cancel each other out – only one will be able to hold the field of battle. Whilst this is intended to be a concrete description of what occurs between two conscious subjects, the look is also used by Sartre to render metaphorically all situations in which I feel myself, abstractly, to be object for another consciousness.[6] This dialectic is the theoretical underpinning of Sartre's analysis of the fundamental sexual attitudes.

In love, I attempt to make myself into a special kind of object for the gaze of the Other: a fascinating object. I attempt to become the objective foundation of the Other's freedom – a sort of secretly active passivity (see *EN* 417).[7] This attitude fails principally because the tenability of the position is eroded by the constant possibility that the Other may choose to regard me not as 'everything in the world', but as just another object 'against a background of world' (see *EN* 426).

In desire the aim is to appropriate the freedom of the Other through a two-way exchange, or double-reciprocal incarnation, as Sartre puts it. By caressing the Other, I attempt to force him into passive identification with the body. Simultaneously, through the return of the caress, I am 'objectivised' to the same degree. The failure of this mode of desire resides in the inability to maintain the delicate balance of object and subject. The desiring subject may, for example, become caught in the trap of its own pleasure: unable to remain sufficiently cold, aloof, indifferent, it is affected by 'trouble' – like clear water turning cloudy, consciousness is befuddled by the invasion of physical sensation.

The failure of either of the above attitudes results in a retreat into one or other of the two *really* fundamental attitudes: masochism and sadism. Masochism is the desire to be pure object for the gaze of the Other; sadism is the reverse of this. It is in this sense that one could describe Sartre's theory of sexuality as being, at heart, sado-masochistic. As in the Freudian pre-genital organisation, the antithesis is between activity and passivity.[8] One should note also the precariousness of these positions: they are characterised by an extreme fragility, such that the active attitude may at any moment crumble into the passive and *vice versa*.

At this stage it is not possible to identify the two poles of the antithesis as 'masculine' and 'feminine' unless these two terms are to de divorced from genital determinations and reduced to the active–passive dichotomy. The most that can be asserted is that, if Sartre does indeed have a theory of sexuality – which is by no means certain – 'masculine' and 'feminine' are to be seen, ultimately, as attitudes of consciousness towards the Other, the world and the body.

As I have already pointed out, Sartre insists that physiological factors do not have an ultimately determining influence on sexual behaviour. But it would be misleading to suggest that the body has no role to play in Sartre's account. The difficulty lies in establishing what this role might be. In the passages of *L'Etre et le néant* where he deals explicitly with sexuality, the role of the body is played down; it is an area of shade, almost a blind spot. The descriptions of love, desire, and so on, present all the appearances of a battle of consciousness wherein the body represents either a weapon to be wielded, or a chink in the somatic armour allowing access to the psychical core.

It is necessary to return to chapter 2 of *L'Etre et le néant* in order to throw some light on the relationship between the body and consciousness, and on the part played by the former in sexuality, especially in determining the attitudes labelled masculine and feminine. There are two important passages to look at: 'je *suis* mon corps dans la mesure où je *suis*; je ne la *suis pas* dans la mesure où je ne suis pas ce que je suis; c'est par ma néantisation que je lui échappe' (*EN* 375). The relationship is one of radical non-coincidence. Consciousness creates itself in a moment of nihilisation: the *pour-soi* arises through the nihilisation of a certain *en-soi*. In other words, the body is constantly gone past (*dépassé*) and is, as such, the past (*le passé*). In its eruption towards its own possibilities, the *pour-soi* nihilates what it *is* and projects itself towards what it *is* not yet. Within the unity of the same project, the *pour-soi* flees one *en-soi* in a futile attempt at recoincidence with another: the aim of human reality is to achieve the impossible perfection of being that is described as *en-soi-pour-soi*, or God. In more prosaic terms the aim is to occupy, simultaneously, the positions of object and subject. One further point to note from the above passage is the image of escape: the body/past represents a prison that has always been in place and which will forever threaten reimprisonment. The second passage (*EN* 376) concerns the body as facticity. The 'body' should be taken, writes Sartre, to include my *birth*, inasmuch as it determines the way in which objects reveal themselves to me; my *physiological structure*, because, through it, the world is revealed as docile or resistant; my *character* and my *past*, inasmuch as all I have lived then becomes my 'point of view' on the world. All of these terms underlined by Sartre are factors which are seen by psychoanalysis and sociology as contributing strongly to gender identity. One could argue that this passage contains, in embryonic form, the foundation for Sartre's later theory of *le vécu* and perhaps even the starting-point for the much more sophisticated socio-psychological apparatus deployed in *L'Idiot de la famille*. But how much weight does Sartre accord to these factors in *L'Etre et le néant*? Since they are nihilated by consciousness, they come to nought. What was done to the subject as a child – the perhaps traumatic limitations imposed by the body, the socio-cultural conditioning, and so on – is 'assumed' by consciousness and transcended towards a brave new world.

Sartre is, of course, framing an ontology, and this context goes some way towards explaining why he should play down these factors. Nevertheless, this confident dismissal of the whole weight of the past on the subject, the studied ignorance of 'le physiologique', do seem to betoken a desperately optimistic voluntarism.

Where does this leave gender development? The only preliminary definition available at this point is that 'masculinity' and 'femininity' are modes of behaviour in which is manifested the manner in which the individual has assumed his given situation. Not particularly helpful. Elsewhere in *L'Etre et le néant* new light is cast on this question, and I shall be returning to these aspects in the latter part of this chapter.

The optimistic vision of this virgin consciousness joyfully negating its past and making light of its embodiment was not to last. Already in the *Cahiers pour une morale* Sartre was describing childhood as 'indépassable'; in the biographies of Baudelaire and Genet, he was drawn back to childhood and its potentially disabling effects on the ulterior development of the free subject. But it is *L'Idiot de la famille* that, in many ways, represents both the culmination of Sartre's theorisation of sexuality, and his final word in the dialogue with Freudian psychoanalysis.[9] The sheer volume and complexity of *L'Idiot* precludes anything like an exhaustive analysis of Sartre's account of Flaubert's sexuality. I shall attempt to give a very brief summary highlighting elements of progress or variation in relation to the theory of *L'Etre et le néant*, and elements that indicate a certain continuity.

The principal shift of emphasis is derived from Sartre's growing enchantment with Marxism. The starting-point is that – unlike in *L'Etre et le néant* – the past is never *dépassé*; it is caught up in a process of ongoing dialectical totalisation that is nothing other than the life of a human being as it is lived. Put simply – and nothing is simple in *L'Idiot* – this means that the subject reacts to the world and each new circumstance on the unalienable basis of what has happened to him in the past. It is with the eyes of the past-become-present that the subject must seek to integrate his present circumstances into a new totality. When achieved – and this moment is purely notional – this new totality becomes the basis for all future reintegrations. Sartre uses the image of a spiral to convey this return of the past, at a higher level of integration, throughout the subject's existence.

Theoretically, any moment of existence could provide an adequate point of departure for Sartre's attempted 'comprehension' of Flaubert. As it is, he begins with infancy. It is here that the *rapprochment* with Freud, and more especially Lacan, is at its most evident. Sartre uses a schema rather similar to Lacan's entry into the Symbolic Order to describe Flaubert's traumatic entry into language. Astonishingly, we read Sartre lamenting the lack of reliable evidence concerning Flaubert's breast-feeding and potty-training. Indeed, Sartre appears to have accepted the descriptive accuracy of Freud's stages of sexual development. The oral phase and the union with the mother's breast are of central importance to his analysis.

Sartre situates the determining factors in the development of Flaubert's sexuality firmly within the family unit: everything is decided by the conduct of the mother and, later, the father. In reconstructing the 'fable' of this childhood, Sartre finds it necessary to give a character study of the parents, embracing factors such as the mother's hypothetical Oedipal attachment to her father; her supposed desire for a baby daughter rather than a son; the socio-economic situation of the family; the father's ambiguous translation from a family of rural veterinarians to landowning urban *grande bourgeoisie*, and so on. This regressive totalisation is, of course, virtually infinite. The fundamental assertion is that Flaubert's much-vaunted 'native wound' is nothing other than a *passive constitution*, and the whole of the first volume is devoted to the reconstruction of this constitution.

Put simply, Flaubert is feminised by his mother. She – like her counterpart in *Les Mots* hoped for a daughter in order to 'correct' her own sad childhood. She produces a doctor, Achille.[10] No more fortunate, alas, the second time, she produces an idiot – Gustave. Sartre imagines that this disappointment affected the way she tended the child: she was more like a skilful nurse than a doting mother; Gustave was 'précautionneusement manié', but nothing more (*IF* 136) This combination of prompt, almost professional, satisfaction of hunger, and lack of tenderness, 'imprints' Gustave with an enduring passivity: he is transformed into a pot-plant. The interesting point is that Gustave's feminisation is brought about through the organism. His passivity is first and foremost *physiological*. In plotting Gustave's sexual development, Sartre gives infinitely more consideration to the role of the body than he did in *L'Etre et le néant*, where, as we have seen, the body was dealt with at best schematically, and at worst passed over in silence. He even goes so far as to suggest a kind of organic complicity on the part of Gustave: 'l'organisme, *sous l'action de facteurs purement physiologiques*, peut "s'ouvrir" à l'émotivité passive' (*IF* 59; emphasis added).

The passivity (which Sartre explicity identifies as femininity) transmitted to the child by the coldly efficient ministrations of his mother, is confirmed and compounded by the child's relation to his father. Sartre claims that Gustave, erroneously, blamed his father for the passivity with which his mother had infected him. In Sartre's version the intervention of the father is perhaps secondary but no less decisive. He is responsible for the ambivalence of Gustave's later 'passive activity' – or sadomasochism – in sexual relations, in that he places him in a double-bind situation. By engendering him second, he makes of him, even before his birth, a minor, and thus disbars him from the (albeit crippling) identification with the paternal imago that the elder brother, Achille, is able to effect. He is destined for a relative existence: the condition of women, in fact, in a patriarchal society governed by omnipotent fathers. Interestingly enough, it is the withdrawal of the father's attention when Gustave is about seven that finally precipitates him into a state of pre-neurosis. Cast out from the Eden of paternal justification, Gustave is condemned to activity by the father; by this same father who by conceiving him second had already condemned him to passivity. Add to this the feminisation at the hands of the mother, and we have a picture of a terrible 'Catch 22'.

Even from this schematic description it is clear that this analysis begs many questions. For instance, Sartre imagines, oddly, that the structure of a 'semi-domestic' family, as opposed to a 'conjugal family', precludes the development of the Oedipal aggression which could have masculinised Gustave. I shall have more to say about Sartre's treatment of the Oedipal triangle in a later chapter.

Needless to say, Sartre's analysis is infinitely more complex than the above summary suggests. I have dwelt only on aspects that enable us to appreciate the distance covered since *L'Etre et le néant*. The suppression of physiological factors in the earlier book is remedied to a large extent in *L'Idiot de la famille* – so much so that Sartre comes to sound in places like a biological determinist. This would be a misleading and unfortunate impression to convey. Sartre's guiding principle is broadly Marxist: we make ourselves on the basis of what has already been made of us. It is at the level of this 'making of ourselves' that the free project reappears. The dialectic between the moment of passive receptivity and that of active self-definition is encapsulated by Sartre's insistence that we perceive ourselves now as 'hommes de hasard' (passive receptors), now as 'fils de nos oeuvres' (active agents) (*IF* 60). In light of this, Flaubert's neurosis, which crystallises around the fall at Pont l'Evêque, is at one and the same time the inescapable *product* of traumatic infantile experiences, and the *orientation* of an existence towards the future, on the basis of this past. This much simply confirms Sartre's previous comments on Genet's homosexuality as a solution that the child invents at the moment of suffocation.

One final point must be made before we can return to *L'Etre et le néant*: Sartre's discussion of masculinity and femininity in *L'Idiot* remains, still, within the framework of the distinctively active/passive reduction. His sidestepping of the Oedipal conflict – of which more later – condemns him to this impasse. It is as if, *as a theorist*, Sartre had stalled in the pre-Oedipal phases.

As I have shown, the analyses of *L'Etre et le néant* do not really add up to a theory of gender development. The sexual difference itself is swept under the carpet and replaced by a kind of ontological hierarchy. The virile attitude is that of the *surgissement* of consciousness itself towards its object (transcendence); the feminine attitude lies presumably in the failure of the conscious project (immanence).

The above use of the words 'virile' and 'feminine' may appear premature. The time has come to demonstrate the grounds on which I would assert that these terms correspond to ontological categories and that, furthermore, an ontological hierarchy is clearly established between these terms in Sartre's theoretical discourse. The passages I shall be examining not only shed light on Sartre's conscious theorisation of the sexual difference, but also, fascinatingly, invite us to read in his discourse the return of the very Freudian thematic, articulated as a phantasmatic[11] *mise-en-scène*, which is so sweepingly dismissed elsewhere.

THE DIFFERENCE IN THEORY

In 'De la Qualité comme Révélatrice de l'Etre' Sartre confronts the Viscous with his own psychoanalytic method. Inasmuch as images of viscosity are very much part of Sartre's own poetic imagination, this section could be viewed as an attempted self-analysis. It is important to bear in mind that Sartre's overriding concern throughout this analysis of the Viscous – and later 'holes' – is to demonstrate that the significance of qualities of the world is first and foremost *ontological*, and in any case *presexual*. So one would expect that, if Sartre is not to have recourse to 'sexual considerations' (see *EN* 661), neither need he have recourse to the language of sexuality. This is far from being the case.

Sartre attempts to demonstrate the 'rigorous objectivity' of this method through the example of snow – the significance of this choice will emerge later. We can say that snow is hard, compact, that it is made up of isolated granules and that it melts at a certain temperature. This much appears to be an objective statement. But, if I want to determine the human significance of this melting, I have to compare it to other objects, located in other regions of experience. These terms of comparison – ideas, friendships, and so on – which can also be said, in French, to 'melt', are claimed to be equally objective (*EN* 662). Now this recourse to comparison and to linguistic usage is wholly consonant with the phenomenological method. Nevertheless, there is a considerable difference between saying that 'snow melts at 4° Celsius' and saying 'money melts in my hands'. The latter is a clear metaphor and, as such, demands a human subject to make the association. To this extent Sartre has already abandoned the realm of pure objectivity. Further,

> Cette liquidité . . . nous renvoie à une certaine possibilité permanente du *compact granuleux* . . . de se métamorphoser en *fluidité homogène* et différenciée. . . . Et nous saisissons ici dès son origine et avec toute sa signification ontologique l'antimonie du continu et du discontinu, *pôles féminins et masculins du monde.* (*EN* 662)

We are brought up short by this last phrase. One could understand that the granular nature of snow could lead to its being qualified as 'differentiated' or even 'discontinuous', and that liquid should be seen as 'undifferentiated' or 'continuous', but why should the discontinuous be 'masculine' and the continuous 'feminine'? Moreover, if objective qualities can, and must, be described in *pre-sexual* terms, why have recourse to the lexicon of sexual difference? What emerges from the above passage is that not only is the 'compact granuleux' threatened with the transformation into 'fluidité homogène', but by the same token the masculine pole is equally liable to crumble into the feminine pole. In the same way as the granular has its secret fluidity, so the masculine has its hidden femininity.

The Viscous is disturbing because of its profound duplicity: it initially appears to be a substance 'qui peut *se posséder* par le glissement'. But in the very next instant its duplicity is revealed. It has the worrying property of being able to 'figer la liquidité, c'est-à-dire, à *absorber* le Pour-soi qui devrait le fonder' (*EN* 669; emphasis added). It appears now that the feminine also has its secret masculinity, that it is active through its very passivity: a trap. At any rate, the Viscous is 'louche', it is the very image of an emulsifying liquid – browning, seasoning and thickening all in one go!

The purely liquid also has its masculine and feminine sides: when the liquid is 'l'être partout fuyant' it is masculine, but when it emulsifies it is feminine. At this level of analysis the Viscous is called upon to represent nothing less than consciousness frozen in its flight.

But at the same time, the obsession with an insidiously masculine femininity is vividly evident in the following:

> [Le Visqueux] donne donc d'abord l'impression d'un être qu'on peut *posséder*. . . . Seulement, au moment même où je crois le *posséder*, voilà que, par un curieux renversement, c'est *lui* qui me *possède*. C'est là qu'apparaît son caractère essentiel: sa mollesse fait ventouse.   (*EN* 670; emphasis added)

If, out of horror at this curious reversal, I attempt to detach myself from the Viscous, it sticks to me, sucks me in. It is an 'activité molle, baveuse et féminine d'aspiration' (*EN* 671). One could quote, with pleasure, at much greater length: these passages are amongst the most powerful and lyrical in *L'Être et le néant*. Indeed this 'poetry' marks the point at which Sartre's intended unambiguous use of the philosophical register collapses. The trinary structure of the last phrase above is motivated not simply by a desire to define: the emphatic repetition so reminiscent of Garcin's fulmination against Estelle in *Huis Clos* (*HC* 84) exudes sexual disgust. The text, otherwise invested with a strong authorial *vouloir-dire*, seems to take on a life of its own under the pen of the author, as if the horror of the Viscous, which 'lives obscurely' under the fingers of its would-be possessor, had transferentially reproduced itself in a text designed to 'master' it.[12]

So the Viscous is explicitly given as feminine: it is a 'revanche douceâtre et féminine' (*EN* 671) – but a revenge against whom, for what? Again, if the significance of qualities is pre-sexual, why employ the word 'feminine'? This is far from being an isolated instance. The sexual metaphors become more and more pervasive as the analysis progresses. Honey melting back into a pot is 'comme l'étalement, le replatissement des seins un peu mûrs d'une femme qui s'étend sur le dos' (*EN* 670). It seems here that the whole woman is the incarnation of the Viscous. The position evoked is clearly one of offering; the woman is to be penetrated, but beware: penetration could be dangerous since the *real* nature of the woman is figured by the viscosity of her breasts, which stand, metonymically, for her whole person. Penetration is the ultimate horror, but even contact with the Viscous may lead to feminisation (*EN* 672).

It would be premature at this stage simply to translate Sartre's text into a different psychoanalytic metalanguage. It is, of course, quite possible to grasp the analysis of the Viscous – even its proliferating sexual content – in terms of Sartre's own theory of sexuality. It will be recalled that the body is an aspect of facticity, and I suggested earlier that 'masculinity' could be seen as a certain way of assuming this facticity. It is now possible to be more specific: the masculine attitude is simply the assumption of a given situation that transcends that situation towards its own possibilities. The feminine attitude is the attitude of a consciousness whose transcendence is curtailed, a consciousness of passive consent, and which constitutes itself as bodily nature.

All of this remains within Sartre's terms of reference, but, if one were to argue – reductively *for the moment* – that Sartre's ontologising of sexuality is in fact an attempted rationalisation, an attempt to displace through a powerful theoretical discourse a network of anxiogenic images, then these passages take on a different light. It is almost as if what is elsewhere suppressed from the theoretical account (the dismissal of Freud's theory of gender identity, for example) returns here to claim its rightful place.

The truly obsessive and persistent image of the feminine in Sartre's writing is not just the Viscous, but a supine, naked woman beckoning and threatening in one and the same gesture. As will become increasingly clear as I pursue this image through new areas of discourse, the threat is one of castration.

Whilst sexual desire leads to the feminisation of the subject through contact with the object of desire (see further Chapters 4 and 5), cognition, or, as Sartre puts it, the desire to know, is explicitly given as a masculine activity: it equates to appropriation, or possession, *at a distance*. I showed earlier that 'regarder' and 'être regardé' are to be viewed, respectively, as masculine and feminine positions. It is with this same dialectic of the look that Sartre commences his description of the human significance of cognition: 'La vue est jouissance. Voir, c'est *déflorer*' (*EN* 638). And the images commonly employed to describe the relation of knower to known object appear to express a certain 'viol par la vue' (ibid.). In fact this is only a nominal rape – that is to say, a rape accomplished without recourse to penetration: rape at a distance. This non-assimilation of the subject to the object characterises Sartre's description of sadism. Indeed, when Sartre describes sadism one could be forgiven for supposing that he is merely describing what psychoanalysis identifies as the component instinct scopophilia. Once again, Sartre detects a pointer in common linguistic usage: the object must be chaste, virginal, covered (in order to be discovered): 'l'objet non connu est donné comme immaculé, comme vierge, comparable à une *blancheur*. Il n'a pas encore "livré" son secret, l'homme ne le lui a pas encore *"arraché"*' (*EN* 638). So, if knowledge is the rape of an immaculate virginity, the knower is 'le chasseur qui surprend une nudité blanche et qui la viole de son regard' (*EN* 639). But the drawback is that the object of this desire (virginal) is destroyed (debased): desire destroys its object. The ideal of this desiring consciousness would be to debase the object whilst preserving it intact at the same time – a case of 'having one's cake and eating it'![13]

The parallel is drawn here with the attitude of the lover to the loved one. The lover dreams of entirely assimilating the loved one, while the loved one retains his/her integrity. This parallel is not in itself surprising, since the descriptions of love and desire are founded on the self-same dialectic of the look as underpins these descriptions of cognition.

But these images appear to have other, less obvious, determinants. Freud talks of the two currents that run through our sexual lives: the affectionate and the sensual (identified with sacred and profane love). If, at puberty, these two currents fail to unite, this will deter or prevent accession to mature genitality. The Sartrean series of (1) virginal object, (2) virginal object debased, (3) virginal object restored to its immaculate state could seem to correspond to the type of object choices that, for Freud, indicate this failure of the two currents to unite: the object that is loved (venerated) cannot be desired (debased), and the object that is desired cannot be loved. A divorce is thus introduced into the heart of the object choice itself. These two kinds of object correspond, furthermore, to two primitive images of the mother: as provider and friend, and as object of sexual desire. I shall suggest in my next chapter that these two images inform, to a degree, the fictional representations of women in Sartre's work. But my present concern is with their intrusion into the theoretical discourse.

Running parallel to the images of the debased/intact object, is to be found a play on 'indifference'. The term 'indifférence' has already been encountered in connection with the Viscous. The English 'indifferent' has connotations that are missing in French (mediocre, poor), but likewise fails to translate the wordplay that is available in the French 'indifférent'. This term can mean 'unaroused', in the specifically sexual sense, but under Sartre's pen it is drawn perilously close to the related term 'indifférencié', meaning 'not different from'. Sartre describes the known object as 'impénétrable, intransformable, entièrement lisse, dans une nudité indifférente de corps aimé et vainement caressé' (*EN* 640). The object is clearly impenetrable because it lacks *holes*; it is not just the marble body of a frigid statue, but a woman stripped of her sexual difference; an androgyne, perhaps, but one that possesses neither male nor female genitals. It is necessary that the object remain *different from* the subject by being 'indifférent', that the object remain cold, untroubled. What would happen if the object were to lose its 'indifférence', if it became aroused, even returned the caress or the look? At this point Sartre's text is marked by a blank. I suspect that the unavowed danger is not the assimilation of the object by the subject – as Sartre would have it – but the

Theorising the Difference

reverse: that the polished marble statue will abruptly split asunder and reveal an organ of its own; that the passive, desexualised object harbours secret desires of its own.[14]

This anxiety is present, but displaced, in the text. It can be read through the distortions operating in the story of Actaeon, the exemplary and mythical knowledge-seeker. The distortion is double. First, Actaeon is made initially more virile, more active. In Sartre's text he becomes an active seeker after knowledge: 'Actéon écarte les branches *pour mieux voir* Diane au bain' (*EN* 639; emphasis added). This apparently scopophilic Actaeon owes little to Ovid and much to a peculiarly Sartrean phantasy. Second, and most significantly, Sartre's text is silent as regards the terrible fate that befalls the hunter. He is punished by Diana for having contemplated her 'nudité blanche'; transformed into a stag, he is torn apart, dis-membered by his own hounds. The hunter becomes the hunted, the looker becomes the looked-at. We already know that, for Sartre, to be object of a gaze is to be passivised; it is also, apparently, to be *emasculated*. It is as if Sartre had interpreted half the myth in a classically psychoanalytic manner (the accidental discovery being interpreted as an unconscious desire to see), but that he had suppressed the other half – the dis-memberment or castration that is attendant upon this violation.

It is with good reason that the fate of Actaeon is passed over in silence in this account. It is the same reason as dictates that the object must remain the 'Belle Indifférente': the fear that the (feminine) object could either *assimilate* or *castrate* the masculine subject.

It is precisely this anxiety that underpins the analyses of the Viscous. The latter is double; it appears to be an object which can be possessed by surface contact, by sliding, but its reality is far more sinister – it threatens the possession of its possessor.

The horror of dilution or dissolution is also associated with this network of images. Sartre insists that consciousness cannot dissolve and assimilate its object. However, a reading of the Actaeon complex such as the one I have just given helps to deconstruct statements such as 'Husserl ne se lasse pas d'affirmer qu'on ne peut pas *dissoudre* les choses dans la conscience' (*Sit I*, 39). It is as though Sartre were erecting a *garde-fou* against the unthinkable: that masculine consciousness could be assimilated by its feminine object; in other words, that masculine should crumble into feminine. This horrifying prospect is glimpsed in the passages on cognition, but it is even more manifest in the much less controlled style of Sartre's short paper: 'Une idée fondamentale de la phénoménologie de Husserl: l'intentionnalité': 'Car [l'arbre] m'échappe et me repousse et je ne peux pas plus me perdre en lui qu'il ne se peut diluer en moi' (*Sit* I, 39–40). In this extract it is the tree that symbolises the feminine object which must remain outside, different and *indifférent*. The tree, or part of it, also appears in the section of *L'Etre et le néant* currently under consideration. The root offers the disturbing appearance of the partially assimilated object; it is already merged with the earth that feeds it, but 'elle ne peut utiliser la terre qu'en se faisant terre, c'est-à-dire, en un sens, *en se soumettant* à la matière qu'elle veut utiliser' (*EN* 644; emphasis added). The masculine attitude ('utiliser') is thrown into jeopardy and compromised. Once again the possessor, by a 'curious reversal' is possessed.

Sartre states that sliding is the opposite of becoming rooted down. If 's'enraciner' denotes feminisation, one would expect 'glisser' to denote a masculine activity, and such is indeed the case. He discusses the case of skiing over yet another 'nudité blanche', this time a virgin field of snow. This is an extension of the 'rape at a safe distance' metaphor, which is characteristic of the cognitive activity. In this description of sliding we encounter some familiar distinctions: 'le glissement est *action à distance*, il assure ma maîtrise sur la matière sans que j'aie besoin de *m'enfoncer* dans cette matière et de *m'engluer* en elle pour la *dompter*' (*EN* 644; emphasis added). It is almost as if the skier were performing a kind of imaginary penetration. The snow has to reorganise itself, 'in depth', in order to support the weight of the skier bearing down on it: it is, therefore, 'troublée', but the skier remains uncompromised; he does not actually penetrate. In purely sexual terms, the overriding impression is one of manual masturbation rather than full coitus.

So sliding is action at a distance, just as a 'viol par la vue' is rape at a distance. The sadistic current is plain enough: the Sartrean sadist seeks to produce arousal in his victim whilst remaining safely buttoned up himself.[15] The aim of the skier is to ensure his mastery over his object, but simultaneously to avoid any possible reversal of this power relationship: 'sans que j'aie besoin de m'enfoncer . . . pour la dompter'.[16]

We have already seen from the passages on the Viscous that to be bogged down symbolises the collapse of subject into object.

Like snow, the Viscous appears to be smooth and polished, but *it* cannot be possessed through these qualities that make sliding possible – they are pseudo-qualities which mask its real, sinister nature. We cannot slip over the Viscous; it sucks in those who would try. The sadistic attitude of the skier is perhaps the ultimate masculine position for Sartre, but there is no stable mediation between it and the masochistic or, for Sartre, feminine pole – only a constant recuperation of one position by the other. The Viscous could be seen as this recuperation in progress, even to the point where the choice in Sartre's texts is not between a specific masculinity and a specific femininity, but between masculinity and emasculation, for the feminine is given as an emasculated maleness. this is all vividly conveyed by the Viscous, which is not – as is sometimes argued – reducible to an image of original femininity, but is in fact the image of 'la conscience enlisée': clear, lucid, *masculine* consciousness muddied by the contamination of substance; the turgescent member abruptly floored by flaccidity.

The only way to avoid this fate is to keep moving, to remain vigilant and to avoid compromising contact. This emerges from Sartre's account of what happens when the skier stops and tries to appropriate the snow: 'j'enfonce dans la neige jusqu'aux genoux; si je prends de la neige dans mes mains, elle se liquéfie entre mes doigts' (*EN* 643). There is no need to labour this point; the duplicity of the feminine object is obvious: the snow is apparently virginal, white, frigid, but its reality is more threatening; any attempted possession will be punished by engulfment.

These echoes of anxiety centred on engulfment and castration take on a startling resonance in the section of *L'Etre et le néant* where Sartre analyses the 'human significance' of holes.

Holes are a topic of some importance, for it is precisely over the question of the *significance* ascribed to the various bodily orifices (oral, anal, and so on) in psychoanalysis that Sartre chooses to confront Freud with his own 'existential psychoanalysis'.

Sartre's chosen orifice is the anus. We now possess an early version, in the *Carnets de la drôle de guerre*, of his reflections on this topic. [17] In *L'Etre et le néant* Sartre equivocates over the process whereby one discovers oneself to be holed. On the one hand, he states that we discover we are holed in the 'field of the Other', specifically through the words and actions of the mother (see

EN 675).[18] But elsewhere this discovery is apparently made by the child alone (EN 675). If my own body can never be an object for me, the objective qualities of this body have to be discovered in the field of the Other (for example, in the language of the mother). But in that case I can never *experience* my body as holed except by accepting the judgement passed on it by the Other for whom my body *is* an object in the world. I shall return to this problem shortly, but simply note for the moment that the hole is given explicity as *feminine*, although Sartre has still not seen fit to define this term in any but a circular fashion. In the *Carnets* we read that 'le trou est souvent résistance. Il faut le forcer pour passer. Par là, il est déjà féminin' (*Car* 189). Two points arise from this. First, how can the hole be *already* feminine if Sartre is bent on bringing out, precisely, its pre-sexual significance? Second, this use of the term 'feminine' appears once again to rely on a sado-masochistic schema: the masculine attitude is to violate, to force entry; the feminine attitude is to offer a (token) resistance. In subsequent pages, this masculine activity returns in the form of filling holes, which is described as a 'travail d'artisan', but one whose consequences are far from satisfying: 'Ainsi, boucher le trou, c'est . . . subir la passion du Pour-soi pour façonner, parfaire et sauver la totalité de l'En-soi' (*EN* 675). What is initially conceived of as a virile activity ends with a sacrifice. Once more, castration is the price of penetration. Nowhere does this emerge more clearly than in Sartre's treatment of the vagina. There is one particularly important passage that must be quoted at length:

> l'obscénité du sexe féminin est celle de toute chose *béante*: c'est un *appel d'être*, comme d'ailleurs tous les trous; en soi la femme appelle une chair étrangère qui doive la transformer en plénitude d'être par pénétration et dilution. Et inversement la femme sent sa condition comme un appel, précisément parce qu'elle est 'trouée'. (*EN* 676)

If, as Sartre has argued, we only learn that we are holed in the field of the Other, the woman is holed because she is seen, by the Other, to be holed. How then is one to understand a phrase such as '*en soi* la femme appelle une chair étrangère . . .'? There is doubtless a degree of oscillation here. Men, too, are essentially holed beings – why should it be only women who suffer this essentialist condemnation? The secret belief is that woman *is* holed in the way that a table *is* a table, whereas man is only holed should he choose to accept this as a judgement passed on him by the Other.

If we return to Sartre's earlier remarks on sexual differentiation, the nature of this contradiction comes into clearer focus. Having said that sexual difference (male/female) is on the side of facticity, he insists that the differentiation into two genders (masculine/ feminine) cannot be ascribed to something as contingent as somatic configuration. But now, having equated the vagina with any *gaping thing*, having said that it is therefore an 'appeal', that woman feels her very condition as an 'appeal', he is implicitly creating a feminine essence: 'to be holed'.

Moreover, the anxiety-provoking aspects of the feminine are impossible to overlook: the penis penetrates but is then *assimilated*. At this stage the anxieties of engulfment and castration appear to be conflated. The more relaxed style of the *Carnets* allows this to surface better than the relatively controlled discourse of *L'Etre et le néant*. the hole is the 'symbole des refus pudiques et violés, *bouche d'ombre, qui engloutit et assimile*' (*Car* 190; emphasis added). This is a nodal point. I have suggested the possibility of reading the passages on the Viscous, cognition, sliding and holes as variations on the theme of castration anxiety. But this seeming divorce between subtext and surface text is not quite as straightforward as it could appear. For the whole thrust of Sartre's writing on sexuality is directed towards an explicit displacement of the explanatory value of the Oedipus and castration complexes as theorised by Freud. For Sartre, what lies beyond the Oedipus complex – should it exist – is that point wherein consciousness comes face to face with itself and dissolves into mist: the original choice.

Immediately after the passages in *L'Etre et le néant* that we have just looked at, on the vagina, Sartre writes, 'Sans aucun doute le sexe est bouche, et bouche vorace qui avale le pénis ce qui peut bien amener l'idée de castration: l'acte amoureux est castration de l'homme – mais c'est avant tout que le sexe est trou' (*EN* 676). The vagina is a hole before it is the female sexual organ. So the idea of castration, in its proper sense of a threat to the male organ,[19] depends on the universal and essential property of the hole – namely, that it involves penetration and threatens dissolution of the penetrator. It is in this ontological sense that the sexual act can be viewed as a castration: the vagina, thank heavens, is *just* a hole, and the penis is *simply* a hole-filler! The ontological fate of any filler of holes befalls the penis, but not *as a penis*: as a hole-filler. But, even if we were to accept this ingenious, and not wholly implausible, proposition, a crucial shift occurs in Sartre's account – a shift that undermines one's confidence in the theoretical discourse. In the passage quoted above, what began as 'passive béance' is suddenly transformed into 'bouche vorace' swallowing the penis. In the gulf that separates these two images, I suspect there lurks the figure of the Archaic Mother and her cannibalistic threat of incorporation.

Since the Viscous appears to be the archetypal image called upon to draw together all of these phantasmatic strands, it seems fitting to close this chapter by returning to that image. The horror of the Viscous is given as a universal human reaction (*EN* 672). In support of the universality of this claim, Sartre claims that even tiny infants show revulsion in the presence of the Viscous (*EN* 667) – and this presumably to demonstrate that ontology has primacy over sexual considerations (or that the latter are ultimately reducible to the former), since very young children are as yet ignorant of sexual matters and could not possibly see in the Viscous the symbol of their future castration. The assertion is manifestly ungrounded. One has only to contemplate a baby joyfully smearing itself with honey or jam in order to sense the error of this statement. Moreover, Sartre later goes on to state that the horror of the Viscous – although derived from a universal definition of consciousness – is not, in fact, universal; a love of the Viscous is also a possible human project: 'qui suis-je donc moi qui, à l'encontre, aime le visqueux? A quel projet fondamental de moi-même suis-je renvoyé si je veux expliciter cet amour d'un en-soi enlisant et louche?' (*EN* 676).

As will become obvious in the next chapter, there is only one answer to this 'qui suis-je donc?': *feminine* or, despite Sartre's non-sexist disclaimers, a *woman*. It is not surprising that this question is allowed to hang fire.

2
Representations

I am concerned in this chapter neither with the discussion, in anthropomorphic terms, of the motives and behaviour of certain 'character types', nor with the structural analysis of the 'character effect'. I shall be looking at three main groups of Sartrean creatures – drawn from the fiction, drama and biographies – in order to indicate, in the first instance, how they relate to Sartre's theorisation of sexuality examined in Chapter 1. These groups are the *femmes-marécages*, the *femmes-mirages*[1] and the *Genitors*. This selection is necessarily reductive, but by no means wholly arbitrary.

The *strategies* that Sartre employs in these representations are obviously connected with his views on sexuality and, more generally, human reality. For example, if the bourgeois of Bouville are represented in terms of solidity, massiveness, lack of reflection, and so on, it is because, at one level, Sartre sees them as representatives of a particular brand of bad faith: their bad faith consists in hiding their contingency from themselves, and others, beneath a mask of necessity. Turning a deaf ear to the chattering of their consciousness, they give themselves the unshakable self-sufficiency of a rock. But in the last section of this chapter I shall show that the *schemas* underlying these representations partake of a different scene: they are roles to be assumed in that *mise-en-scène*, or scenario, of desire that psychoanalysis calls a phantasmatic.

It would be wholly mistaken to assume that these two levels of representation are dissociated: they do not simply coexist in Sartre's texts. It would be equally mistaken to suppose that the phantasmatic level is the hidden reality of the surface level: the text is not equivalent to the manifest content of a dream; it is an organised and coherent set of relationships directed *outwards* towards the world and the reader. It does have its latent, or sub-, text, but the problem consists in attempting to articulate the nature of the relationship between these two levels of representation and, by extension, the two levels of analysis that they solicit.

SWAMP AND MIRAGE

Il n'y a pas de femmes belles, il n'y a que des laides déguisées.

In her *A propos de Sartre et de l'amour*, Suzanne Lilar coins the terms *femme-marécage* and *femme-mirage* to encapsulate the attributes of two groups of Sartrean female characters. In the present context, these terms denote schemas, not strategies. These schemas preside over the creation of the fictional characters and consist in a small number of transferable attributes. The schema that underpins the figures of the *femme-marécage* includes traits such as fleshiness, annexation to a natural world of repetitious cycles, and, above all, viscosity. The *femme-mirage* is in many ways the positive counterpart to this: this generative schema includes acorporeality, frigidity, unreality, beauty, and so on. But scarcely any single character is a function of just one of these schemas: transformations occur in the characters that involve a transfer of representational traits, and I shall be examining the significance of these transformations in the last section of the chapter.

As Roquentin purges himself of his melancholy between the sheets of Françoise's bed, it is aspects of her physicality that are the favoured terms of description (*OR* 71).[2] Epidermal contact provokes a surrealistic nightmare where the *patronne*'s body, and more especially, one supposes, the 'jardinet' of the public triangle, is metamorphosed into a seething jungle (*OR* 72). At one point Roquentin formulates the essence of his discovery thus: 'l'existence est un plein que l'homme ne peut quitter' (*OR* 158). Participating in the proliferation of Nature, women, in Sartre, are part of this plenum. They are also synecdochically extended to represent the whole of it. The barmaid at the Brasserie Vézelize appears to Roquentin like a human fruit-tree, smiling secretively as her breasts blossom and fill her blouse: 'Et la femme continuait à sentir sa gorge exister dans son corsage, à penser; "mes nénés, mes beaux fruits", à sourire mystérieusement' (*OR* 159). She is the privileged site of a natural activity which takes its course through her but over which she has no control. The female characters in Sartre are very often seen, or phantasised, to adopt an attitude of compliance or complicity to this vegetative process.

Flowers and blossoming are frequently tinged with negative

overtones. In a sense, the flower is a false transcendence: its blossoming is like a slow erection, but the end product remains soft.[3] But, if the flower is viewed negatively by the male, it is seen as the natural ally of the woman in her rather sinister projects of seduction. When Marcelle believes she is about to ensnare Mathieu into a life of married bliss, she leans over, the text notes, takes a rose and inserts it into her coiffure (*OR* 687). Eve, in *Les Jeux sont faits*, makes a precisely analogues use of a rose in her attempt to seduce Pierre from his world of virile demands.

There is doubtless a kind of internal consistency in this attitude towards the body. As a theorist, Sartre sees the body as the 'contingency that consciousness exists', and yet the women tend to be 'existed by'[4] their bodies. By contrast, the male characters, overwhelmingly, experience their bodies either with disgust or as an obedient, honed, instrument. In both cases it is a question of viewing the body as an instrument for transcending the present and taking off into the future; as a means of fashioning a world of new instruments and concrete projects. When the body is viewed with disgust, it is because it is perceived as an hindrance to the realisation of this virile project. I use the word 'virile' in the sense established in Chapter 1, where we saw that, ultimately, the masculine attitude for Sartre is to be equated with the explosion, or *surgissement*, of consciousness towards the world. In the case of the female characters under consideration, physical descriptions proliferate almost to the point of self-parody: they are identified with their bodies. And it is always the body in its most contingent, fleshy aspects (obesity, flabby buttocks, pendulous breasts, and so on) which is the prime determinant of this group of characters.[5]

So in Sartre's image these bodies participate in the proliferation of Nature as it continues its course unchecked. The female characters will often adopt one of two attitudes towards this state of affairs: they see themselves as willing or rebellious victims

Madame Fleurier in 'L'Enfance d'un chef', as seen through the eyes of the inquisitive Lucien, finds herself totally identified with her body: 'elle *était* cette grosse masse rose, ce corps volumineux' (*OR* 329; emphasis added). She is the first of many Dianas surprised at her ablutions. Marcelle, too, suffers an atrocious narrative condemnation. She is 'pis que nue, sans défense, comme une grosse potiche' (*OR* 397). Her flesh is rarely the source of pneumatic bliss; far more often it gives rise to a cloying horror. It is 'molle et beurreuse' At this point it is worth pointing out that the word 'chair' (flesh) is almost exclusively reserved for the female body.

But at least Marcelle has the fleeting saving grace of having once been a firm-bodied young woman. In contrast, Sarah is condemned without right to appeal. She is one of the most dis-graced characters in Sartre's fictions. She is unctuous and compliant, oozing a kind of creeping generosity. As seen by the committed Brunet, her maternal protectiveness strips her of any political hardness, and for Mathieu she is an object of some disgust. He gazes in horror as her flapping yellow kimono gapes open to reveal her sagging paps (OR 432) – to possess large soft breasts is already a moral failing!

Lola is a rather complex character and is not readily classifiable according to any single representative schema. Initially, however, she is portrayed in heavily physical terms. For Mathieu, the predatory sensuality of her face is immediately, and brutally, evident (OR 499). And, rather than simply the softness of her breasts, Boris feels 'L'*épaisse* douceur de ses seins' (OR 427). Most notably, her lips take on the attributes elsewhere associated with her breasts: instead of being thin or drawn, or full or round, they are enormously heavy and clearly the source of some foreboding for Boris, giving him an impression of 'une nudité moite et fiévreuse' in the middle of an immobile plaster mask (OR 416). This evocation of Lola's lips has its positive counter-image in *Le Sursis* where Irène is described as being 'un peu boulotte avec une chair mate, un peu trop tendre, un peu moite' (OR 1068). Once more, flesh is the determinant. But she is saved from outright condemnation by having 'une toute petite bouche aux commissures lasses' (OR 1068). The fleshiness which so nearly disgraces her is absent from her face. But she too hovers between two representations. Her *eyes* hold Nature at bay, but eventually she must close them and, when she does, Nature encroaches and reappropriates her face 'comme la nature reprend les jardins abandonnés (OR 1080). Body and vegetative nature are here explicitly equated. In *Les Mouches*, Clytemnestre is defined as body before she even makes her entrance (*Mou* 128). This tendency for the female characters to be defined as body *a priori* is so pervasive that a complete enumeration would be tedious almost to the point of hilarity: it is the repetition of the same.

So the *femme-marécage* is a part of Nature to the extent that her body is annexed to the natural world. This representation is achieved not just through metaphors of vegetation, but also through monotonous concentration on those aspects of the physique which are, for Sartre, most contingent and fleshy.

A further aspect of this representation is the concentration on odour.[6] At the level of Sartre's representational *strategies*, odour appears to function as the paradigm for the relation of consciousness to its own facticity: one feels responsible for one's own smell, but one is not the foundation of that smell.

The female smell *par excellence* is the sweet odour of stagnation and rotting flowers, especially violets. The waitress at the Café Mably, in *La Nausée*, emits a stench which is 'semblable à l'odeur de violette que dégagent parfois les corps en décomposition' (*OR* 68). The smell is, obviously, a smell of nature and is qualified – lest we be tempted to find the scent of violets pleasant – as the stink of death and decomposition. Once more, it is Marcelle who is the most complete victim of this particular strategy. Just as Clytemnestre was condemned as body before her appearance on stage, so Marcelle is pre-scented as an odour (*OR* 395). She is the locus of a mysterious natural process: 'C'était plutôt pénible de l'entendre parler de sa voix d'homme, pendant qu'une forte sombre montait d'elle (*OR* 397). It seems that female characters in Sartre only ever smell intransitively. The above phrase is an interesting give-away. What is 'pénible' for Mathieu is the *contrast*: the word 'homme' forces the reader to identify the smell as feminine, since the structure of the phrase ('pendant que . . .') invites a contrast. She talks like a man (that is, *pretends to be* a man), but the overriding impression is one of femininity – the smell is a stronger determinant of gender than the voice.

The smells of women are never clear, bright honest smells such as wine, garlic or tobacco (the 'male' smells in Sartre): they are 'sombres', 'vagues', 'lourdes', 'épaisses' or 'tristes'. The coenaesthetic overtones of these terms invite us to identify women as belonging to a twilight zone lying somewhere between the clarity of consciousness and the sinister opacity of the object-in-itself. This experience is double-edged (smells can resemble colours and *vice versa*); the sense experience is, in fact, an hesitation between the two, or rather a disturbing simultaneous perception of both. In *La Nausée*, we read that the black of the chestnut root 'débordait de loin la vue, l'odorat et le goût' (*OR* 155). Similarly, the light in Marcelle's room is 'morte et rose comme une odeur refroidie' (*OR* 463).

Interestingly enough, the female characters appear to be largely unaware of their smell: it is the male characters who notice and react to it. It is, for example, Mathieu who describes the smell in Marcelle's room as the smell of illness, sweeties and lovemaking (*OR* 696). But the most crushing olfactory condemnation comes from the homosexual Daniel. Marcelle is now 'pourrie'; the air in her room will be 'irrespirable' (*OR* 530). She is transformed, almost comically, into one large odour: 'Marcelle était une épaisse odeur triste déposée sur le lit, en boule, qui s'effilocherait au moindre geste' (*OR* 561).

But these female smells do not invariably disgust the males. On his first meeting with Jessica, Hoederer remarks that Jessica smells sweet and that she should not wear that perfume when visiting his sex-starved bodyguards (*MS* 100). But on this occasion Jessica has left her Chanel at home: it is her natural smell. Hoederer's reaction to this is 'tant pis' – even when the smell is pleasant, it remains dangerous. It is the very femininity of Jessica, concretised in her odour, that threatens the masculine world of action and commitment. This scene prefigures the catastrophe when the last smell to titillate Hoederer's nostrils is the smell of woman: 'C'est trop con', as he, perhaps punningly, remarks!

It is possible in this episode to glimpse a feature which will develop considerable importance when it is time to look at the transformations wrought in these portrayals. Woman is a trap. The serene beauty of Jessica is akin to the smooth surface of sinking sands. The promise of Jessica's odour is in reality a threat: the enticing smell of a rose conceals the putrescent stench of rotting violets. I shall return to this later, but enough has been made of these olfactory references for the time being.

It is not simply that Sartre sees women as being closer to nature – although this may also be the case. The body may be annexed to the natural world, but it also makes a *victim* of its owner. The waitress in the Café Mably is quite literally a victim of her body. She suffers from a – typically – unspecified disease: 'Elle a une maladie dans le ventre'; beneath her skirts she is gently rotting away, whilst a melancholy smile plays on her lips (*OR* 67). Although a limit case, this character is in many ways archetypal. The smell in Marcelle's room is also that of illness. The above quotation is slightly ambiguous: 'ventre' could mean 'intestines' or 'belly', but it could also mean 'womb'. This second meaning is surely predominant in the case of Marcelle – and Ivich after her fall from grace – where pregnancy is viewed by Mathieu and Daniel as a kind of organic rotting from the inside out. Through pregnancy, both Marcelle and Ivich become unwitting victims of Nature. The body is taken over by a parasite. Pregnancy is regarded by Marcelle as a blessing and by Ivich as a curse, but, whatever *their* reaction to this recuperation by Nature, they are condemned irrespectively at the level of the narration. It is the male character who is particularly horrified by this self-assertion on the part of the reproductive cycle. Mathieu thinks with distaste, 'dans une chambre rose, au fond d'un autre ventre, il y avait une cloque qui gonflait' (*OR* 437). A previous mysterious illness had already reduced Marcelle to the confines of her body, obliging her to remain indoors as much as possible. Now control of the body is further removed from her grasp. The rhythm of her life has become her matinal vomiting (*OR* 464). Although in the first instance a victim of Nature, she is later seen, for once from the inside, to be open to Nature, willing its fulfilment, willing it to take its course through her: complicity and submission, therefore, to the tyranny of the natural cycle.

Mathieu's desire to abort the embryo is readily comprehensible within the framework provided by the novel's surface themes: it is a rejection of a commitment he finds abhorrent, the refusal to take out a mortgage on a future that he wishes to keep open. But it is *also* the refusal of the gastric intimacy of the womb and its viscous contents. Clearly also, it is a rejection of paternity, and the determinants of this rejection will become abundantly clear in later chapters.

Like Mathieu, Daniel is outraged by Marcelle's pregnancy. She is simply 'cette lourde femelle', a feeding-bag for a gluttonous parasite, 'chair graisseuse et nourricière, garde-manger' (*OR* 568).

So many 'mysterious illnesses' afflict Sartre's female characters. Madame Darbédat, in 'La Chambre', is confined to her room like Marcelle by an obscure ailment. We are doubtless intended to view these 'maladies' as the outcome of a *choice* on the part of the victims. But such areas of obscurity are a strange lapse for a novelist. Perhaps we should assume that illness, for Sartre, represents yet another false transcendence: a false change towards death, rather than a self-realisation. The reaction of Madame Darbédat is quite typical. Limited first to her room, and within her room, to her mortal shell, she turns from the future and lives in the past. She is fat with congealed time, 'alourdie de souvenirs' (*OR* 235). This refusal of human time and the acceptance of the circularity of natural time, stagnation, is captured, of course, in the image of the Viscous that was encountered in Chapter 1.

We saw in *L'Etre et le néant* that the Viscous is the twilight region between immanence and transcendence; the feminisation of an erupting masculine consciousness through contamination by substance. It is also the recuperation of the human order of work, projects, transcendence by Nature itself: if we do not act quickly and constantly, we find ourselves sinking knee-deep into a fetid swamp. Nature may appear to allow itself passively to be domesticated, but its submission is laziness: it awaits the day when it will strangle the temple of Technos with its creeping tendrils – Bouville metamorphosed into Angkor Watt. Inasmuch as the *femme-marécage* embodies the determinants of the Viscous, this fate is not a mere abstraction: the *femme-marécage* threatens engulfment of a very specific kind. At one end of the representational scale, the *femme-marécage is* the Viscous; she may also betray her 'real' nature through a seemingly innocent propensity for viscous substances. Rirette in 'Intimité', the passive woman who longs to swoon in the embrace of an iron-muscled gorilla, is betrayed by her taste for sticky Port (*OR* 289). One thinks also of Madame Darbédat's self-indulgence in Turkish delight: this 'chair vitreuse' with its 'parfum de croupi' filling her mouth (*OR* 234). Apart from the ambiguous texture of the substance itself, one should note the epithet 'croupi' – stagnant and musty. The stagnant pond is covered in slime; not only is it unchanging, but there is a certain duplicity about it: the calm surface belies the horrible world of microscopic organisms that lurks beneath. Naturally, it is also pink: the non-colour *par excellence*. Between the safe, sterile virginity of white and the violence of red, pink is a colour – like the mauve of Cousin Adolphe's braces in *La Nausée* – that cannot decide what it wants to be. Incarnadine is also the colour of flesh, bringing us back round to the '*chair* vitreuse' of the Turkish delight. This characterisation by taste is a hallmark of Sartre's style. The same strategy, in reverse, is also employed in the case of Ivich, who is horrified by the viscosity of her drink.[7]

What is more interesting are those points where the female characters are themselves seen to embody the Viscous. It is significant that they are rarely, if ever, viscous-for-themselves: they are seen to be viscous, cloying, damp, sticky, and so on, by the male characters.[8] This revelation inevitably provokes a reaction of disgust mingled with revulsion. This is the full horror of the *femme-*

marécage, who is the embodiment of the Viscous and who threatens to bog down, suck in, engulf and – if the hypothesis I broached in the previous chapter is correct – *castrate* the representatives of virility.[9]

In the *Lettres au Castor* (for example, *LAC* I, 401, 434; II, 137) Sartre accepted de Beauvoir's criticism that he was being too harsh on poor Marcelle. If the text that resulted was an edulcorated version, one wonders how Marcelle appeared in the original version. It falls, characteristically, to Daniel to give Marcelle her name: 'Marcelle, c'était un *marécage* . . . les idées *s'enlisait* dans sa tête, elle n'existait qu'en apparence' (*OR* 530; emphasis added). The implication is that existence – in the active sense of ex-sistence – is the mere appearance, and the underlying reality is a sinister, consuming 'vie'.

Estelle, in *Huis clos*, suffers the same condemnation. She is perhaps the most typical of Sartrean *femmes-marécages*. Doubly a woman (*est Elle*) and only superficially a star (Stellaire), she is outwardly urbane and beautiful, hence unreal. But the veneer soon melts off and her real nature shows through. When this surface veneer of beauty and unreality is pierced, Garcin is revolted by what he sees: 'Je ne veux pas m'enliser dans tes yeux. Tu es moite! Tu es molle! Tu es une pieuvre, tu es un marécage' (*HC* 84). This is the definitive and archetypal reaction of the male character when confronted with the revealed image of the swamp-woman. Following this intuition Garcin is destined to pass eternity oscillating, like Mathieu,[10] between a 'conscience haineuse' (Inès), and a 'femme immobile' who threatens constant engulfment. In other words, these male characters are caught between two diametrically opposed images of the feminine. One of these we have now met with; the other is the *femme-mirage*.

If the *femme-marécage* is too physical, too 'natural', too fertile, the *femme-mirage* appears to be her antithesis. In this schema, images of acorporeality, virginity, frigidity and sterility abound.

In many ways Lulu in 'Intimité' represents the opposite pole to the Marcelle who longs to feel the velvety hands of her lover roaming over her buttocks (*OR* 656). Not for Lulu the swooning passivity of the satisfied woman, for it is through her body that she feels herself vulnerable to domination: 'Ils vous prennent pour un instrument dont ils sont fiers de savoir jouer. Je déteste qu'on me trouble' (*OR* 306). Within the framework provided by Sartre's text, Lulu's frigidity is clearly intended to be seen as more willed than real. Her bad faith consists in her clinging to the belief that she is constitutionally frigid, whereas – as the above quotation makes plain – her 'frigidity' does not *prevent* her from feeling sexual pleasure. It is, rather, a freely chosen denial of pleasure. But the significant point is this very refusal. She refuses the complicity of her body, and refuses fertility (*OR* 280). She experiences her body as an obscene excrescence, a certain intimate vulnerability that must be overcome. But, at the level of representation with which I am concerned, Lulu is the precise antithesis of the schema of the *femme pâmée*. At its deepest, her 'frigidity' represents a refusal to feel the desire of the Other in her body (see *EN* 90). In her attitude to the 'physiological', Ivich is not dissimilar to Lulu. She suppresses the demands of her body of a constant and exhausting tension: 'elle oubliait tout, elle se fuyait . . . , elle oubliait de manger, elle oubliait de dormir' (*OR* 446).[11]

We should note in passing that 'elle se fuyait' is a notation normally associated with the transcendent structure of consciousness itself. This flight is the very opposite of immanence, just as Ivich is the opposite of the (literally) in-dwelling Marcelle. As with Lulu, her body is experienced as vulnerability: 'J'ai horreur qu'on me touche', she snarls at Mathieu when he is bold enough to make an advance (*OR* 449). It is she who hurls the worst Sartrean insult at Lola, whose brutal physicality scandalises her: 'c'est une sale bonne femme, une femelle' (*OR* 597).

Once again, sexuality is a key determinant in this representation. Even when Mathieu begins to desire Ivich, it is uncertain whether this desire is directed at the flesh-and-blood Ivich herself, or at an iconic Madonna. This introduces a second determinant in the representation of the *femme-mirage*. If the *femme-marécage* is felt to suffer from a surfeit of reality, her counter-image teeters constantly on the brink of extinction. At the level of conscious intention, this representation can certainly be linked with Sartre's ideas on the imaginary and the art object. *L'Imaginaire* was one of the few works that he never rejected as inadequate. Even *L'Idiot de la famille* is dependent to a large measure on the framework provided by this 1939 work. Sartre's argument in *L'Imaginaire* centres on the status of the imaginary object. The latter is not to be regarded as a content of consciousness that may be summoned up, perused at leisure and reflected upon: it is the correlate of a 'conscience imageante'.

The result of this phenomenological position is a dichotomy: on the one hand, the real world as it yields itself to perception, unlimited, rich and inexhaustible; on the other hand, the impoverished, schematic world of the imaginary – there is never anything more in an image than is put there by the intentional consciousness responsible for its constitution. But it is Sartre's remarks on the art object that are of interest to us. Beauty is not of this world: 'Ce qui est "beau" . . . c'est un être qui ne saurait se donner à la perception et qui, dans sa nature même est isolé de l'univers' (*Imag* 363). And, since sexual desire, for Sartre, is an engagement with a *real* object, it follows that a beautiful woman cannot be the object of desire: the great beauty of woman kills the desire one might feel for her; in order to desire her one needs to forget that she is beautiful and 'take a dive' – 'car le désir est une plongée au coeur de l'existence dans ce qu'elle a de plus contingent et de plus absurde' (*Imag* 372–3). This would require further commentary. The dichotomy itself is dubious even within the phenomenological frame of reference that Sartre adopts: the existence of a realm of pure perception untainted by the imaginary is at the very least debatable. The dichotomy is, however, real and very operative in Sartre's work, but it is possible that it could be determined by other factors. In effect, the imagination/perception schism reproduces the duality of the sacred and the profane love objects, familiar in psychoanalytic theory. The sacred object may be admired or worshipped – Ivich, for example, is referred to as 'une idole' – but not desired. To desire the object is to debase it and take the plunge: a fall not just into the humdrum world of perceived reality, but also, perhaps, into the open arms of the dreaded *femme-marécage*. I shall return to this 'fall' later, but for the present moment it is worth examining the beauty–unreality aspect of the *femme-mirage*.

There is a certain 'mise en abyme' effect in Sartre's representations of many of his female characters: they are works of art within a work of art. A woman may be 'sensual', 'pretty', 'attractive', and so on, but if she is 'belle' she belongs firmly in the category of the work of art, which is the very antithesis of Nature on Sartre's representational scale. Conversely, if a woman is to be viewed as a sexed body, she must first fall from that state of grace described as beauty. What immediately sets Electre apart from the inhabitants of Argos is her beauty. 'Tu es belle. Tu ne ressembles pas aux gens d'ici', says Oreste (*Mou* 126). Inès greets Estelle with the words 'vous êtes très belle' (*HC* 29). Hoederer to Jessica: 'Je croyais que tu serais laide . . . c'est regrettable' (*MS* 88). And Goetz to Hilda: 'Tu es belle. La Beauté, c'est le Mal' (*DBD* 224). It is a curious fact that Sartre denigrates the real and the imaginary with almost equal severity. There is no doubt about the meaning of Eve's beauty: it is a trap, a double trap. On the one hand it leads the male into a state of desire in which this beauty will melt away to reveal the too-fleshly woman beneath – the *femme-marécage*. But, on the other hand, if the male remains on the plane of aesthetic contemplation, he is equally guilty: to place himself on this plain, he has to flee the real world of concrete demands and de-realise himself. All of these themes – beauty, the trap, duplicity, and so on – are resumed in the figure of the actress.

As early as *La Nausée*, the Anny that Roquentin remembers[12] had 'cette fidélité puissante au moindre trait de son image' (*OR* 73). Her hotel room is decorated like an elaborate stage set and Roquentin must de-realise himself in order to enter the set. He has to create a role in order to bring about the 'perfect moments'. With Anny, the aesthetic attitude is elevated to the status of a categorical imperative (*OR* 175). As Eve, in 'La Chambre', enters Pierre's psychosis, the room is transformed into an hallucinatory nightmare. Her father notices her heavy make-up and her 'air de tragédienne' (*OR* 244).

Although Ivich is not an actress, she appears to Mathieu to possess the fragility of a work of art. Her physical appearance is given not in terms of flesh but rather as the marble sterility of the art object: 'elle semblait peinte et vernie, comme une Tahitienne sur une toile de Gauguin, inutilisable' (*OR* 448). In contrast to the flabby thighs of Marcelle or the sagging breasts of Sarah, she has a 'petit corps rageur et frêle' (*OR* 600). Mathieu's detached contemplation of this object is reproduced in the reader: Ivich is only ever seen from the outside, never from the inside by means of the free indirect discourse.[13]

From Anny in Sartre's first published novel, to Johanna in *Les Séquestrés d'Altona*, we turn full circle. Johanna too is an ex-actress. She is sent by the Father to Frantz's room, made up, in a fine dress, beautiful. Frantz is under no illusion as to why she is there: 'tout est là, camarades: "sois belle et tais-toi", une image . . . l'absence, la Beauté' (*Séq* 169). She is, like Ivich, a mirage, 'un piège à beauté' as Frantz puts it (*Séq* 175). Far from representing the temptation of the flesh, she embodies the temptation of the imaginary.

There is little point in multiplying examples. Whenever a female character is represented in terms of a refusal of physicality, a rejection of nature, a predilection for the unreal or beauty, we are dealing with the schema of the *femme-mirage*. This name is well chosen: such characters appear to offer a salvation akin to that of an oasis in a desert, but if one approaches them they vanish. Or, rather, they are transformed: the pool of fresh translucent water does not so much disappear as reveal itself to be a brackish mire. The third section of this chapter will deal with the strikingly similar sets of circumstances under which this transformation occurs. But, for the full significance of these transformations to be grasped, a third figure has to be introduced into the organisation of representational schemas.

THE GENITOR

Il baise, tue, prie et ne pense pas.

What do a nineteenth-century Bouvillois arms-manufacturer and a twentieth-century *tante-mâle*[14] have in common? At first sight, not much, perhaps; on closer inspection, rather a lot – for Sartre. Sartre's representations of the doyens of the French bourgeoisie have a double articulation. First, these characters incarnate a kind of ontological sin, a certain bad faith described in *L'Existentialisme est un humanisme*, where Sartre gives the name 'salauds' to those who attempt to demonstrate that their existence is necessary, whereas, in reality, it is contingency itself (*Ext* 84–5). Second, bourgeois ideology has sought to translate this ontological falsehood into a socio-economic reality: the bourgeoisie, in its own self-representation, is so 'natural', so eternal, as to cease to be a mere class at all – the bourgeois has monopolised the very concept of Humanity. So Sartre's portrayal of the bourgeois *milieux* relies on social observation underpinned by ontological – and later Marxist historical – insights. From this point of view, then, it is not surprising that a certain stereotypical sameness pervades fictional representations of these characters, be they labelled 'chefs', 'hommes de bien', 'honnêtes gens', 'justes' or 'salauds': Charles Schweitzer would not be out of place exchanging dominical greetings on the Rue Tournebride, and Gerlach would find his way into the 'Petit dictionnaire des grands hommes d'Altona' as surely as his stern countenance would look down from a portrait in the local art gallery.

But there is a substratum to these representations, and at this level – the level I identify as the phantasmatic – these stalwart pillars of society are liable to cohabit with some rather strange bedfellows. The answer to the question with which I opened this section is that, at this level of textual organisation, the *grands bourgeois* and the *tante-mâle* are, functionally, virtually identical.

But this is to anticipate an argument which I shall not be able fully to develop until the final chapter of this work. Perhaps the best starting-point is *La Nausée*.

Before meeting the bourgeois in person we are introduced to an even more perfect example: the statue of Gustave Impétraz – perfect because dead, set in stone. If the project of the *salauds* is to convert themselves into fascinating statues within their lifetime, on his death Impétraz has simply achieved his apotheosis. He continues to live, to exude a fascination (or a repulsion) as he did in his lifetime. A giant in his life, he remains a giant in death. He casts a spell over all who survey him. This is Roquentin's intuition as he contemplates this colossus with a mixture of horror and awe (*OR* 36). This spell seems to be woven primarily around women. He is the God who sanctifies the prejudices of these women, the giver of the laws they so gratefully receive (cf. *OR* 36). But far from being bewitched by the statue's spell, Roquentin is repulsed by it: 'Une sourde puissance émanait de lui: c'est comme un vent qui me repousse: Impétraz voudrait me chasser de la cour des Hypothèques' (*OR* 37). Even in death Impétraz is anything but impotent. The courtyard is his personal seraglio where his female admirers come to pay homage to his phallic presence, and where Roquentin is an interloper. It is important to note the sexual element, which is never absent from the representation of this figure. The underlying sexual content is here condensed into the smoking of a pipe.[15] Roquentin is struggling to keep his pipe alight in the face of the wind which, he feels, emanates from Impétraz. His desire to face up to this colossal presence is justified by the desire to keep the pipe burning and to smoke it to the end. The admixture of awe and horror inspired in Roquentin by these *gens de bien*, of whom Impétraz is the incarnation – or rather the 'bronzification' – was even more apparent in many passages cut from the typescript before publication (see *OR* 1755–6).[16] The dominant impression is one of ambivalence: fear and loathing tempered by awe, and held at bay by a rather desperate defiance.

The set-piece of the visit to the museum art gallery reproduces this confrontation. Here again the *salauds* are outside of the limp flux of contingent reality and hardened in the Imaginary: the statue had the actual hardness of bronze, the portrait the aesthetic hardness of the work of art where nothing is superfluous or contingent. Once again Roquentin feels threatened and harassed, but this time he will exact his revenge and depart triumphant. He comments on the portrait of Blévigne that all that would be passed down to posterity would be 'une face menaçante . . . un geste superbe et des yeux sanglants de taureau' (*OR* 111). The favoured terms of representation are socio-ontological. The canvas immortality of these *salauds* is simply the logical extension of their 'necessary' existence, justified by and founded upon the concept of rights: 'Car ils avaient eu droit à tout: à la vie, au travail, à la richesse, au commandement, au respect, et, pour finir, à l'immortalité' (*OR* 99). Whilst Roquentin is experiencing the limp, formless flux of existence, they have spent their lives denying this truth by conferring upon themselves the perfect hardness of a mathematical concept. Parrotin, for example, had the simplicity of an idea: all that remained in him was bones, dead flesh and pure right (*OR* 106)!

The *salauds* in Sartre's work are given a body to match their existential pretensions: if they aspire to the solidity of oak, then they mysteriously acquire a physique which reflects and emphasises their pretensions. Pacôme has small feet and delicate hands, but 'de larges épaules de lutteur' (*OR* 101). His eyes, like those of a statue, are unsmiling.[17] Rogé has the stature of an epic hero 'des bras comme des cuisses, cent-dix de tour de poitrine' (*OR* 80). His power, too, resides in his 'gros yeux noirs et impérieux' (ibid.). This *Impé-* prefix often occurs in connection with the *salauds*; the connotations of imperiousness and domination are clear enough.

If the *salauds* appear solid, dense and impenetrable, this is doubtless a function of the narrative perspective. By contrast, the chosen narrator invariably suffers from the unbearable lightness of being. He is the outcast from the clan, the son driven away from the primal horde by the jealous father, and returning to exact revenge, armed not with a cudgel and staff and in the company of his brothers, but quite alone and equipped only with his intellect and a pen. The ambivalence surrounding these granitic figures derives from this fact of perspective. The fact that the *salauds* may appear to be both laughable and awesome arises from the oscillation of narrator: now attracted, now revolted. The *salaud's* self-sufficiency is at one and the same time envied and denigrated as a lie – there exists a constant temptation to *identify* with this figure.

The episode in the art gallery has a distinctly Oedipal flavour to it. A confrontation is being staged between the father and his less-than-welcome errant son – a son who will not return to the fold. Indeed, Roquentin projects this sinister desire to recuperate onto the face of Parrotin, which is, in itself, devoid of any such significance (*OR* 105). The context of this confrontation is provided by the comminatory presence of the 'Mort du célibataire' at the entrance to the gallery.[18] The conflict unfolds at the level of paternity: the one thing that all these good folk have in common is that they were Genitors: none had died unmarried, without issue, without succession (*OR* 99). It is as though the watching eyes ('je sentais *sur moi* le regard de cent cinquante paires d'yeux' – *OR* 99; emphasis added) really were the *sur-moi*: Roquentin's superego condemning him for some transgression of the Law of the Father.

Not all of the *salauds* in *La Nausée* are beings of canvas, bronze or marble. Docteur Rogé is a real and noisy presence as he crashes into Chez Camille. Whatever private anguish or solitude had been gnawing at Monsieur Achille is abruptly swept aside: his individuality is recuperated by Rogé's summary classification 'un vieux toqué'. The good doctor is a professional of experience. He is one of those – like Achille-Cléophas in *L'Idiot de la famille* – who know man as if they had made him themselves (*OR* 82); the Imaginary father endowed by the child with superhuman powers. The reason for accepting the judgement of the Genitor is the warm glow of justification – one is presented with an immutable essence. The punishment for rejecting it by asserting one's own singular desires is to be cast out like a wayward son: 'leurs meilleures histoires sont celles d'imprudents, d'originaux qui ont été châtiés' (*OR* 84).[19] Again, Roquentin's attitude towards Rogé is strangely ambivalent. Initially he is relieved by this massive presence, willing to accept his deliverance. But soon resentment and anger take over, working a transformation in the appearance of this colossus.

The schema presiding over the representation of the Genitor now has most of its principal elements: massivity, solidity, power over women, a simultaneous threat and temptation to the young male character normally responsible for the narration. It is perhaps unnecessary to accumulate further detail in this respect. However, a brief examination of some other Sartrean works will serve to illustrate the deep permanency of this figure in Sartre's literary corpus.

Both Darbédat in 'La Chambre', and Jacques in *Les Chemins* share the physical well-being characteristic of the *salauds* – they are literally 'bien dans leur peau'. 'Quelle vitalité!' thinks Darbédat's wife, disparagingly, as he bursts Rogé-like into her room. His strength appears to increase as he bounds up the stairs on the way to his Thursday meetings with his poor son-in-law. His physical well-being and sexual attractiveness seem to go hand in hand (see for example Mademoiselle Dormoy's comment, *OR* 240). As with the bourgeois of Bouville, the exterior is hard and the interior is profound silence (*OR* 249). Jacques, too, is 'insolent de santé', and 'très droit, un peu raide' (*OR* 500). These qualifications not only suggest propriety, moral rectitude, physical strength, but also participate in that group of images through which dumb *being* is regarded as a permanent erection, and existence something approaching a global detumescence: a cubist canvas set next to Dali's melting watches. Like a latter-day Impétraz, Jacques too poses as the fount of all wisdom, the guardian of the holy scrolls. To his wife, he is 'La Science, l'Industrie et la Morale' (*OR* 1312).

Philippe's stepfather must surely be the arch representative of the Genitor in Sartre's work. He is the very incarnation of aggressive masculinity: 'il baise, tue, prie et ne pense pas' (*OR* 1271). His imagined sexual prowess is a particular source of resentment to Philippe: 'les femmes l'adorent parce qu'il sent le bouc' (*OR* 1271). One of the models for the relationship between Philippe and the General is that between Baudelaire and his stepfather, General Aupick. Given the projective, or empathetic, procedure that Sartre adopts in *Baudelaire*, Aupick could be seen to be as much or as little – of a fictional creation as Impétraz or Monsieur Fleurier. The nature of Sartre's enterprise in *Baudelaire* means that some of the *explicit* distance that separates the novelist from his characters is eroded in the biographical work. Sartre imagines that Baudelaire entertained profoundly ambivalent attitude towards his stepfather. He at once despises Aupick and admires him; he rejects bourgeois morality yet subjugates himself to it: 'Dans la mesure, en effet, où il s'est délibérément *soumis* à la Règle divine, paternelle et sociale, le Bien l'*enserre* et l'*écrase*' (*Baud* 121; emphasis added). Significant terminology. Aupick is the incarnation of this societal *Bien*, and Sartre visualises Baudelaire's conformism as the *sexual* submission to a crushing male presence: he is possessed by this severe Genitor. This is the starting-point of another thread of textual analysis: the Genitor as pederastic father. To follow this thread will lead to an analysis of the complex and pervasive equation that Sartre establishes in *Saint Genet*, between the *justes* and the male homosexual. This thread will also lead to the surgical, gimlet gaze of Achille-Cléophas in *L'Idiot de la famille*. But this exploration will have to wait until Chapter 5.

To submit, for Baudelaire, consists in denuding himself before the severe gaze of the General (*Baud* 77). It seems that in Sartre's work this severity is particularly apt to find itself cast into the shape of a general, or a *chef*, or – a father: one is reminded of the 150 pairs of eyes gazing down disapprovingly on Roquentin from the wall of the art gallery. A typical ambivalence underlies this image: the child feels both guilty and afraid under the gaze of the father, but at least he feels *something*.

This talk of Genitors in connection with stepfathers could appear out of place. The stepfather is, after all, a stand-in, a substitute. But I would maintain that the stepfather is uniquely capable of bringing about a resurrection of Oedipal resentment and ambivalence. When the stepfather arrives late on the scene – as was the case with Aupick, and indeed Mancy – his position as usurper is foregrounded dramatically. Now, the feeling that the father is the usurper of the child's exclusive attachment to the mother is present in the normal Oedipal triangle, but it is naturalised there by the social sanctity of the conjugal bed. 'Father' is, after all, a position, and one which will be occupied sooner or later whether the natural father is present or absent.[20]

Sartre's theatre also has its share of *salauds*. Not all occupy centre stage like the awesome Père of *Les Séquestrés*. In *Les Mains sales*, they are present as shadowy figures in Hugo's bourgeois background. Hugo's father never appears, but he is ever-present as a negative principle: the arrival of Karsky is akin to an abrupt return of the repressed, so extreme is Hugo's reaction. Although Hugo revolts against his father's legacy, it is this very legacy that ensures that Hugo will not pass from revolt to revolution. At other times the *salauds* appear as almost humorous stereotypes: the Good Ol' Boy white supremacists of *La Putain respectueuse*, for example.

The bourgeois *salauds* of *Les Mouches* have a firm grip on the bodies and souls of the Argives – Egisthe is a very bourgeois king, and Jupiter a very bourgeois king of the gods. Egisthe is basically no different to the exalted inhabitants of Bouville's Coteau Vert. Just as the *chef* preserves the social hierarchy by fooling those below him into believing that he is the source of all wisdom and the guarantor of all security, so Egisthe plays the figurehead of order. The guardians of Order in Bouville are merely the descendants of forefathers who have now been deified: the statue of Impétraz has the status of idol, and the portraits in the gallery fill the Sunday visitors with religious awe. Egisthe, too, does the bidding of a *deus absconditus* who has left only his statue for worship. He transforms himself into a concrete superego: he wishes every one of his subjects to feel 'jusque dans la solitude, mon regard sévère peser sur ses pensées le plus secrètes' (*Mou* 199). He seems to be aiming for that impossible synthesis: to be a fascinating object which is its own foundation, or God. In this context, Jupiter is the archetypal *salaud*, the original Genitor who has spawned countless generations of paternal tyrants through his example.

The symbol of the statue alerts us to another of Jupiter's descendants, to be found somewhat closer to home – in the Schweitzer household itself. In *Les Mots*, Sartre's brilliant and devious rewriting of his childhood, Poulou is born into a cycle of paternal 'saloperie'. He was spared the rod of his own genitor – who had the courtesy to opt for early retirement – but had ample opportunity to witness the conduct of the arch-*salaud* himself, Karl Schweitzer. The latter seems to have furnished Sartre with such a stock of character traits, idiosyncrasies, anecdotes, and so on, that one suspects he may lie behind every *salaud* to issue forth from Sartre's pen.[21] To mask his own contingency and approaching death, Charles surrounds himself with an aura of necessity (*Mots* 80). To predicate oneself with necessity is to attempt the metamorphosis into a living work of art. Like all the *salauds*, Charles tries to petrify himself, to turn himself into his own statue: 'il raffolait de ces courts instants d'éternité où il devenait sa propre statue' (*Mots* 23). God is the perfect example of a self-sufficient object of which he is the continuing foundation. And Karl does not stop short of attempting to deify himself; he bore such a close resemblance to God the Father, writes Sartre, that he was often mistaken for him (*Mots* 21). The flowing white beard, the buffoonery, the likeness to a statue – all of these cannot fail to recall the Jupiter of *Les Mouches*. Like the *salauds* of *La Nausée* who explain the new by the old and the old by the older still, Charles lives in an external repetition of the same: he no longer goes to concerts; he stopped reading new material when Victor Hugo died, and now simply rereads. The impressionable Poulou is in danger of falling victim to a kind of creeping atavism, as an old man, frozen into the bourgeois ideology of the mid-nineteenth century, attempts to impose his ideas on him (*Mots* 56). But this threat of an atavistic recuperation is only the dark side of a temptation, for another *salaud*, Monsieur Simonnot, is clearly the object of Poulou's envy. He has the slow deliberation of an ancient statue creaking into unexpected motion: 'il . . . dirigeait son regard intérieur sur le *massif granitique* de ses goûts. Quand il avait obtenu le renseignement demandé, il le communiquait à ma mère, d'une voix *objective*' (*Mots* 78; emphasis added). Suffering from the intuition of his own contingency, Poulou is intensely envious of this rock: 'Ma jalousie ne connut plus de bornes le jour où l'on m'apprit que Monsieur Simonnot, *cette statue*, ce *bloc monolithique*, était par-dessus le marché indispensable à l'univers' (*Mots* 79; emphasis added). We return, once more, to the prime signifier – the statue–phallus.

I began this section by placing the Genitor at the head of the series of *salauds*, *chefs*, *justes*, and so on, as the figure who ultimately subsumes all the O/others. It is therefore appropriate to conclude with *Les Séquestrés d'Altona* and the archly named Père. This nomination turns a father into The Father, every father there ever has been or ever will be. His attributes are, by now, all too predictable: the power over women, the cynical manipulation of what he knows to be a role in order to maintain his power. His instructions to Werner on how to become a leader echo those of Monsieur Fleurier to his son: in order to command, simply take yourself for someone else (*Séq* 30). Just as Mathieu, Roquentin, Oreste and Philippe, to name but four, play out a constant confrontation with the world of bourgeois morality,[22] so the characters in *Les Séquestrés* come up against the pervasive influence of the Father at every turn of the plot. What has previously been a symbolic problematic is now given dramatic consistency; whereas Roquentin was free to storm out of the gallery, Mathieu free to reject both paternity and Jacques's brand of morality and die – he supposed – in freedom, Frantz remains a function of the paternal will; even his death has been foreseen. Previously the young central 'hero' was able to escape the clutches of the paternal vampire through his lucidity and his violence, but here even that lucidity, even that violence, have *already* been recuperated.

FROM THEMATIC TO PHANTASMATIC

Le Dur est creux.

It would be useful briefly to take stock at this point. It could be objected that the foregoing analysis amounts to little more than a fairly stable thematic taxonomy. After all, the figures of woman as virgin and whore, the sacred and the profane, are hardly unique to Sartre's fiction; they are to be found in the literature and myth of all ages and all cultures.[23] Are not Sartre's stereotypical representations of the *bourgeois salaud* simply the stock-in-trade of the fictionalist? As long as we remain at the level of a thematic, these objections are, at least in part, justified. But this apparently stable thematic is only a first stage of analysis. Laplanche and Pontalis write *à propos* of the phantasmatic in psychoanalysis, 'This should not be conceived of merely as a thematic – not even as one characterised by distinctly specific traits for each subject – for it has its own dynamic, in that the phantasy structures seek to express themselves, to find a way out into consciousness and action, and they are constantly drawing in new material.'[24] To posit the existence of a phantasmatic level of organisation in a body of work such as Sartre's is to work on the assumption that the phantasy level and the work's surface thematic are almost seamlessly imbricated. The *reconstruction* of this phantasmatic involves the tracing of a movement. Working at the level of representation, this requires a *parti pris* of suspicion with regard to seemingly stable surface structures such as those suggested by the term 'stereotype'.

In this final section, then, I shall be examining the dynamic of these typically Sartrean representational patterns, in particular the moments in which the mirage melts into mire, and the statue – the cipher–signature of the Genitor – turns out to be a hollow man, a stuffed man.[25]

If the imaginary is the favoured domain of the *femme-mirage*, her transformation is marked by a plunge into reality. There are, for example, two Annys in *La Nausée*: the romanesque Anny of Roquentin's previous acquaintance, who was capable of de-realising her room, herself and Roquentin through a kind of magical incantation, and the Anny that Roquentin goes to meet in her hotel room in Paris. This Anny is now 'grasse' with a 'forte poitrine' (*OR* 161). One could object that this is simply a realistic effect of the ageing process, and, in a sense, this is correct. But one has to grasp what 'ageing' can signify for Sartre. Anny has ceased to 'temporalise' herself; she is turned back towards her past and away from the future. It is as if the physical degeneration were the cipher for an attitude of *laisser-aller*. Once the virile tension is slackened, Nature floods back over her in the way that weeds invade an abandoned garden.

An analogous process affects Marcelle, but this time it is recounted in the opposite direction. Marcelle was not always the rather flabby, slightly sinister reclusive of the narrative's present. At one point, Mathieu contemplates a photograph of her and sees a slip of a girl, dressed in mannish attire (*OR* 396). Turning away from the photograph, he sees the Marcelle with the flabby thighs and heavy breasts; the contrast could not be more explicit. But the contrast is not simply between a young woman and a woman past her prime: it is almost as if the gender-markers had changed. Marcelle in the photograph has a man's hairstyle, a man's jacket, a man's flat-heeled shoes; she is hard and slim: the aesthetic trick of the photograph has cleansed her of her too-heavy femininity. The contrast is pressed home further when Marcelle remarks ruefully, 'C'est marrant.' It is as if she no longer had the moral right to say this; in the photograph 'elle aussi devrait dire: "C'est marrant"', avec la même désinvolture gauche, la même audace sans aplomb. *Seulement, elle était jeune et maigre*' (*OR* 396; emphasis added). This contrastive phrase structure is reminiscent of the passage where we saw Marcelle talking like a man but smelling like a woman.

This quasi-moral fall from one representational schema into another is something that has already occurred before the commencement of the narrative, as it were: Marcelle is already a swamp, and her fall is conveyed retrospectively. But the fall continues and deepens. Significantly enough, it is with pregnancy that Marcelle puts herself beyond salvage. She may be flabby, she may be confined to the dimensions of her body through her mysterious illness, but with pregnancy this body falls totally into Nature. She slows down like a liquid turning viscous: 'ses gestes avaient perdu leur raideur aggressive, ils s'étaient empâtés et alanguis' (*OR* 772). Abruptly, it is images of the natural world that serve to define her: her breasts have begun to sag, tiny droplets appear around the nipples, droplets that are 'blanches et salées comme des fleurs' (*OR* 442).

I have already emphasised the antithesis between Marcelle and Ivich, the swamp and the ice-maiden, the cloying reality and the untouchable art object. But Ivich, too, falls as a result of a kind of narrative revenge. Interestingly enough, it is pregnancy again that occasions this fall. In a fit of panic and resentment, she gives herself to a fellow student and is, statistically, very unfortunate: she conceives. This pregnancy and its premature termination are not, however, narrated: they occur in the interstices between volumes 2 and 3 of *Les Chemins*. The first we hear of it is through Boris's reflections on her miscarriage: 'par le fait, Ivich avait beaucoup vieilli et enlaidi depuis sa fausse couche' (*OR* 1188). Gone are the unreality, the beauty and the youthfulness that are the hallmarks of the ice-maiden. This character who had been previously devoid of odour has been mysteriously recuperated by her body; now she is surrounded by an odour of fever and *eau de toilette* (*OR* 1189). She feels betrayed by this body, which had acted without her consent, and is now ashamed of it, adopting high necklines and low hems. It is true that she does not have the complicity towards her fate that Marcelle shows – even the miscarriage could symbolise a rejection of her assigned place in the reproductive cycle. Nevertheless, the condemnation remains: she is transformed in and through the narrative itself despite her angry refusal of this change.

There is one further aspect of Ivich's transformation: if her miscarriage enables her to escape the clutches of the patriarchal order in the short term, she is none the less felt, by Boris, to have been recuperated by this order. She has joined the ranks of the Father's handmaidens; she is a married woman, reflects Boris, with in-laws, a family car and a hubby at the front (*OR* 1194). This observation is, perhaps, simply a reflection of Boris's predilection for rather naïve social categorisations. But, at the same time, it touches a very deep obsession in Sartre's work. The quasi-incestuous intimacy of Boris's relationship with Ivich has been shattered by her treachery: she has gone over to the other side, to the camp of the father. It is precisely at this point that Ivich becomes a swamp, attempting to hold back the young male. Boris is striving to be free through action, but Ivich suddenly represents a force that would hold him back, drag him down, suck him in. It would be no exaggeration to say that this attempt to curtail the explosive pro-jection of a virile consciousness is sensed as being tantamount to a castration.[26]

The suddenly revealed viscosity of the female character is so often the corollary of the male characters' suspicion that she wishes, secretly, to hold him back. Most typically, Estelle becomes 'octopus', 'swamp' precisely when Garcin perceives her sinister intentions. Less obviously, Brunet senses the hidden viscosity of Zézette, as he imagines her draping herself around Maurice's neck to prevent him from going off to war (*OR* 747). Eve, in *Les Jeux sont faits*, is never more insidious than in the instant when she tries to make time stand still for her and Pierre – to keep him from his virile duty. The same functional role is played by the postmistress in *La Mort dans l'âme* with regard to the soldierly Pinette. As she clings round his neck he exclaims, 'tu me casses les couilles!' (*OR* 1295). 'Casses' or 'coupes', one wonders.[27]

There is one further common denominator in these metamorphoses, and probably the most telling: when the ice-maiden melts, she melts into mother. The parallel between Ivich and Electre is most striking in this respect. The final act in Ivich's transformation is Boris's horrified realisation, 'A présent, ses yeux restaient mornes . . . dans ces moments-là, elle ressemblait à leur mère' (*OR* 1194). This process in *Les Mouches* is given explicitly as a recuperation by the patriarchal order. Jupiter gives voice to the silent admonishment that Roquentin reads on the faces of the portraits in the art gallery: 'Rentre dans la Nature, fils dénaturé!' Like Roquentin, Oreste refuses, but Electre submits. The symbol of her treachery is the donning of the soiled robes of her dead mother. This ending has already been prepared, like a fatality: early in the play Clytemnestre remarks to Electre that, although the latter may hate her, she nevertheless resembles her (*Mou* 135). It comes as no surprise, then, that, when Electre returns to the paternal fold, Oreste should note, 'tu es encore belle, mais . . . où donc ai-je vu ces yeux morts? Electre . . . tu lui ressembles; tu ressembles à Clytemnestre. Etait-ce la peine de la tuer?' (*Mou* 218). Poor Electre has joined the blue-rinse set.

Quite specifically, both Ivich and Electre are suddenly perceived to be the father's property. Clytemnestre herself was not an autonomous figure – she had simply been the mouthpiece, the transmitter of the Law of the Father (*Mou* 135).

It is at this point that a curious but persistent network of images forces itself on our attention; a web that extends from Sartre's first published novel to his last (*L'Idiot de la famille*!). We have seen that Ivich and Electre both inherit the dead eyes of their mother. Precisely the same image occurs in *L'Age de raison*: as Mathieu gazes on Odette, he realises that she is Jacques's thing; when Jacques is there Odette's face is impassive, indefinable, 'comme celui d'une statue aux yeux sans prunelle' (*OR* 828). When Johanna, in *Les Séquestrés d'Altona*, agrees to do the Father's bidding, Werner asks, 'où est ton regard? Tu as des yeux de statue: blancs' (*Séq* 96). All of these images lead back to the courtyard of the library in *La Nausée* and the imposing phallic presence of Impétraz. But they also look forward – at least in terms of the composition of the Sartrean *oeuvre* – to *Les Mots*; not only to the statuesque grandfather Karl and the monolithic Simonnot, but also to the anxiogenic figure of the phallic mother: the 'jeune géante' who tends Poulou, and the petrifying Vénus d'Ille who so impressed the young child (see *Mots* 82–3).[28]

But I am, perhaps, guilty of pre-empting my own conclusions. Before continuing it would be wise to recapitulate. The transformation from *femme-mirage* to *femme-marécage* shifts what could be seen as a banal thematics onto the plain of a not-so-obvious phantasmatic. This metamorphosis could be expressed in terms of any number of binary oppositions, many of which figure in Sartre's own theoretical discourse: hard to soft, discontinuous to continuous, clear to clouded, and so on. But perhaps the best image to capture the abrupt and startling revelation of viscosity attendant upon these transformations is that of Oedipus waking up in horror to the realisation that his bedfellow of many a year was his mother. It is the moment when the axe falls on desire, abolishing the object and clogging the drive. It is the moment of a split in the maternal imago, a split which throws desire back onto an aporia: 'where they love they may not desire, where they desire they cannot love'. Furthermore, since the figure of the Father is clearly related in some way – through the statue images – to this transformation, it is perhaps not too premature to speculate that we are dealing with the intrusion of castration anxiety into the dialectic of desire. The metamorphosis of the Genitor should cast some light on this shadowy nucleus.

The portrait-gallery episode in *La Nausée* could be seen as a 'return leg' of a tie whose first leg had seen Roquentin defeated and driven out by Impétraz. The bourgeois of the gallery are endowed with the same mysterious sexual power as the phallic giant: Blévigne does not merely stand out from the canvas in a lifelike fashion; he *is* the phallus himself, as the imagery makes clear: 'il était raide comme une trique et jaillissait de la toile comme un diable de sa boîte' (*OR* 110). In the face of this gigantic erection Roquentin might well feel flaccid, but this time round he is armed with knowledge and lucidity. The portrait was a *trompe l'oeil* and Blévigne was a virtual midget: the phallus turns out to be a rather pitiful prosthesis. If this cutting-down-to-size of Blévigne reads like a symbolic castration, this impression can only be confirmed by the nature of the fore-pleasure Roquentin experiences as he prepares to wield the knife: 'une douce *jouissance* m'envahit' (*OR* 108; emphasis added). This castration motif is continued in the language used to describe the death of Blévigne's son: 'une rose coupée, un polytechnicien mort' (*OR* 112). The mythical fertility and sexual potency of the Genitor[29] is thus effectively neutralised. Blévigne's potent seed turns out to be blighted, and instead of a mighty oak a fragile flower emerges. For the revenge to be complete, the power over women which is one of the constants of the representation of the Genitor is nullified: Blévigne's wife was a domineering giant. Rogé, the colossus who 'saves' Roquentin and Monsieur Achille, is not allowed to retain his statuesque solidity either. As Roquentin contemplates the doctor, the veneer of immortality melts and the truth is revealed to Roquentin's joyful gaze: Rogé is a dying man (*OR* 84).

My metaphor of the melting varnish was suggested by a parallel incident, again in *La Nausée*. Roquentin succeeds by force of will in annihilating the terrible gaze of Rémy Parrotin so that only a 'résidu cendreux' remains. I shall quote the passage at length, since the images it employs will later (in Chapter 5) take on considerable importance:

> Parrotin offrait une belle résistance. Mais tout d'un coup *son regard s'éteignit*, le tableau devint terne. Que restait-il? *Des yeux aveugles*, la bouche mince comme un serpent mort et des joues. . . . Les employés de la S.A.B. ne les avaient jamais soupçonnées. . . . Quand ils entraient, ils rencontraient *ce terrible regard*, comme un mur. Par-derrière, les joues étaient à l'abri, blanches et molles. (*OR* 106; emphasis added)

One day as Parrotin lay gently slumbering, a moonbeam caressing his nose, Madame Parrotin, Roquentin imagines, had dared to look him in the face: 'toute cette chair était apparue sans défense, bouffie, baveuse, vaguement obscène' (*OR* 106-7). From that day, Madame Parrotin had taken over the reins of command. This passage has a rich variety of subtexts. One could note in passing the thematic similarity with the Blévigne episode. In both cases, Roquentin phantasises that the wife comes to 'wear the trousers'. Related to this, however, is the theme of the look. It is the 'terrible regard' of the Genitor that paralyses the *célibataire* – simultaneously demanding that he return to the paternal fold, and laying down the limits of his desire. The transgression of these limits will entail the threat of castration. But, if the look of the Genitor can be the agent of castration, the meaning of Roquentin's 'lucidity', *his* destructive gaze, must be the resentful reversal of this paternal malediction. In other words, the Genitor is deflated, symbolically, by the sharpness of the son's gaze. Although these may be elements of the phantasmatic architexture of Sartre's literary edifice, they are not for all that the *explicit* reference points of this passage. The revelation of contingent flesh that Madame Parrotin has when her husband's gaze goes out can be related easily to certain analyses of *L'Etre et le néant*. Obscenity is the revelation of the 'pure contingency of presence' embodied by *flesh*. The eyes mobilise a face, bringing it to life and masking this pure contingency of presence. This is why Parrotin's employees do not register his swollen, fleshy cheeks. When the eyes are turned off, the face is recuperated by Nature, returned to its primary obscenity.

This image of rampant Nature also finds a place in *La Nausée*, and it is again associated with the vengeance that Roquentin would call down upon the heads of the founding fathers. What would they do, these bourgeois who make money, make laws, make marriages, and have the immense stupidity to make children? What will they do when Nature invades their 'belle cité bourgeoise', when inanimate becomes animate, and the animate is frozen to stone; when they wake up on a blue earth in a forest of rustling penises as high as factory chimneys? This apocalypse is not simply a vision; it is a wish fulfilment: 'Eh bien oui! Que cela change un peu, pour voir, je ne demande pas mieux' (*OR* 188).

But a few years later this apocalypse does take place. It is called the Second World War. It is witnessed with approval and anguish, by Daniel and Mathieu respectively, in *La Mort dans l'âme*. The way in which this historical *débâcle* is narrated is, amongst other things, a further chapter in the debunking of the Genitor. Indeed, the whole of this third volume of the intended tetralogy is like a systematic deflation of the father's authority. The virility of the Husband and Father, the inflexible Law of the bourgeoisie, are all torn down and supplanted by a violent machistic sexuality. In place of the chain of procreation, and re-creation of the father, we find the sadistic phantasy of ejaculation at a safe distance: the rifle which spits bullets like a penis ejecting sperm. Mathieu chooses to be an assassin rather than son of his father; it is an 'énorme revanche' (*OR* 1344). Doubtless Mathieu would have preferred to have at the end of his sights a nice fat family man such as the one Hilbert guns down in 'Erostrate', or Philippe's stepfather, the General; or perhaps Jacques. He has to make do with the German soldiers, but that is not what he *sees*: 'il tirait sur l'Homme, sur la Vertu, sur le Monde: la Liberté, c'est la Terreur' (*OR* 1344) – the time-honoured values of Parrotin and Blévigne. The specific targets are even more revealing: one shot for not having robbed Lola (disregard for property and ownership); one shot for not having ditched Marcelle outright (blunt refusal of paternity); one shot for not having slept with Odette (transgression of the incest taboo).

But there is a further complicating factor in all of this which makes it more than a simple 'Oedipal' murder. Mathieu's *'énorme revanche'* is not just against a Moses-like figure of paternal severity: he is revenging himself also out of resentment. The father has not been Father enough. The whole episode of the belltower is set up and prefaced by a significant desertion – the desertion of the officers: ' "Que c'est vide!" pensa Mathieu. Quelqu'un d'*immense* avait brusquement décampé, laissant la Nature à la garde des soldats de deuxième classe' (*OR* 1281; emphasis added). When 'Quelqu'un d'immense' takes his leave, an 'énorme revanche' is clearly called for!

The Nietzschean *Gotterdämmerung* aside, this structure of desertion by the father, followed by his retroactive destruction, has an exact parallel in *Les Mouches*. Before reducing Jupiter to impotence, Oreste too experiences the death of Pan, except here Pan wears a Schweitzeresque beard and does conjuring tricks: 'Hier encore . . . tu étais mon excuse d'exister et le monde était une vieille entremetteuse qui me parlait de toi sans cesse. *Et puis tu m'as abandonné*' (*Mou* 233; emphasis added).[30] The bare bones of the parallel are these: a figure representing an originary Genitor first abandons, and is then symbolically destroyed by, a young male who is always portrayed as *already* marginal to the society presided over by this patriarch.[31]

Many readers have seen the belltower episode as a kind of apotheosis, the triumphal end of Mathieu's road to freedom. But, despite the impression of liberation through violence, I would contend that the liberation is factitious. I shall show later that Mathieu does not liquidate the father: *he ingests him*, and the father lives on inside him, possessing him from the inside out. The most revealing intertext to this whole episode is doubtless *Saint Genet*. It is in that work that we are able to witness both the mechanism of the transformation of the Genitor (the revelation that 'le Dur est creux'), and the accompanying phantasy of the pederastic father, which functions at once as an element in, and a negation of, this phantasied metamorphosis. But the appropriate place for that investigation will come in Chapter 5. I shall conclude the present chapter with a brief examination of two other Sartrean biographies: *Baudelaire* and *L'Idiot de la famille*.

In his study of Sartre's existential biographies, Michael Scriven notes that during the late 1950s and early 1960s the father-figure assumes an explicit and powerful significance in Sartre's thinking: 'It is through the father figure that the contradictions of an entire class are mediated in the context of family relations.'[32] The insight is similar to that of Michel Contat in his *Explication des Séquestrés d'Altona*, where he states that 'le Père représente le monde en tant que celui-ci est traumatisant pour l'individu parce qu'il le confronte à la nécessité qui nie la liberté'.[33] But what neither Contat nor Scriven points out is the extent of the *implicit* significance of this figure in Sartre's work well before the late 1950s. It is true that the father-figure became increasingly foregrounded as time wore on, but it remains to be seen just how thoroughgoing Sartre's *prise de conscience* regarding the unconscious ramifications of this figure in his own works really was.

It has become something of a truism to say that Sartre's biographies tell us more about the biographer than about his subjects.[34] But, given the method Sartre adopts, this should not really have surprised anyone. The biographies are all explicitly presented as *fabulations* around their supposed subjects, exploiting a highly empathetic, even projective, procedure. In this sense, they are not so much classical artist-biographies as investigations of the limits of epistemology itself. Sartre is concerned with the displacement of (analytical) *explication* in favour of a dialectical model of *compréhension*, in which the boundaries between subject (biographer) and object (artist) are necessarily blurred. *Baudelaire* is an early and fairly naïve attempt, but *L'Idiot de la famille* represents a very sophisticated – if at times mind-buckling – achievement. In any case, the proximity of the biographer to his nominal object is far greater than that between the novelist and his fictional creatures.

In both *Baudelaire* and *L'Idiot* – as indeed in *Les Mots* – Sartre presents us with a childhood of the artist in which a central position is occupied by the family constellation. If this *parti pris* appears to have Freudian inspiration, then that appearance is partly deceptive: Sartre is choosing to take on Freud and the post-Freudians on their home territory.[35] I shall provide the merest skeleton of Sartre's analysis. In *Baudelaire*, we are presented with the picture of a mother–infant dyad, an Eden of organic unity: 'il se sentait uni au corps et au coeur de sa mère par une sorte de participation primitive et mystique; *il se perdait* dans la douce tiédeur de leur amour réciproque' (*Baud* 18; emphasis added). This is an ambiguous Eden. Total security, but a security paid for at the price of suffocation: the child, literally, lost *himself* in this harmonious dyad. Moreover, one should not be taken in by this pleasant-sounding 'douce tiédeur': it is rather too close for comfort to a whole array of similar Sartrean formulations that conjure up, quite unambiguously, an explicit anti-value. One thinks, for example, of the 'moite intimité gastrique' in Sartre's paper on Husserl ('Une idée fondamentale de Husserl: l'intentionnalité', *Sit* I 39–40) or of the images of viscosity discussed in Chapter 1.

Baudelaire's body is not his own: it is an organic extension of his mother's. He is 'lavé, habillé, par de fortes et belles mains'. Here the ambivalence is further driven home: when the child finally takes cognisance of his body, he wakes up to find that he is a doll! The term *manié* – reserved in Sartre for the mother's treatment of the infant – is a very highly charged word. Its meaning lies somewhere between 'handled' and 'manhandled', and it is the term which epitomises the crippling attentions of Madame Flaubert towards young Gustave. Whereas this handling is still, at least apparently, pleasant in *Baudelaire*, it takes on sinister overtones in *L'Idiot*.

In point of fact, Sartre seems to arrive at this version of the mother–infant dyad through a dialectical admixture of inductive and deductive reasoning. He posits the cold efficiency of Caroline towards Gustave on the basis of her probable attitude, derived in turn from an 'objective' analysis of her own relationship with her father and of the socio-economic situation of the Flaubert family unit. He also deduces this attitude from the evidence of Flaubert's own writings and whatever contemporary testimonies he can locate. In any case, what emerges, both with Charles and with Gustave, is that the infant is *feminised* at a crucial stage: either by contagion (the 'participation primitive et mystique') or by objectification ('maniement'). Hence the ambiguity of these Edenic beginnings.

But Baudelaire the infant could hardly be conscious of this fate, since it was being inscribed into his very body. Knowledge only arises, in Sartre's version, with the intercession of General Aupick. The child is savagely separated from the mother and he reacts with resentment. He revindicates the separate existence to which he has been condemned, against his mother and Aupick: 'Si vous vouliez plus tard *m'attirer à vous et m'absorber de nouveau*, cela ne serait plus possible' (*Baud* 24; emphasis added). At this stage the die has been cast and Baudelaire's choice has been made. The consequences that Sartre draws from this choice, with regard to the poet's sex life and his attitudes towards qualities of the world, are strangely familiar – at least to readers of Chapter 1.

First, Baudelaire's feminisation against his mother's body, and at the mother's hands, is now experienced as a quality of his own body: 'cette énorme fécondité molle, [Baudelaire] a surtout horreur de la sentir en soi-même' (*Baud* 137). His reaction to this recuperation by nature is the cult of the dandy, the predilection for synthetic beauty and sterility: 'Le blanc est la couleur du froid, non pas seulement parce que la neige est blanche mais surtout parce que cette absence de couleur manifeste assez bien *l'infécondité et la virginité*' (*Baud* 148; emphasis added). Here again is the characteristic split between fecund and sterile, debased and virginal: the *femme-marécage* and the *femme-mirage*. This passage reads like a commentary on Sartre's own representational schemas, but it also suggest a rationale for their transformations: Baudelaire's ambivalence is translated by an oscillation between a nostalgia for the original dyadic intimacy and a dread of engulfment by this 'énorme fécondité molle'. Moreover, the image of the *femme-mirage* can be seen to function as a defence mechanism: it is the negation of the mother-as-fecund, that is to say as object of Another's desire.

This ambivalence is also characteristic of Baudelaire's attitude towards the father-figure. He alternately rejects the authority of

Aupick, belitting him, and craves his severity. It is as if he could find no median order between two conflicting imagos of the father, and that the predominance of one immediately triggered its replacement by the other.

The issue is further complicated by Sartre's suggestion that Baudelaire carries within his own body not only the mother, but also the father. He writes that what Baudelaire detests in paternity is 'cette continuité de vie entre le géniteur et les descendants qui fait que le premier, compromis par les derniers, continue à vivre en eux d'une vie obscure et humiliée' (*Baud* 134). So Baudelaire rejects possession by both mother and father. The evident solution to this 'difficulté d'être'[36] is one that I shall have occasion to discuss later: the myth of autogenesis.

The hero of *L'Idiot de la famille* is likewise condemned to a perpetual tension between the active and the passive, to an eternal inability to identify himself with either an active or a passive role. The terms of Sartre's description are worth closer attention: 'Il bondit à pieds joints par-dessus sa naissance et va chercher les causes de son "anomalie" dans sa préhistoire et, plus loin encore, dans un *fiat* prononcé par l'autre absolu . . .' (*IF* 215). Gustave's bitterness is so deep and so tenacious that it *determines* in him a lifelong disgust for procreation and a predilection for sterility. What Sartre is discussing here is the question of who is to blame for Gustave's 'affective castration' – mummy or daddy? On the one hand, the mother, like Baudelaire's, had conditioned the child to passivity. But, on the other, Gustave's *status* is the direct result of an ante-natal choice: the choice of his father to constitute him as bourgeois and second-born. It is interesting that Sartre imagines Flaubert confused as to who the agent of his 'castration' might be. Sartre, too, appears unable to make up his mind. A view of castration as a kind of 'Catch 22' permeates Sartre's work: if the father is present he is inevitably a 'bad father'; if he is absent he leaves the child to the tender mercies of an archaic 'bad mother' who threatens engulfment, or a phallic mother who threatens castration. It is as if Sartre had no capacity to imagine identification as anything other than total: identification means *becoming* rather than *occupying the place of*. In leaping forward from 1947 to 1971 I have skipped over a significant text: the *Scénario Freud*. It is a delicious irony that the one 'character' Sartre is able to *show* overcoming this problem of identification with the father is the Sigmund Freud of the screenplay. 'It was my turn to play the role of father',[37] says Freud at the end of the synopsis of the screenplay

(*SF* 570). Of course, it is one thing to grasp intellectually the difference between the good and the bad father, but it is at least arguable that the confusion between these two figures remained *operative* in Sartre's texts long after this intellectual *prise de conscience*.

Many elements of the phantasmatic substructure of Sartre's texts are now becoming apparent. These elements can be seen to be active in both the theoretical discourse and the fictions. If we regard the phantasmatic as a kind of *mise-en-scène*, then these elements resemble players lit simultaneously from back and front. On the one hand they participate fully in the authorial *vouloir-dire* – they are perfectly integrated into the scene which the author wishes to project to the audience, or the reader. At the same time, they are illuminated by a very dim light that has percolated through from another scene.[38] To continue this metaphor, it is clear that, for this backlighting to become apparent, the frontlighting has to be momentarily switched off. And so it is that, in a first reductive movement, I am concerned presently with this other scene.

The fact that these images are overdetermined cannot be too strongly stressed. They are, for example, dually determined by their simultaneous participation in an authorial *vouloir-dire* and a certain *vouloir-taire*. Taken only as figures from the unconscious phantasmatic, their overdetermination is, as it were, manifest. The *femme-marécage* is both the figuration of the engulfing mother and the figuration of the mother perceived as object of illicit desire – because already desired by the absolute Other. In both cases castration anxiety is apparent, although the agent of this castration would, strictly speaking, be different in each case. The *femme-mirage* is, at one and the same time, a representation connected with the 'affectionate current' of love, and a defence against castration anxiety: the desexualisation of the *femme-marécage* figure, the disavowal of the subject's own desire.

Similarly, the crumbling of the Genitor from phallic statue into hollow statuette is both an expression of the deeply resented *inadequacy* of one father-figure, and a rejection of the equally deeply feared *severity* of another, conjured up to redress the shortcomings of the first.

So at this stage a picture of the desiring subject has emerged, caught in a maelstrom between the Scylla of a castrating father and the Charybdis of an engulfing–castrating mother. It is the inherent instability of this dynamic that lies at the heart of the transformations in the representational schemas.

3
Theorising Desire

In his preface to the *Scénario Freud*, J.-P. Pontalis writes, 'Il me paraît incontestable que Sartre a su rendre sensibles, et donc d'abord sensibles à lui, un certain nombre de phénomènes dont la notion de mauvaise foi . . . ne suffit plus à rendre compte' (*SF* 16). De Beauvoir tells us that Sartre originally 'wrought' the notion of *mauvaise foi* in order to account for these phenomena within the framework of a philosophy of consciousness. It is probably true that Sartre was eventually able to recognise the inadequacy of the idea of bad faith in accounting for such phenomena as parapraxes and hysterical symptoms, but it is far less certain – on the evidence, for example, of *L'Idiot* – that he ever fully accepted the explanation proposed for such phenomena by the Freudian notion of the dynamic unconscious.

In this chapter I shall be giving an account of Sartre's theorisation of desire. This account reads at times like a dialogue of the deaf between Sartre and the dead father – Freud. To trace the history of Sartre's theory of desire is also to mark the trace of a *rapprochement* between Sartre and psychoanalysis. But this coming together resembles that of the Lacanian Subject and his Truth: they are destined only ever to converge asymptotically. Indeed the *rapprochement* – despite the existentialism–structuralism polemic of the 1960s – is greater between Sartre and Lacan than between Sartre and the father of psychoanalysis.

In *La Transcendance de l'Ego* and *Esquisse d'une théorie phénoménologique des émotions*, Sartre can be seen laying the foundations for his theory of consciousness. His overriding concern in these two early works is to establish the absolute autonomy of the conscious mind: consciousness is freedom itself. The very nature of this undertaking would clearly involve the demolition of any competing theory which sought to establish limits to this autonomy, or to suggest that consciousness could be subject to extraneous, determining forces. Freudianism, with its stress on the unconscious mind and the disruptive power of unconscious desires, was obviously one such theory. In fact, from his first theoretical work to his last, Sartre worries away at the problem of desire. The two most intractable problems were the source of desire and the agent of desire. That is to say, where does desire arise, and who desires?

Simone de Beauvoir reports near the beginning of *La Force de l'âge* that she and Sartre had read only very little Freud before the war – the *Interpretation of Dreams*, the *Psychopathology of Everyday Life* and possibly the *Introduction to Psychoanalysis*. And that they had grasped the letter rather than the spirit. Their classical Cartesian education had rendered them quite incapable of even beginning to grasp the fabulously complicated mental processes adumbrated by Freud in, for example, his forgetting of the name Signorelli.[1] This lack of thorough reading, coupled with a basic philosophical block, are evident in the naïveté of some of Sartre's objections to psychoanalysis in his earlier works.

But his first targets in *La Transcendance de l'Ego* were somewhat closer to home: his chosen adversaries are La Rochefoucauld and his erstwhile *Maître à penser* Edmund Husserl. For La Rochefoucauld, behind a multitude of apparently contradictory desires there always lies an egoistic organising principle: the ultimate locus of desire is the *moi*. In this conception, altruism is a mere illusion, since the telos of any given act is, literally, self-interest (*TE* 38).

Sartre also detects a tendency to 'egotise' desire in the later work of Husserl. The problem that both La Rochefoucauld and Husserl – and indeed Sartre himself – are grappling with, is a real one: what makes a desire 'mine', rather than simply a depersonalised, abstract desire? Husserl's solution, argues Sartre, was to reinstate, surreptitiously, a *moi* behind every consciousness. This is conceived of not as a direct motivating force but as a subtly pervasive influence: an entity whose light, or *Ichstrahl* (*TE* 20), falls onto each object that comes under our attention and imparts to it a kind of glow of desirability or non-desirability. Now, it is precisely this unifying, transcendental ego *behind* consciousness that Sartre is at pains to discredit. His phenomenological conception of consciousness renders the unifying and individualising role of the *je* quite useless: 'C'est la conscience, au contraire, qui rend possible l'unité et la personnalité de mon Je' (*TE* 23).

Sartre is effectively removing desire from the opacity of the ego and reinstating it as a fundamental structure of consciousness: consciousness chooses itself as desire. By comparison, the ego is a secondary and constructed self, appearing at the level of reflection.[2] At this point Sartre brings in a distinction that he was never to renounce – inasmuch as it is still a central plank in his analysis of Flaubert in *L'Idiot* – the distinction between 'pure' desire and 'poisoned' desire. The former corresponds to the very explosion of consciousness towards its object; the latter arises when we seek to make the desiring consciousness an object of knowledge: 'C'est le point de vue que j'ai pris sur [mes désirs] qui les a empoisonnés . . . avant d'être "empoisonnés", mes désirs ont été purs' (*TE* 43). This nostalgia for an Edenic original purity of desire is evident in Sartre's descriptions of the bond between the desiring subject and its object: he talks of them as being united in an indissoluble dyad (*Esq* 39). Not dissimilar, in fact, to the 'indissoluble intimité de la mère et du nourrisson' (see Chapter 2 above).

This is the foundation for the notion of bad faith: consciousness can afflict itself with 'forgetfulness' – it 'forgets' that it is the source of all desire and instead ascribes these desires to the ego, whose relative opacity enables consciousness, then, to remain 'ignorant' of its own desire.

This move on Sartre's part does not, however, solve the problem of the subject of desire. Logically speaking, if desire is 'unreflected' (that is, corresponding to spontaneous consciousness), then the only desire I can recognise as *mine* is one that is, by definition, 'poisoned', since it is now an object for reflection. All desire is pure until it is poisoned by our attempt to apprehend it reflexively. It will be seen, in subsequent chapters, that this split between the pure and the impure has resonances that extend far beyond Sartre's theoretical lucubrations.

La Transcendance de l'Ego and *Esquisse* could be seen as the opening battles in Sartre's crusade to establish his theory of consciousness, and, in the process, to establish desire as a structure of consciousness. In *La Transcendance*, Sartre attacks the notion that the ego is the source of desire. He goes on, in *Esquisse*, to combat the Freudian conception that locates desire in the unconscious mind. Both theories are antagonistic to Sartre's position in that they posit a mental region which acts upon consciousness whilst remaining inaccessible to inspection by the latter.

Sartre begins in *Esquisse* by pointing up the similarities between his and Freud's views of affectivity: both see emotion as an organised response; both therefore posit a kind of finality to emotion; the question hinges on whether this finality is conscious or unconscious – 'Ce qui est en question ici, c'est le *principe même des explications psychanalytiques*' (*Esq* 35). He has in mind here the principle which sees present actions as being explicable by reference to the past, which sees consciousness as subject to *causal pressure* from unconscious desire (*Esq* 37). In *Transcendance* the 'fait transcendantal' that Sartre sought to eliminate was the transcendental ego, here it is the unconscious desire. Of course, Sartre is overstating the apparently deterministic nature of Freudian psychoanalysis. The process whereby a symptom is formed is in fact far more 'dialectical' than Sartre cares to see: the symptom is a compromise between desire and its repression, but also a response to a present situation as well as future expectations. Freud's two errors, according to Sartre, are his basic conception of desire as an entity outside consciousness, and his view of consciousness, which allows for it to be *acted upon* by something extraneous to itself. Sartre was making things easier for himself by using the blanket term 'fait de conscience' to cover such diverse phenomena as simple parapraxes and hysterical paralysis.

Since dreams were Freud's royal road to knowledge of the unconscious, Sartre chooses this ground on which to launch his attack. For Freud, the manifest content of the dream is the result of a compromise between a desire seeking to express itself and a repressive agency attempting to prevent this expression by means of censorship. The censorship has at its disposal the processes of the 'dream work': condensation, displacement and so on. These are the forces responsible for the garbled message that finally intrudes into consciousness in the form of the manifest dream images. Sartre's position is to dismiss this account on the basis of the two 'errors' mentioned above. It is not until *L'Etre et le néant* that he shifts ground slightly and pursues a more fruitful line of attack centred on the location of the censorship.

On the question of the neurotic symptom, Sartre admits that 'le fait conscient *symbolise avec* le complexe exprimé',[3] but goes on to point out that the relationship of symbolisation implies an immanent relationship of comprehension between the two *relata*. We shall see that this notion of 'compréhension' was destined for a great future in Sartre's theoretical writings. In *Esquisse*, however, it is almost a verbal distinction: a desire which is axiomatically 'compréhensible' but equally axiomatically unknowable in its pure state is to all practical purposes unconscious.[4] Sartre's own contribution to the problem of dream symbolisation was the difficult notion of 'fascinated consciousness' (cf. *Imag* 326). But the inadequacy of this concept – even for Sartre himself – is brought out well by Pontalis: 'Bien plus mystérieux encore pour le philosophe le saut de la conscience dans l'inertie: comment diable la transparence peut-elle "choisir" l'opacité?' (*SF* 17).

If the ultimate finality of desire is to be sought in consciousness itself, two questions arise. First, how is it that consciousness can be manifestly unaware – in desire, disgust and other affective states – that it is organising itself as a response? Second, how is it that consciousness is often quite unaware of the meaning of this organised response? An answer to these questions was already present in *Transcendance*: affective consciousness is originally unreflected (*Esq* 38). This unreflected consciousness cannot posit, simultaneously, itself and its object at the level of self-knowledge. The only way this consciousness can know itself is through the qualities it bestows on the world outside itself: it apprehends itself, on the world, as 'une qualité des choses' (*Esq* 42). The status of these qualities – an example of which would be the Viscous – is ambiguous. They are *subjective* to the extent that they are conferred on objects by the unreflected consciousness; they are *objective* inasmuch as consciousness is only able to apprehend them as objective qualities of the world. This effective dissolution of the subject/object dichotomy means that consciousness is its own captor: it is confined within a notional space bounded only by its own ontological limits. It cannot withdraw within itself in order to doubt that it is outside in its object: 'Elle ne se *connaît* que sur le monde' (*Esq* 55).

So, in establishing desire as a 'fait de conscience', Sartre rejects those theories that place the source of desire in a transcendental stable self (La Rochefoucauld, Husserl), but also those that root desire in the *soma*. The latter would be the case with James and the associationists, who view emotion as the apperception by consciousness of physical modifications, but also to some extent with Freud, who regarded libido as having organic roots.[5]

In all of this, the place of the body is not easy to define. If the unconscious – were it to exist – is unable to act on consciousness in Sartre's account, then the same must be true of the body in its inert materiality. To admit that desire has its roots in the *soma* would be tantamount to opening the door on another determinism similar to the one he denounces in Freud. None the less, there appears to be a degree of floating in Sartre's theorisation of the body in these earlier works. In *L'Imaginaire*, he writes that, before imaging a voluptuous scene, I was perhaps already in a state of desire; perhaps *my body* had 'une sorte de désir diffus de l'acte sexuel' (*Imag* 268), and states that 'désir, dégoût, existent d'abord à l'état diffus, sans intentionnalité précise' (*Imag* 268). But where, exactly, do they exist? Surely not in consciousness, since intentionality is the very definition of the latter. This state of acute sexual tension is such an empirically observable fact that Sartre could hardly have ignored it; the problem seems rather that he is unwilling to confront the problem of the *psyche–soma* relationship in cases such as this. The notion of a 'désir diffus' which is 'sans intentionnalité précise' is simply meaningless within the framework of Sartre's theory of consciousness.

The Freudian concept of *Trieb*, standing on the borderline between *psyche* and *soma*, is clearly of central importance to this problem, and I shall now turn to *L'Etre et le néant*, where this notion is discussed.

Sartre's main discussion of desire here is to be found in the section on 'fundamental attitudes'. What Sartre has to say about desire is not readily comprehensible without a certain grasp of his general theory of consciousness. It must therefore be borne in mind that all fundamental attitudes – and these include love and desire – have their basis in Sartrean ontology: they are primitive efforts to recuperate an alienated being. And this in two ways. First, the *pour-soi* is defined as *manque* (lack). The *pour-soi* is the negation of the mode of being exemplified by inert matter: the *en-soi*. So the *pour-soi* tears itself away from one *en-soi* and projects itself towards another, which, it is imagined, would restore its wholeness. This is what Sartre means when he says that the fundamental human ambition is to be God: a perfect being which is simultaneously *en-soi-pour-soi*. Second, my being is originally alienated from me by the Other: I have an *objective* existence only in the eyes of the Other, and one that I must remain forever unable to grasp for myself. The Other, therefore, has a perpetual hold over me: 'Autrui a barre sur moi.' Now, far from being a marginal area of human activity on the brink of brute animality, sexual relations are a privileged domain in that they display the exemplary purity of the struggle waged between *pour-soi*, *en-soi* and *pour-soi-pour-autrui*. Roughly speaking, between consciousness, body and Other.

As part of his attempt to bring human sexuality under the umbrella of the ontology, Sartre attacks what he sees as two erroneous features of Freudianism: its biologism, and its stress on the unconscious. The first target is instinct theory.[6]

Freud is guilty of biologism, says Sartre, in that his conception of the 'sexual instinct' relegates sexuality to the status of a physiological contingency: that is, we are sexed beings *because* we possess genital organs. But Sartre stands Freud's unfortunate dictum 'anatomy is destiny' on its head when he wonders, 'Si l'homme ne possédait un sexe que parce qu'il est originellement et fondamentalement un être sexuel, en tant qu'être qui existe dans le monde en liaison avec d'autres hommes?' (*EN* 433). His desire to rescue sexuality from organic opacity probably prompts him to go too far here, but the statement of the problem is undeniably bold. Ironically enough, Sartre uses Freud's theory of infantile sexuality in order to establish the fact that sexuality – as a fundamental human phenomenon – cannot be equated with mere genital sexuality: sexual activity is present in very young children who have no inkling of what genital maturity could itself imply in the way of satisfaction. Similarly, eunuchs do not cease desiring because they have lost the use of their organs.[7] In effect Sartre is establishing a dichotomy in sexual life that was to be an abiding feature in all of his future theoretical developments: on the one hand, a sexual desire that may be physically satisfied (through copulation, masturbation, and so on); on the other, a desire that can only be described *ontologically*. Since consciousness is defined as lack, this desire may never be satisfied, although sexual relations are one means by which human reality attempts to fill the breach in its being.[8] In essence, Sartre is accusing psychoanalysis of confusing these two related but distinct modes of desire in an orgy of 'physiologism'. There is no disagreement over the *manifestations* of infantile sexuality; the difference arises over its *significance*. In psychoanalytic theory, libido is the name given to the specifically sexual drive, the endosomatic, constantly flowing source of stimulation, derived, Freud supposed, from all bodily organs. The libido theory underpins the elaboration of the pre-genital sexual organisation as well as explaining the very possibility of object choice. For Freud, the sexual drive originally attaches itself 'anaclitically' to a more fundamental drive, that of self-preservation. The epitome of this process is the infant suckling at its mother's breast. The pleasurable oral sensation experienced by the infant leads it to wish for repetition of this pleasure *above and beyond* the simple need for nourishment. In this way, the sexual drive attaches itself to a more primitive instinct and a desire is created quite distinct from the need which originally gave it a 'foothold'. Further, and to reiterate from Chapter 1, the phases of infantile development correspond to a pre-programmed growth cycle: the mouth, the anus and the as yet immature genitals, through the activities centred upon them (eating, defecating, urinating and so on) and the attention paid to them by the infant's entourage, become, in turn, sexually charged and are thus constituted as 'erotogenic zones'. That is, they offer a pleasure yield which is specifically sexual. It is important to remember that the 'sexual drive' itself is not knowable: one only ever encounters its representatives/ representations. Thus, 'oral fixation' refers to the insistence in the unconscious of a nexus of *representations* connected with this phase.

It is highly unlikely that Sartre's knowledge of libido theory was, at the time, as thorough as this: it was sufficient for him to know that libido stood on the borderline between the psychic and somatic – libido is 'un résidu psychobiologique qui n'est pas clair par lui-même, et qui ne nous apparaît pas comme *devant être* le terme irréductible de la recherche' (*EN* 631). Sartre's 'irreducible term' in his existential psychoanalysis would be the *choix originel* – the choice of being. Furthermore, to concede that sexuality might have at least some biological determinants, would be to disbar it from the phenomenological ontology, since 'facticity' represents the limit of such an investigation and not its object: 'Pouvons-nous admettre', asks Sartre, 'que cette immense affaire qu'est la vie sexuelle vienne de surcroît à la condition humaine?' (*EN* 433). The answer is an emphatic 'No!'

To recapitulate: if desire has its roots in obscure somatic processes, it is inaccessible to consciousness; if desire is unconscious – which it is, in the final analysis, for Freud – then it is doubly inaccessible to consciousness. Not only this, but in the latter case consciousness would lose most of its cherished prerogatives, as one would be forced to regard it as a constituted object in relation to the hidden, unconscious subject in a chain of cause and effect.

If Sartre succeeds in rescuing desire, at its source, from the 'crémeuses chimies du corps', the body none the less returns with a vengeance when it is a question of establishing the *aims* of desire. Desire is 'L'appréhension première de la sexualité d'autrui'; it is in desiring the other or in apprehending his desire for me that his 'sexed being' is revealed to me. This desire reveals '*à la fois mon* être sexué et *son* être sexué, *mon* corps comme sexe et *son* corps' (*EN* 434). This is also the starting-point for Sartre's discussion of the object of desire. It is worth noting that Sartre uses the term 'transcendent object' indiscriminately, to refer both to what Freud would call the aim of desire, and to its object – for Freud, the specificity of desire resides in its plasticity with regard to aim and object.

First, the aim of desire cannot be to bring about the cessation of an unpleasant state of tension; this would fail to explain the specificity of object choices – we desire *a* woman, says Sartre, not just any receptacle for masturbation (*EN* 434). Neither is the pursuit of pleasure the aim of desire, although the 'homme moyen', Sartre concedes condescendingly, could be forgiven for believing this to be the case (*EN* 435). This 'man in the street', obsessed with his orgasm, and beset by lazy-mindedness and conformism, sounds almost, by implication, like Freud: it is this emphasis on erection and ejaculation that has led to desire being viewed, erroneously, as an *instinct*, says Sartre. Interestingly enough, Sartre feels that he must concede at least some ground on this point. He notes, for example, that the sexual act may provide a release from the tension of desire, when the latter is experienced as painful or tiring (*EN* 435). We have rejoined here the earlier distinction between fundamental sexuality and desire that may be satisfied. Nevertheless, Sartre *is* conceding some kind of physiological basis to desire: why would desire be painful or tiring unless it arose from some kind of physical pressure or tension? If sexual desire can be – at least momentarily – satisfied, it must be, at least in part, physiological.

Sartre avoids these conclusions by falling back on the distinction between 'pure' and 'poisoned' desire, which mirrors that between spontaneous and reflected consciousness. In the case of a desire that may be satisfied, argues Sartre, 'il faut alors que le désir soit lui-même posé comme "à supprimer" et c'est ce qui ne saurait se faire que par le moyen d'une conscience réfléchie. Or le désir est par soi-même irréfléchi . . .' (*EN* 435). In other words, only a second-degree, 'poisoned' desire may be satisfied. This splitting of desire into a fundamental desire and a satisfiable desire achieves very little, since it does not really explain the relationship between the two. It creates a dichotomy as distinctive as the one Sartre takes issue with in Freud (conscious/unconscious), and it does nothing to help explain the physiological process whereby sexual desire is experienced as a tension-to-be-suppressed.

So, if desire is not desire for pleasure or for the avoidance of unpleasure (*Unlust*), or for copulation, or even for its own suppression, what, then, is its object? 'Un corps vivant comme totalité organique en situation avec la conscience à l'horizon' (*EN* 436).[9] A body in situation, haunted by an intuited consciousness. The drift of Sartre's argument up to this point has tended towards the extrication of desire from the opacity of the body (drive, libido, and so on); he is now attempting to retrieve desire from the unfathomable reaches of the unconscious. But the price of this is a certain depersonalisation of desire. It is fundamentally the same problem as the one encountered in *La Transcendance de l'Ego* and *Esquisse*: namely, if desire is pre-reflexive and therefore pre-personal (there is as yet no *je* to speak of), how can I speak of *my* desire? The problem is not really resolved when Sartre confronts this question directly: 'celui qui désire c'est *moi* et le désir est un mode singulier de ma subjectivité' (*EN* 436).

Moi? Surely not the ego, since this only appears as the object of a reflexive consciousness – the original 'conscience qui se fait désir' is pre-personal and unreflected (*EN* 436). Here again, Sartre is countering the psychoanalytic conception of an unconscious subject of desire. It is true that the subject may remain ignorant of his desire *in itself*, but this is not due to its being unconscious; it is because he may never *know* this desire *in itself*: he can only ever know it 'on the world' or 'on its object'. It follows from this that desire only ever appears to the subject in the field of the Other, as desire of the Other. In practice, the pre-reflexive consciousness replaces the unconscious for Sartre.[10]

By and large, Sartre's theoretical account of desire – as sketched above – is less successful than his descriptions of sexual desire. These descriptions are amongst the most convincing, even gripping, in *L'Etre et le néant*.[11] These passages also provide a more plausible account of the role of the body than do the passages which discuss the source, aims and objects of desire in the abstract.

His starting-point is the phenomenon of 'trouble', 'l'homme qui désire *existe* son corps d'une manière particulière. . . . Le désir est défini comme *trouble*' (*EN* 437). This difficult-to-translate term signals a recourse to a kind of ordinary language philosophy quite in keeping with the phenomenological procedure, which is both descriptive and comparative.[12] *Trouble* denotes both sexual desire, and the muddying of clear water as in the English (mis)appropriation of the phrase 'troubled waters'. In desire, then, consciousness precipitates itself into complicity with its own facticity, the body:

'le désir me *compromet* . . . dans le désir sexuel la conscience est comme empâtée, il semble qu'on se laisse envahir par la facticité, qu'on cesse de la fuir et qu'on glisse vers un consentement *passif* au désir' (*EN* 438). The operative distinction is between desire and hunger. The physical pangs occasioned by an empty stomach do not prompt complicity on the part of consciousness: facticity (the body letting me know that it needs food) is transcended by consciousness towards an end – the cessation of hunger by the taking of nourishment. So the lack at the heart of hunger is real and may be filled by a plate of spaghetti, whereas the lack at the heart of desire is both unreal and far more fundamental: it is a lack of being. Thus desire is experienced as the passivity of the *pour-soi* with regard to its own facticity.[13]

Now, this fall into complicity with the body in desire later turns out to be more of a jump. It is a necessary and intrinsic aspect of the project of consciousness in sexual desire: 'Le désir . . . est . . . le pro-jet non-thétiquement vécu de s'enliser dans le corps' (*EN* 439). But, if the *pour-soi* is by definition a flight from inert materiality, one is entitled to wonder why it should permit or, *a fortiori*, seek out this contamination by substance. In fact, consciousness is lured into this complicity by the prospect of an illusory transcendence. This transcendence is none other than the ultimate value which haunts all fundamental attitudes: the *en-soi-pour-soi*, or God. In more prosaic terms: the aim, in desire, is to sink into complicity with the body in order, precisely, to induce this same complicity in my partner. When I caress the Other I seek to induce signs of 'trouble', or sexual arousal, in him which indicate that I have succeeded in forcing him into complicity with his body. I also want him to return these caresses in order that I might experience a similar complicity. This is what Sartre calls 'double reciprocal incarnation'. The aim is ultimately to be *pour-soi* (subject) to the extent that I have forced the incarnation of the Other (object); and, in the same instant, *en-soi* (object) inasmuch as the Other (now subject) has led me into identification with my own body. In this ingenious description the aims and objects of desire are very much ontological: it is a question of realising a certain mode of being.

Unfortunately this notional mode of being is axiomatically impossible. Desire is thus destined to fail, and the reasons for its failure are very revealing. First, I may 'forget' that I am actually attempting to bring about the incarnation of the Other, and topple over into the masochistic attitude – total passivity. Second, I may err in the other direction – sadism – where I use my body wholly as instrument and refuse contact with the Other. The third failure, strangely, is orgasm. The following passage explains why: 'il *se fait* que l'incarnation se manifeste par l'érection et que l'érection cesse avec l'éjaculation. Mais en outre, le plaisir est l'écluse du désir parce qu'il motive l'apparition d'une conscience réflexive *de* plaisir' (*EN* 447).

One could note, parenthetically, the 'phallocentricity' of this account: how would a woman's desire fit into this general description? For Sartre, it is both entirely contingent and somewhat unfortunate that the erection is the index of incarnation, since the erection is an 'unstable structure' – as unstable, in fact, as the hollow statues in Sartre's fictions. Desire has to be pre-reflexive – in this way, the *purity* of desire is safeguarded against the noxious incursions of the ego, on the one hand, and facticity on the other. We have, once again, returned to the distinction between pure and impure desire. This third failure of desire – the poisoning of an original pure desire by the besmirching glance cast on it by a second-degree reflective consciousness – is in fact analogous to the failure of love in Sartre's theory: the lovers' enterprise collapses when they are looked at by an interfering third party (*tiers*).

Sartre's theorisation of desire is intended, amongst other things, to displace the centrality of the Oedipus complex in psychoanalytical discourse. For Freud, the Oedipus complex marks that moment at which desire encounters the Law and must accommodate itself to it. For Lacan, the Oedipal moment – or entry into the Symbolic Order – is the notional point at which desire is definitively deprived of the means of its total articulation. It is also, in Lacanian theory, the instant of primary repression (*Urverdrängung*): that is to say, the formation of the unconscious, as desire, through anticathexis, sinks into this sub-articulate region.[11] There is, nevertheless, something uncannily 'Oedipal' about Sartre's unpsychoanalytical account. I would suggest that this uncanniness arises from a similarity in structure.

Fundamental desire is aprioristically doomed to failure in *L'Etre et le néant*. To this extent, the account is similar to that of psychoanalysis, where the desire that *must* come to grief is the one that locks the mother and child in the mother–infant dyad. But the reasons for this failure reproduce a classic Oedipal pattern: the intercession of the Law of the Father (here the reflexive consciousness, interceding like a third party); the necessary identification with the mother or with the father (here the passive or active orientations: masochism and sadism). It is probably equally significant that neither pole is allowed to hold firm in Sartre's version: the desiring subject oscillates continually between masochistic and sadistic attitudes before the ultimate orgasmic collapse.

Having advanced this suggestion, I would draw back to leave the reader a degree of freedom to react. I am not arguing that the validity or otherwise of Sartre's *theorisation* of desire is necessarily undermined by the discovery that it reproduces an Oedipal pattern. If this were so, one would be forced by the same token to disqualify the authority of Freud's discourse: it has been argued that Freud's quest for knowledge, resulting in his 'discovery' of the Oedipus complex, simply repeated or re-enacted the quest for knowledge that motivated Oedipus.[15] Ironically enough, Sartre himself shows this rather well in his *Scénario Freud*, where he centres the screenplay on the part played in Freud's 'discovery' of the unconscious by the agonistic relation to his father(s). This is, however, a point to which I shall return.

Before leaving *L'Etre et le néant* it is necessary to return briefly to the problem of object choices. 'The finding of an object is in fact the refinding of it': this Freudian aphorism emphasises the radical difference between Freudian psychoanalysis and Sartre's projected existential analysis. Love objects are always bound to previous object choices – ultimately unconscious ones – going back to earliest infancy, which determine, or at the very least condition, any ulterior choices. In dismissing the idea that consciousness may be *acted upon* by anything outside itself, Sartre leaves himself in a difficult position: if desire emanates neither from a stable self (ego) conceived of as a more-or-less fixed bundle of tastes and tendencies, nor from an established unconscious affectivity, what *motivates* desire as to the choice of its objects?

Now, Sartre does not dismiss the dimension of the past with regard to this choice of objects. But the Sartrean past, unlike that of Freud, is one that is constantly remodelled by consciousness and summoned forth into the present, rather than one which wilfully irrupts into it: 'La conscience se choisit désir. . . . Mais nous avons montré . . . que le motif était *suscité à partir* du passé et que la conscience en *se retournant* sur lui, lui conférait son poids et sa valeur' (*EN* 441). In this account, the past is that which is, literally, gone past or *dépassé*. This last term implies that the past is not simply left behind but carried along with, or integrated into, the project of consciousness. The notion of intentionality combines, therefore, both the past and the future, the motive and its interpretation. If I feel burdened by the weight of the past, it is because I freely choose to confer this weight on it.

There is no place here for the return of the repressed. If the repressed could return, it would be as an invited guest, not as a gatecrasher. Similarly, whereas for Freud what is *done to* the child at an early age is decisive, for Sartre the pressures of the early environment are inoperative except inasmuch as they are 'comprehended' by the subject: 'le milieu ne saurait agir sur le sujet que dans la mesure où il le comprend' (*EN* 634).[16]

This has a ring of plausibility about it. But how far does Sartre really go towards accounting for the uncannily insistent nature of our object choices? A closer examination of the passage quoted above casts doubt on this plausibility. He notes that, 'turning back on it', consciousness confers a value on past motivation. This means simply that the pure/impure dichotomy is maintained in place. The *motif* is only 'knowable' in its degraded and impure state, as an object for a reflective consciousness.

Again, the original desire salvages its purity but at the price of remaining effectively pre-personal, and this leaves the problem of motivation almost intact. In other words, Sartre's solution to the problem is verbal, tautological and perhaps even 'magical'.[17]

There is nothing in the *Cahiers pour une morale* to suggest a fundamental change of position on desire. But, if the general theory of consciousness which provides the underpinning remains the same, the emphasis and perspective certainly undergo some modification. The ethical project deals with a human freedom *in situation*, and it is the limiting factors of this notion of situation which Sartre is forced to take more fully into account. In practice this means that Sartre is obliged to accord greater importance to the body-as-facticity, and to the place of the alienating Other in the subject's world.

If one were to map these two aspects back onto the problematic of *L'Etre et le néant*, it would be seen that they continue, in the *Cahiers*, the two-pronged attack on Freudianism: on instinct theory (desire as somatic phenomenon) and the unconscious (desire as Other).

The ontological primacy of desire, established in *L'Etre et le néant* now appears to have acquired the status of universally accepted truth: '*on sait* que le désir est désir de posséder la transcendance de l'autre comme pure transcendance et pourtant comme corps' (*Cah* 240; emphasis added). And, in the case of a farm labourer who raped a small girl, the ontological ambition of the labourer's desire is seen to form the irreducible bedrock of this conduct: what makes the desire irresistible, claims Sartre, is the aspiration to the Absolute that lies at its heart (*Cah* 187).

Nevertheless, we are able to witness Sartre making something of a compromise. There are now, it seems, desires that straddle the previously well-policed frontiers between need and desire: 'ces désirs-besoins venant du corps' (*Cah* 252). In other words, despite a steadfast effort to safeguard the ontological purity of desire, Sartre finds his account drifting progressively towards the dreaded domain of facticity.

The comments on the Other in the *Cahiers* throw some interesting new light on Sartre's attitude toward the Freudian unconscious. The pure/impure distinction is taken up once again. Sartre repeats that any given desire is always, in itself, pure. Taken in isolation, it contains the very germs of human reality: the affirmation of transcendence, freedom, the *dépassement* of the given situation, and so on. Its impurity is of a secondary nature: 'Il n'est *illégitime* et *impure* que secondairement s'il est *empoisonné* par la volonté d'être et par *la présence en lui de l'Autre*' (*Cah* 433; emphasis added).[18] Desire is experienced, secondarily, as *perverted*, when the other slips into the heart of my desire itself, with the result that what is most fundamentally my true self, or *ipséité*, is experienced as other. But the Other is no longer, or no longer only, the ahistorical, eternal 'Other' of Sartre's earlier ontology. This Other is now also an historically determined figure. In 1947–8 Sartre was 'en route vers le concret': it is capitalist society that effects the most radical alienation of man – the fact that the Other is experienced *a priori* as hostile within the context of scarcity (*rareté*), and, worse, that one no longer recognises oneself in one's work.

The poet–ethnologist Michel Leiris is also enlisted in Sartre's crusade against the unconscious. Sartre notes in the *Cahiers*, 'l'inconscient comme dernier type d'aliénation: à comparer au zar' (*Cah* 426).[19] Leiris writes, in *L'Afrique fantôme*, that the *zar* are a society of male and female spirits, organised into a hierarchy with kings and lords, and servants and slaves – a society, indeed, in every way similar to that of the living. It is a parallel society, a society of 'black doubles' who are, crucially, able to *see* the living, whilst the latter are unable to see them. In the Christianisation of the myth, it was God who created this society. Sartre sees this as a symbol of the petrifying power of the look: God is endowed with the evil eye; he has condemned the visible (the living) to be possessed by the invisible (the dead), and not only to be possessed, but also to be 'regardés et habités par ceux qui ne peuvent être ni regardés ni habités' (*Cah* 378). So the *zar* are the concretisation of the look of the Other which is everywhere felt but never seen. *Les Jeux sont faits* is Sartre's own version of this very myth. What seems to have gripped him in Leiris's account of the *zar* is the notion of *possession* – a possession which translates the parasitic presence of the Other at the very heart of being.

Interestingly enough, Sartre argues that the 'myth' of the Freudian unconscious is simply the latest in line of a series of metonymic displacements of this fundamental alienation, which, although ontologically founded, manifests itself in different forms at different historical moments. Confusion and mystification can arise because we conceive of our own consciousness on the model of the Other: 'ces contenus de conscience, ce fleuve de la conscience qu'on introduit en nous puis cet inconscient freudien: c'est l'Autre' (*Cah* 444). The 'vraie subjectivité et l'ipséité de la personne' (a tautology if ever there was one!) are still to be sought in transcendence and in the circuit of consciousness (*Cah* 430).

Two longish passages from the *Cahiers* will serve to indicate how far Sartre still is at this period from any kind of acceptance of a Freudian notion of unconscious desire.

> Chez Freud l'acte libre ou le désir conscient se croient libres mais c'est une illusion de la conscience. En fait ils sone *explicables*[20] par la libido inconsciente. . . . La description est parfaitement exacte et nous fait conclure au déterminisme. Sauf en ceci que l'ordre psychique inconscient n'est autre *qu'une autre conscience.*
>
> (*Cah* 206)

This 'other consciousness' is, again, the correlative of impure reflection, and is increasingly designated by Sartre as a *false consciousness*:

> L'espèce aussi me ressaisit par derrière, au sens où chacun de mes actes *pour moi* unique et libre est saisi par l'autre qui est

derrière moi[21] comme explicable par l'espèce. Aussi est-elle perpétuellement assimilable à un dehors de ma conscience et, comme j'intériorise nécessairement ce dehors en le pensant *mien*, à un inconscient qui est sens profond de mon conscient. (*Cah* 102)

So the Freudian unconscious is at one and the same time a believable *myth* of our alienation, and – inasmuch as it is false but widely believed – a further *manifestation* of our alienation. Freud is both alienator and alienated, mystifier and mystified. There is, of course, another possibility: if Freud were fully conscious of the mystification he disseminated, he would also be a monumental *salaud*!

It is sometimes argued that the work Sartre carried out on the *Critique de la raison dialectique* was a necessary prerequisite for the writing of *L'Idiot de la famille*. The latter is indeed more sophisticated, and more Marxian, than the previous biographical enterprises. However, it appears to me that the instruments of analysis in *L'Idiot* are at least implicitly present in *L'Etre et le néant* and even explicitly envisaged in the *Cahiers*. *L'Idiot de la famille* is a thoroughgoing attempt to describe the process of interiorisation of the exterior, and exteriorisation of the interior, referred to in the last passage quoted above. In *L'Idiot* this is called *personnalisation*.

The growing emphasis on childhood is also already present in the *Cahiers*. Referring directly to Lacan, Sartre notes, 'il y a une autre aliénation (et capitale) qui se trouve dans toutes les sociétés: c'est celle de l'Enfant' (*Cah* 380).[22] And, ten years before *Questions de méthode*, Sartre is setting forth the central place of 'psychoanalysis' (here envisaged as a kind of ontologised Freudianism) in any possible account of this period of alienation. He gives a remarkably accurate summary of the project of *L'Idiot* more than twenty years before its publication (*Cah* 287), a summary taken up in the *Critique*: 'la psychanalyse, à l'intérieur d'une totalisation dialectique, renvoie d'un côté aux structures objectives, aux conditions matérielles et, de l'autre, à l'action de notre indépassable enfance sur notre vie d'adulte' (*CRD* 96).

L'Idiot de la famille, which Sartre worked on intermittently from as early as 1956, is a monumental effort to square the circle, an effort to syncretise Marxism and Freudianism, an effort to subsume both, ultimately, under a distinctly Sartrean ontology. The resulting

2800 pages – always elusive and at times impenetrable – could be seen as the result of the kind of 'stress' that Sartre analyses in Flaubert: the more-or-less successful integration of 'foreign bodies' into an ongoing totalisation. Inasmuch as Sartre was seeking in *L'Idiot* to comprehend the insertion of an individual in the cultural order, to understand the mechanisms whereby an individual's family drama becomes 'de-territorialised' within the wider historical process, the work could have borne the Marcusian subtitle of 'Eros and civilisation'. As a project, it presents the twin characteristics of being urgently necessary and massively self-indulgent. Its great length and sheer difficulty mean that it will never, directly, be the instrument of liberation for men attempting to understand their insertion in history that Sartre hoped it would be – at best it will filter into popular consciousness via vulgarisations and commentary. The present intellectual climate in France, however, does not permit one to imagine this happening in the foreseeable future.

Sartre's use of psychoanalysis in *L'Idiot* was controversial from the beginning, and generally outraged the psychoanalytical establishment, who saw in it a web of misrepresentation and naïve misapprehension.[23] I believe that Sartre's appropriation of psychoanalysis is somewhat more subtle than, but perhaps just as perverse as, these reactions suggest. The difficulty of defining Sartre's relation to psychoanalytic theory in *L'Idiot* is compounded by the fact that this relation involves blind-spots and lacunae that one would like to call upon psychoanalysis itself to illuminate. There is a risk of falling into a sort of critical *mise en abyme*.

In the pages that follow, then, I shall give only the most schematic account of Sartre's use of psychoanalysis, limiting myself to aspects which represent a development of issues looked at in the preceding pages of this chapter.

Even the most cursory perusal of *L'Idiot* is sufficient to reveal that the tone of Sartre's references to psychoanalysis is very different from in earlier works, where he was content to dismiss it as stuff and nonsense. There are constant references to Freud and to post-Freudians such as Lacan and Mannoni. The authority of 'analysts' is frequently evoked in support of his theses; the text positively bristles with psychoanalytic terms such as 'fetishisation', 'disavowal', 'denial', 'valorisation', 'castration', 'Oedipus complex', 'phallus' and 'phallic mother'. Both the descriptive *and* the explanatory authority of psychoanalysis find themselves both ratified *and* rejected in the text. On occasions, the arrival on the scene of Freud is heralded with the enthusiasm normally reserved for the parousia. But Lacan appears to have furnished Sartre with more operating categories than Freud.

'On entre dans un homme comme dans un moulin', writes Sartre. But, despite the apparent arbitrariness of the point of departure, it is very significant that he chooses to commence his account with 'l'apprentissage des mots' (*IF* 13). It is the stress on language in the Lacanian rethinking of Freud that provides Sartre with the means of effecting a *rapprochement* with psychoanalytical theory. And this is due, at least in part, to the fact that Sartre himself had long viewed human relations in terms of a symbolic exchange. The opening section of *L'Idiot* could be read as a fairly orthodox account of how Gustave failed in his insertion in the Symbolic Order and became stalled in the Imaginary. These Lacanian terms denote a linguistic version of the Oedipus complex. The dyad of mother and infant is dissolved by the entry into language (the Symbolic Order), where the child acquires the mediation (the paternal metaphor as name-of-the-dead-father) which provides access to subjecthood, and undergoes alienation with regard to his own desire. The picture that Sartre gives of Gustave, who is initially incapable of distinguishing between the 'puissance magique' and the 'pure valeur signifiante' of words (*IF* 20), puts one in mind of the process of 'foreclosure' in which the subject becomes bound to the non-distinction between signifier and signified.[24]

The accession to the Symbolic Order – which can be regarded as being analogous to the 'happy' outcome of the Oedipus complex – also involves the transition from *being* the phallus to *having* the phallus: in the Imaginary, the child phantasises itself to be the maternal phallus – that is to say, that which would make the mother whole again. In relinquishing the desire for the mother through the paternal interdiction, the child identifies with the father inasmuch as the latter is felt to *have* the phallus and to be able to use it in a socially normalised way. The fact that Sartre is working, to some degree at least, under Lacanian inspiration is indicated by passages later in the work where the question of the maternal phallus resurfaces, and where Sartre explicitly states that Gustave *still* desires to *be* the mother's phallus: 'tout se passe comme si le fétiche était à la fois l'incarnation et la négation du phallus maternel' (*IF* 720).

The sections 'Le miroir et le rire' and 'Le miroir et le fétiche' could be read as attempts to integrate the Lacanian mirror-phase and entry into the Symbolic Order into a properly Sartrean framework. It should be noted in this respect that Sartre had arrived at his own version of the mirror phase as early as *Saint Genet*; even earlier, in fact, if one draws the lessons implicit in the notion of Ego as a self constructed from imaginary identifications, adumbrated in *La Transcendance de l'Ego*.

Given this seemingly dramatic *rapprochement* with mainstream psychoanalysis, of which I have indicated but a few instances, it will perhaps come as a mild surprise to readers unfamiliar with *L'Idiot* that Sartre *nowhere* in this work admits the existence of the dynamic unconscious. On the contrary, Sartre spends an immense amount of time constructing an ideational framework capable of accounting for the manifestations of the unconscious in a non-psychoanalytical manner. The third volume of *L'Idiot*, in particular, provides the most interesting sidelight on Sartre's ambivalence vis-à-vis psychoanalysis as a method of interpretation. Analysing Gustave's 'neurosis', and in particular the fall of Pont l'Evêque, Sartre sets out to demonstrate 'l'intentionnalité fondamentale' of his neurosis (*IF* 1467). The term *intentionnalité* is clearly intended to indicate that the neurosis of Gustave is oriented towards the world, and towards the future, at least as much as it is 'pushed' from the past. The Freudian concept of 'gain from illness' also pointed not just to the satisfaction that could be derived from neurotic symptoms, but to the fact that they were always, at least in part, a response to a difficult situation in the present. But in Freud this is conceived of primarily in economic terms: the neurosis 'compromises' with the pleasure principle. Sartre's version is rather more radical in that it implies, through *intentionnalité*, that the neurosis is potentially wholly conscious.

We have seen that the dichotomy employed to explain away the unconscious in the earlier works was that between *connaissance* and *conscience*. The 'motif' of desire is *unknowable* by essence, since a cognitive consciousness makes of it an object and thus denatures it. What is *known* is the denatured object of a second-degree reflective consciousness. Although 'unknowable' in itself, desire was still transparent to consciousness because it was a mode of consciousness itself. In *L'Idiot* Sartre has nuanced his position somewhat. The working opposition is now that between *connaissance* and *compréhension*, within the unity of the *vécu*. The following passage makes this clear:

> La compréhension est un accompagnement muet du vécu . . .
> une saisie obscure du sens d'un processus par-delà ses significa-
> tions. . . . C'est l'aurore d'une réflexion mais quand celle-ci
> surgit, avec ses outils verbaux, il est fréquent qu'elle fausse le
> 'compris': d'autres forces entrent en jeu . . . qui le déviéront ou
> la contraindront à remplacer le sens par un ensemble lié de
> significations . . . . (IF 1544)

On the face of it, this sounds almost like a commentary on the Lacanian subject alienated from its desire in language;[25] that desire is unknowable in language and loses itself in metonymic displacements along the signifying chain ('un ensemble lié de significations'). Except here, this desire is anything but unconscious. In fact Sartre is falling back on the notorious old distinction made in *Qu'est-ce que la Littérature?* between *sens* and *signification*. Desire is not susceptible to a direct formulation in language (*signification*); at best it may be evoked 'poetically' (*sens*). What started as a relatively unproblematic apprehension by consciousness of its own project, has ended up as an obscure, almost coenaesthetic, intuition forever deprived of the ability to formulate itself. It should be noted that this endeavour to formulate desire is here analogous to the intervention of a reflective, or impure, consciousness. Sartre says he will call this 'pre-reflective'. In *L'Etre et le néant*, though, pure reflection was already a 'dumb accompaniment' to a state or action: a non-thetic self-awareness. Presumably Sartre makes this further distinction in *L'Idiot* because the term 'reflection' theoretically covers both its pure and impure modes.

In both cases, an Other is responsible for the deviation or perversion of my originally pure desire.[26] With the mention of this Other who, situated sometimes behind, sometimes within, the subject himself, 'forces him from behind to be' (see *OR* 122) we are moving dangerously close to the chasm of a dizzying *mise en abyme*. For this Other is given a name in *L'Idiot*: it is the arch-father himself, Achille-Cléophas. I can only hint at what I sense to be the beginning of an infinite regress of mirror-identifications by noting that the Freud of the *Scénario*, the monster of lucidity with the piercing, visionary eyes,[27] is reincarnated in the terrible father of *L'Idiot*. Achille-Cléophas takes on the guise of Sigmund Freud; his gaze is that of a surgeon, but also that of a psychoanalyst: 'Les rêves, les songes et les mensonges que son regard a violés, désarticulés, ce sont ceux de Gustave. Celui-ci, plus d'une fois, a vu sa vie profonde "tomber à ses pieds en tronçons"' (*IF* 459). The father is guilty – like Actaeon – of committing a 'viol par la vue'. The father is, quite simply, *guilty*.

In the *Scénario Freud*, Fliess asks Freud 'Ainsi la névrose des enfants résulte de la perversion des pères?', and Freud looks embarrassed by 'cette simplification grossière de ses théories' (*SF* 289). Freud may well look embarrassed, but I would suggest that this 'crude simplification' which makes of the father the sodomiser of his sons is anchored very firmly in Sartre's own phantasmatic universe (see Chapter 5).

There would obviously be a great deal more to say about Sartre's theorisation of desire in *L'Idiot*. I shall, for example, have occasion to return in a later chapter to the use and misuse of that psychoanalytic cornerstone, the Oedipus complex, in this work. I have simply sought to bring out a few points that underline the degree of continuity to be found throughout Sartre's work with regard to the unconscious. At its very simplest, Sartre's attitude resembles one of disavowal: 'yes, I know, but . . . .'

It seems fairly likely that Sartre had, by the time of writing *L'Idiot de la famille*, arrived at an *intellectual* acceptance of the Freudian unconscious. But this is not to say that he had begun to recognise the products of his own unconscious. If the analogy between Achille-Cléophas and Freud himself holds any water, then a bizarre twist has occurred whereby the notion of the unconscious itself – as well as its principal champion – have themselves become implicated in that network of phantasies that is called a phantasmatic. In this way, *L'Idiot* resembles a monstrous monument to the power of transference: Sartre is summoning up the creatures that inhabit his own unconscious in an attempt to put to flight the vampires that, he imagines, were lodged in that of Gustave Flaubert.

I suggested at the end of my discussion of *L'Etre et le néant* that Sartre's attempt to theorise desire as a structure of consciousness could be seen as an attempt to salvage the original purity of desire from a double-headed danger: *recuperation* by the body, and *perversion* by the Other. This dreadful alternative, between two versions of castration in fact, will provide the broad organising principle of the last two chapters of this work.

It is important to rectify, pre-emptively, a possible misconception even before it begins to take hold. We have the coexistence in the same textual space of a strongly directed theoretical discourse *and* a network of images which – when placed in relation to each other, and this is the labour of interpretation – betray their origins in another scene. It would be wholly inappropriate to regard Sartre's theoretical discourse as being analogous to the manifest text of a dream which has been determined in its every detail by the latent text of the phantasm. It would be equally wrong to view Sartre's theoretical discourse as the controlled product of a perfectly conscious *vouloir-dire*. There is a commingling, an intertwining, a cross-fertilisation. What must be established is the *relationship* between what is said and what is striving to be said. This is doubtless a relationship characterised very often by interference or even by flat contradiction, but a relationship that is, in the final analysis, *productive*. It is with this in mind that I turn now to track the paths of desire traced outside the lines of the theoretical discourse.

4
The Staging of Desire

Sartre's reputation has suffered in a fashionable backlash following his death. It seems that he was a 'political illiterate', his biographies are 'unreadable', his plays mere *pièces à thèse*, his novels either *romans à clef* or sterile dramatisations of obscure theories. In the latter criticism lies a strange misapprehension. To argue that a novel – any novel – is a sterile dramatisation of an already elaborated theory is to assume that the theoretical discourse has automatic primacy; it is also to assume that the ultimate source of authority for a text resides with its author. After structuralism and post-structuralism this is an odd position to defend.

Nevertheless, there is no doubt that *La Nausée* – described by Sartre himself as a 'factum sur la contingence' – anticipates many key elements of the philosophy elaborated in *L'Etre et le néant*. There is equally little doubt that many scenes from *Les Chemins* appear to be stagings, or *mises-en-scène*, of the theory of sexual desire discussed in my last chapter, and I shall be looking at a few of these episodes shortly. But these *mises-en-scène* of desire also constitute the dramatisation of a different desire.

I have already referred to this double dramatisation. I should like this time to draw an analogy with a mode of dramatic production invented by the Oulipo. The idea is to construct a play which is in fact two, or more, quite different plays being acted out on the same stage at the same time, in such a way that the surface continuity of a single unified action is maintained.[1] The play here is on the notion of context: a single utterance will have two radically different functions depending of which 'stage' it is perceived to emanate from. As is often the case with Oulipean products, this is a game which illustrates, obliquely, a serious point – here, the overdetermination of dramatic or literary language.

Critics have not been slow to point out that physical sex in Sartre's novels and short stories is, more often that not, squalid, sadomasochistic and tinged with an unmistakable disgust.[2] This will come as no surprise to readers of *L'Etre et le néant*. As we have seen, the aim of desire is never that which is attained in actual intercourse: the true finality is either submerged by a reflective consciousness of pleasure, or irretrievably lost in its fixation at one or other pole of the sado-masochistic oscillation.

The episode in 'L'Enfance d'un chef' where Lucien seduces, or is seduced by, Maud reads like a concrete illustration of this theoretical position (*OR* 379). Since desire is essentially pre-reflective, the first apprehension of this state of desire is a reflective consciousness of what has 'already' occurred: the thickening complicity of consciousness with its own facticity that Sartre calls 'trouble'. The first active step by Lucien is the caress: consciousness making itself body in order to incarnate the Other. Characteristically, there is no lingering description of the rapture of orgasm. Like a coy American television movie, the scene cuts to 'afterwards'. But this is not coyness on Sartre's part, it is a narrative necessity: simply, there is no *personal* consciousness there to record the moment of its own submersion. Thinking back on the scene, Lucien is vaguely aware more of the frustration of his desire than of its consummation; what he had desired of Maud was her seriousness, her dignity, her disdain for the male of the species – in short, 'tout ce qui faisait d'elle une personne étrangère, vraiment *une autre*, dure et définitive, toujours hors d'atteinte' (*OR* 380). The object of Lucien's desire had always been this elusive alterity. He had sought to capture it in the way that we say a photograph really 'catches' a person's living expression whilst at the same time freezing this attitude on the photographic paper. This other face of Maud had 'l'air habillé',[3] the distinction being that between the body apprehended in movement, in its instrumentality, and the body grasped for what it *is*: gratuitous flesh. The radical otherness of Maud is precisely what, paradoxically, Lucien's desire destroys:

> Et tout ce vernis avait fondu sous son étreinte, il était resté de la chair, il avait approché ses lèvres d'un visage sans yeux, nu comme un ventre, il avait possédé une grosse fleur de chair mouillée. Il revit la bête aveugle qui palpitait dans les draps avec des clapotis et des bâillements velus et il pensa: c'était *nous deux*. (*OR* 380)[4]

This is a 'copybook' example of the failure of Sartrean desire: Maud, as indicated by the extinction of consciousness falls into the masochistic role, and Lucien himself, made flesh, is lost in a welter of pleasure wherein the fundamental aim of desire disintegrates.

The sadistic attitude is just as much a failure as masochism. This aspect is graphically illustrated by Pierre in *Le Sursis*. He has lost the superiority he enjoyed over Maud (another Maud!), by virtue of being the prestigious other: Maud has realised that he is a coward. This image of Pierre-the-coward that she carries everywhere is the equivalent of a voodoo doll which symbolises possession by the Other: Pierre has been dispossessed of his being; only a dramatic repossession will serve his purpose, and the instrument will be sex. He seeks to bog down this condemnatory other consciousness in flesh, in the same way as a witch-doctor captures an enemy's soul in a waxen effigy: 'faire monter lentement le trouble du ventre à la tête, empâter ses petites idées claires, je te baiserai, je te baiserai, j'entrerai dans ton mépris, je le crèverai comme une bulle' (*OR* 891).[5] It would be hard to imagine anything much farther removed from a loving desire, and yet the same structure is revealed in Mathieu's relationship with Marcelle: it is not desire that Mathieu feels for Marcelle but 'l'envie de voir cet esprit rétif et anguleux fondre comme une aiguille de glace au soleil' (*OR* 404). But Mathieu *does*, precisely, 'desire' Marcelle – in Sartrean terms. He wishes to melt this spiky other consciousness just as Pierre wishes to burst Maud's contempt like a bubble.

Marcelle is initially passive, 'les yeux clos, pesante, défaite' (*OR* 404), but when Mathieu looks up again she has 'les yeux grands ouverts et fixes': her 'esprit rétif et anguleux' still shines out defiantly. The conflict passes to the physical level:

> Il la renversa sur le lit – il lui caressa les seins. . . . Marcelle soupira, les yeux clos, passive et gourmande. Mais ses paupières se crispaient. Le trouble s'attarda un moment, posé sur Mathieu comme une main tiède. Et puis, soudain, Mathieu pensa 'Elle est enceinte.' Il se rassit. (*OR* 408)

Here, as in *L'Etre et le néant*, a reflective consciousness kills desire. But it is not a consciousness of pleasure: it resembles more the interposition of a third person pointing an accusatory finger at Mathieu – he is guilty of that most heinous of Sartrean crimes: he is a father-to-be.

All of these aspects of desire (incarnation, *trouble*, failure) come together in the long and unerotic description of sex between Boris and Lola: we see sexual desire passing through all its stages, like so many stages on the *via dolorosa*, before ending in its 'passion' – that is to say, orgasmic failure.

Initially, it appears to be the *image* of Lola that attracts Boris; the artificial Lola, the Lola who wears a tragedian's mask; he now prefers 'la peau de Lola, elle était si blanche qu'*elle n'avait pas l'air vrai*' (*OR* 416; emphasis added). But Lola is not content with being worshipped from afar. She calls upon Boris to imitate the lover of *L'Imaginaire* and take a dive into the heart of existence. Once the plunge has been taken, Boris has only to let himself go – to *become* body. Nevertheless, the prospect of incarnation is not exactly viewed with joyful anticipation: 'Une fois qu'on était dedans, ça pouvait gazer, mais *avant*, on ne pouvait s'empêcher d'avoir peur' (*OR* 428).

Boris's main fear seems to be loss of control. Despite his efforts to remain in control, he finds himself caught up in the swirl of the orgasm and becomes nothing more than a reflective consciousness of pleasure – although it must be said that it is a peculiarly displeasurable kind of pleasure: 'Une onde pâteuse montait de ses reins à sa nuque.' He tries to resist, but in vain: he is lifted up on the wings of pleasure and cast down onto the body of his lover in the moment of orgasm. His consciousness is nothing more than consciousness (of) pleasure, a 'tournoiement rouge et volupteux' (*OR* 429). The last expression is interesting. At the simplest level it refers to the red glow imparted to Lola's room by the neon sign outside the window. At another level it refers back, through the blood association of 'rouge', to the execution of the bull – an image already evoked by Boris to denote the bloody and drearily predictable conclusion of his desire (*OR* 428). The image appears to be heavily overdetermined. On another level the blood-red death of the exhausted bull conveys the conventional 'little death' of the orgasm, but one also has the uneasy feeling that somewhere in all of this Lola has become the matador. In other words, in this exemplary description of Sartrean desire, a different desire, and a different dread, begin to emerge. Boris's fear is not simply that of a lucid consciousness faced with the momentary invasion of facticity: the source of the fear is Lola herself; the Lola who awaits Boris stretched out naked on the bed is no longer the vulnerable over-the-hill *chanteuse*: 'C'était une autre Lola, *paresseuse et redoutable*, elle le *guettait* à travers ses cils' (*OR* 428; emphasis added).[6] Her passivity is only apparent: beneath, there lies a terrible, secret activity. In this instant Lola is metamorphosed into the *femme-marécage*: the surface appearance of passivity, even vulnerability, is a dangerous lure; it hides a frighteningly active principle of assimilation. The phantasy that emerges here has already been seen to underlie many passages in Sartre's theoretical writings (see Chapter 1 above).

In a sense, Boris is 'doing his manly duty', and this expression, used by Mathieu to describe Pinette's seduction of the postmistress in *La Mort dans l'âme*, leads into another instance of the phantasy. Pinette is apparently at his most active: he crushes the woman into the earth, he is the 'soldat glorieux et vainqueur'; but he jeopardises his virility in the very exercise of it. First the rooting-down: 'il tenait la prairie couchée sous son ventre, elle l'appelait, *il s'enracinerait en elle par le ventre*' (*OR* 1282; emphasis added); then the complete assimilation: 'la tête plongea dans la gloire et l'amour, la prairie se referma' (*OR* 1283). The ambiguity of the last phrase is tantalising: a banal image meaning that Pinette's head was lost from view beneath the tall grass; or a worrying image suggesting that the earth swallowed and closed up over him.

This motif of engulfment appears to have its roots in the imaginary dyad – the pre-Oedipal attachment to the mother – and the absence of a strong paternal imago. But the determinants of this phantasy are perhaps not quite so simple. The later orientation of Sartre's work towards the father–son relationship, as evidenced by the *Scénario Freud*, *Les Séquestrés d'Altona* and *L'Idiot de la famille*, was already present as early as 'L'Enfance d'un chef'. The decisive relationship here is that between Lucien and his father. Sartre thought that he was parodying the successful resolution of the Oedipus complex in this story (see Chapter 5), but this was not all that he parodied. The primal scene makes a parodic appearance early in the story with the 'nuit du tunnel' episode, but it reappears, this time at the level of the imagery and almost certainly not as a function of a conscious design on Sartre's part. In the passage quoted above, Lucien 'revit la bête aveugle qui palpitait dans les draps avec des clapotis et des bâillements velus' (*OR* 380). This representation is strikingly similar to the 'beast with two backs' of Flaubert's primal scene, as imagined by Sartre in *L'Idiot*. It also reproduces a classic anxiogenic feature: the parents are one and the same creature; in other words, the scene of parental lovemaking is not just experienced as violent and sadistic by the child who witnesses it, but gives rise to castration anxiety: the father's penis disappears into the mother and is, apparently, engulfed or devoured – in the same way as Pinette is engulfed by the female meadow. The primal scene can be reactivated in the Oedipal phase, when castration anxiety is again predominant: it is in the Oedipal crisis that the child must learn that, from the point of view of the Law, it is he, and not the father, who is the intruder in the conjugal bedroom.

'L'Enfance d'un chef' is a nodal point in Sartre's relation with psychoanalysis, and one whose complexity cannot be overstated. He both uses and abuses Freudian theory in this story. The theory is used to make up for deficiencies in his own theory, whilst being parodied and attacked in favour of that theory: we are asked, implicitly, to view Lucien's flight into inauthenticity more as a conscious choice than as the result of unconscious causality. But at the same time, in the same text, it is possible to read an 'acting-out' of unconscious phantasies whose very existence functions as counter-proof to their explicit denial in the text.[7]

In the sex scene between Lucien and Maud we witness the passage of the virginal object ('toujours hors d'atteinte') to the debased object – the typical pattern of collapse from *femme-mirage* to *femme-marécage*. But there is also a suspicion that this transformation is to some degree connected with the reactivation of the primal scene.

As I turn now to *La Nausée*, a very similar pattern will become discernible in this text ostensibly concerned with the relationship of consciousness to the world.

I believe that Roquentin's nausea is 'readable' in terms of a certain dialectic of desire, a discourse of desire reproducing itself through the medium of a small number of obsessively repeated images and metaphors – images which also operate, as demonstrated in Chapter 1, in the supposedly authoritative discourse of Sartre's theoretical works. I shall centre my reading on the crisis points formed by the major attacks of nausea undergone by Roquentin.

The first attack is precipitated by a specifically sexual disappointment: 'je venais pour baiser', but Françoise is not there, with the result that Roquentin feels 'une vive déception au sexe, un long chatouillement désagréable' (*OR* 24). The nausea follows. The hard edges of the world disappear; time itself becomes limp and melts over external perceptions. It is as if the internal perception of the detumescence of the penis ('une vive déception au sexe') were projected onto the external world, which becomes in turn a presentation of detumescence. Roquentin's ostensible reasons for his continuing relations with Françoise are purely hygienic (*OR* 11). It seems that 'baiser', as opposed to 'faire l'amour' has a purgative, one might almost say, 'therapeutic' effect. But the therapy clearly backfires. When Roquentin does finally fuck Françoise, he has a dream, already touched upon in Chapter 2:

> J'ai laissé aller mon bras le long du flanc de la patronne et j'ai vu soudain un petit jardin avec des arbres bas et larges d'où pendaient d'immenses feuilles couvertes de poils. . . . Les larges feuilles étaient toutes noires de bêtes. Derrière des cactus et des figuiers de Barbarie, la Velléda du jardin public désignait son sexe du doigt. 'Ce jardin sent le vomi', criai-je. (*OR* 72)

The fact that there is some kind of relationship here between nausea and desire is evident enough, but what is the nature of this relationship? The explanation advanced by Michel Contat in his Pléiade edition is only partially satisfying. He points out that psychoanalysis sees dreams in which animals appear as indicating sex with a person who is not desired, and concludes by saying, 'Ce que la patronne a de rédhibitoire pour le désir de Roquentin, c'est qu'elle appartient sans discrétion au règne abhorré de la physis' (*OR* 1767). There are several things wrong with this suggestion. First, unless Contat is suggesting that Sartre is consciously using Freudian dream theory, which seems unlikely, it confuses two separate orders of explanation: the Freudian and the specifically Sartrean. Secondly, it is an argument that puts the cart before the horse. The suggestion is that Roquentin *cannot* desire Françoise *because* she belongs to the domain of Nature, but it seems to me that the images of proliferation and moist, suffocating abundance which form the core of the representation of the *femme-marécage*, rather than indicating the simple impossibility of desire, function as a blanket representation for an object of desire which is definitively forbidden but which resurfaces autonomously. And this *at the level of the text*, not in the dreaming psyche of a fictional character.

The Velléda pointing to her sex could furnish no more concrete indication, as it were, of the anxiety lying behind this complex of representations. And it is precisely this kind of perception that characterises Roquentin's delirious hallucination of the world when he is submerged by nausea. The axis of fecundity–sterility is worth pursuing. The link between fertility and nausea is established, at the level of the imagery, early in the book. Having fled the Rendez-vous des Cheminots, Roquentin heads out into the clear night air. First he must get past the Old Station, whose 'présence a *fécondé* les cent premiers mètres du boulevard Noir . . . *y a fait naître* une dizaine de réverbères' (*OR* 31; emphasis added). He succeeds in getting past by penetrating into a region of cold sterility:

> La Nausée est restée là-bas, dans la lumière jaune. Je suis heureux: ce froid est si pur, si pure cette nuit. . . . N'avoir ni sang, ni lymphe, ni chair. Couler dans ce long canal vers cette pâleur là-bas. N'être que du froid. (*OR* 34)

It is as if Roquentin's temporary antidote to nausea were to banish the representation which provokes it: to escape from the region of fertility into an ideal, inorganic purity or sterility. The passage also re-enacts the myth of autogenesis. In effect, Roquentin is escaping from a sickening *maternal* fecundity into a phantasy of rebirth. His wish to 'couler dans ce long canal vers cette pâleur là-bas' reads irresistibly like a desire to have been not of woman born, and translates a phantasied rebirth owing nothing to the lymphatic intimacy of the womb.

It is, however, in the celebrated *jardin public* episode that the relationship between nausea and desire, as vehiculed through images of proliferation, begins to become clearer. It is to this that I shall now turn.

The deep thematic association between this passage and the dream about the garden that stinks of vomit is underlined by the fact that the Velléda found its way into the dream from this self-same park: the park is watched over by this figure, who is at once worryingly female, petrified and petrifying. This scene is normally viewed as an illustration of the nauseous apprehension of contingency: the uneasy partnership between *soma*, consciousness and the world, and so on.[8] There is no doubt that Sartre *intended* the passage to be read in this way, but I would contend that, in addition, the *jardin public* amounts to the textual figuration of a full-blown castration anxiety, centred on the resurfacing of a banished representation. The melting of varnish, once more, signals the start of a revelation: 'Ce vernis avait fondu, il restait des masses monstrueuses et molles, en désordre – nues d'une effrayante et obscène nudité' (*OR* 151). When the veneer habitually provided by its name falls from the object, what remains is its *frightening* nudity. This falling-away of the name is brought about through the fascinated contemplation of the object, in this case the tree, in much the same way as a name repeated over and over again loses its signifying property and reverts to what it *is* – a collection of sounds. A long passage deleted from the published version of *La Nausée* but reproduced in the Pléiade edition throws interesting light on this point. The above passage originally continued,

> Ce qui m'a souvent troublé devant la nudité d'une femme, c'est la soudaine apparition du sens bestial et secret du corps, au-dessous des signes humains dont se compose un visage. Eh bien, tout à l'heure, c'était pareil. L'aspect humain des objets avait fait place à un drôle de sens. . . . C'était bien un sens, oui. Ça voulait dire quelque chose. Mais . . . je parlerai tout à l'heure de ce sourire des choses, doux, tremblant, un peu pourri: je ne l'ai vraiment compris qu'à la fin, beaucoup plus tard. Sur le moment j'étais gêné, comme si j'eusse assisté à un spectacle que je n'eusse pas dû voir. (*OR* 1784)

The richness and importance of this passage that has fallen victim to 'secondary revision' cannot be overemphasised. It is clear that what is perceived in the present moment has lost its *signification*, but retained a certain *sens*. This much is perhaps explicable in terms of the strange distinction that Sartre was to draw explicitly in *Qu'est-ce que la Littérature?* and reaffirm in *L'Idiot de la famille*, where it becomes central to the notion of *compréhension*, the distinction between prose writing that signifies, and a poetic use of language that conveys a *sense* – that is to say, a pre-linguistic, properly unsayable meaning. But it is the troubled relationship in this excised passage between representation and desire which should retain our attention. Drawing together the context of the image ('le sens bestial du corps') and the closing phrase ('sur le moment j'étais gêné') the conclusion is inescapable: the detached and floating signifier (detached, that is, from its conventional signified) which is only understood *nachträglich* ('beaucoup plus tard') is none other than the so-called primal scene – the banished representation. As I shall show shortly, this latter-day Actaeon who stumbles across the sight he should not have seen is unable to remain outside the spectacle for very long.

Roquentin's enthralled contemplation of an X-rated spectacle has parallels elsewhere in *La Nausée* – for example, when he stumbles across the exhibitionist and the little girl who are riveted to each other by the obscure force of their desires (*OR* 95); and elsewhere in Sartre's work – for example, in the scene from *L'Age de raison* where Mathieu finds himself desiring Ivich for the first time, vicariously, through the desire of another.

What Roquentin sees in the *jardin public* is a nightmarish proliferation:

> Toutes choses, doucement, tendrement, *se laissaient aller* à l'existence. Je compris qu'il n'y avait pas de milieu entre l'inexistence et cette abondance pâmée. Si l'on existait, il fallait exister jusque-là, jusqu'à la moisissure, à la boursouflure, à l'obscénité. (*OR* 151; emphasis added)

The world perceived by Roquentin is deturgescent, castrated, and Roquentin is unable to remain on the outside looking in, safely buttoned up:

> *Je me laissai aller* sur le banc, étourdi, assommé par cette profusion d'être sans origine: partout des éclosions, des épanouissements, mes oreilles bourdonnaient d'existence, ma chair elle-même palpitait et *s'entrouvait, s'abandonnait* au bourgeonnement universel, c'était répugnant. (*OR* 157; emphasis added)

Roquentin, too, is emasculated, feminised; he is submerged by this horrific proliferation. But, as the italicised words make clear, this emasculation goes further: he takes on the attributes of a receptive vagina. This bizarre experience which leaves Roquentin somewhere between a castrato and a transsexual is reproduced in and through the text by Roquentin's radical inability to attribute the predicates of virility to his perceptions – it is as if the symbolic castration had been displaced on to the faculty of perception itself:

> Ce platane avec ces plaques de pelade, ce chêne à moitié pourri, on aurait voulu me les faire prendre pour de jeunes forces âpres qui jaillissent vers le ciel. . . . Impossible de voir les choses de cette façon-là. Des mollesses, des faiblesses, oui. Les arbres

flottaient. Un jaillissement vers le ciel? Un affalement plutôt; à chaque instant je m'attendais à voir les troncs se rider comme des verges lasses, se recroqueviller et choir sur le sol en un tas noir et mou avec des plis. (*OR* 158)

The thematic association between this passage and the Velléda dream is further underlined by the way they are concluded. In the dream, Roquentin wakes up screaming 'ce jardin sent le vomi!'; and, in the *jardin public* scene, 'Je criai "quelle saleté, quelle saleté!" et je me secouai pour me débarrasser de cette saleté poisseuse' (*OR* 159).

It is important to note, with regard to Sartre's conscious intentions in *La Nausée*, that attacks of nausea frequently follow disappointment or the abandonment of a project: for example, the frustration of Roquentin's desire to screw Françoise, or the abandonment of the Rollebon project. This is perfectly explicable in terms of the Sartrean ontology. Consciousness is essentially pro-jective; it explodes towards the future. When this future collapses, it is as if consciousness suddenly flowed back on the present: stripped of its projected reason for being, it is thrown back onto its being without reason, its contingency.

The abandonment of the Rollebon project ushers in the attack of nausea in the Lucienne episode. The aspect of contingency highlighted here consists in the apprehension by consciousness of its necessary link with the body, without being the foundation for the existence of this body which 'has a life of its own'. It is this revelation that opens the floodgates: 'son corps existe encore, sa chair meurtrie. Elle n'existe plus' (*OR* 120). If Sartre was intending to represent the tendency of the body to cloud consciousness under certain circumstances, it is interesting that he chose sexual desire as a typical instance of this – all the more interesting since desire appears in this episode to have no *real* intentional object. As Michel Contat remarks in the *Oeuvres romanesques*, the Lucienne episode is highly revealing of the Sartrean sexual phantasmatic, and would have been even more revealing had the passages that Sartre cut at the behest of his editor remained in the published version (see (*OR* 1777).

In this episode, which I prefer to think of as a scenario, there are four actors – Roquentin, Rollebon, Lucienne and the 'ignoble individu' – and only two roles, rapist and raped, which rotate in a pattern of circular collapse. The starting-point for the scenario is provided by a newspaper article which Roquentin chances to glance at: a small girl, Lucienne, has been raped and strangled; her body has just been found (*OR* 120). This image of the dead girl, raped by an unknown assailant, provokes the delirious reaction. The first identification is with the rapist, and signals a sadistic desire: 'je fuis, l'ignoble individu a pris la fuite, son corps violé. . . . Je . . . voilà que je . . . [bande?] . . . . Violée' (*OR* 120). At this point Roquentin is invaded by his own desire, which is equated, by parallel notation in the text, with the invading presence of existence flooding in on him. The sadistic desire mutates into a masochistic one. Through the metonymic association of 'doigt' (finger and penis), Roquentin slips into the role of the violated child:

> Un doigt qui gratte dans ma culotte gratte, gratte et tire le doigt de la petite maculé de boue, la boue sur mon doigt qui sortait du ruisseau boueux et retombe doucement, doucement, mollissant, grattait moins fort les doigts de la petite qu'on étranglait, ignoble individu, grattait la boue, la terre moins fort, le doigt glisse doucement, tombe la tête la première et caresse roulé chaud contre ma cuisse. (*OR* 120)

The deturgescence of the penis is simultaneously the satiety of the rapist's desire and the emasculation of Roquentin as he is identified with the victim of the rapist. This sado-masochistic identification with rapist and raped recalls the Sartrean paradox that desire has a 'masculine' transcendent aim but is recuperated by the 'feminine' process of incarnation. This dual identification is reinforced by 'je fuis je suis un ignoble individu [rapist] à la chair meurtrie [raped]' (*OR* 121).

The scenario unwinds, then, in the following way: Roquentin on the outside – as an observer of an (imaginary) spectacle – mutates into Roquentin as rapist and thence to Roquentin as rapist–victim, and ends with Roquentin as pure victim of a (homosexual) rape: 'l'existence prend mes pensées par derrière et doucement les épanouit *par-derrière*; on me prend par derrière, on me force par-derrière de penser, donc d'être quelque chose' (*OR* 122).

Now, it is precisely at this point, as Roquentin is being 'taken from behind', that Rollebon makes his reappearance. It was the 'death' of Rollebon, the abandonment of the biographical project, that appeared to provoke the crisis. But Rollebon was more than a simple pretext for the activity which had justified Roquentin's existence. The terms the latter employs to describe the death of Rollebon are laden with resonances deriving from a different discourse: the writings on the father in *Les Mots* and, later, *L'Idiot*. Roquentin writes, 'Tout à l'heure encore il était là, *en moi*, tranquille et chaud et, de temps en temps, je le sentais remuer. . . . *Il pesait lourd sur mon coeur et je me sentais rempli*' (*OR* 115; emphasis add). Rollebon possessed Roquentin from within like a 'parasite sacré',[9] like a baby in the womb, like a stool distending the bowel. It is instructive to compare this passage with *L'Idiot*, where Sartre describes the continuing possession – through total identification – of Achille by his dead father: 'C'est que *le Père réside en lui, inerte pesanteur*, comme la somme de ses impuissances. . . . Il voulait être son père vif; il sera jusqu'au bout son père défunt' (*IF* 128; emphasis added). There are two phantasies,[10] or, rather, two faces of the same phantasy, underlying the Roquentin–Rollebon relationship. The first consists in Roquentin's belief that he is bringing the Marquis back to life; the second reverses this relationship: 'il . . . s'était emparé de ma vie pour représenter la sienne' (*OR* 117;[11] 'représenter' also in the sense of 'repeat' or 'act out again', since Roquentin had followed in the footsteps of Rollebon in Russia, where he too had committed a crime and made good his escape).

In all of this it is Rollebon (*rôle bon*) who has the 'beau rôle'. To recall the analogy I made at the start of this chapter, these theatrical metaphors begin to come into their own. Two dramas are being enacted. The first concerns the dialectic of consciousness and body; the second revolves around the identification, or failed identification, with the father.

In *Les Mots*, identification with, or possession by, the father is viewed with a degree of anxiety, but it is nevertheless seen to be the necessary, if unpleasant, prerequisite of accession to a masculine role and escape from the feminising intentions of the mother. This is clearly one source of the castration anxiety in *La Nausée*: when the identificatory imago disappears, the nauseous collapse of masculine into feminine, as in the *jardin public* episode, follows – as if automatically. The phrase 'Rollebon est mort. Antoine Roquentin n'est pas mort' (*OR* 122), which concludes the Lucienne episode, mirrors the phrase which opens it: 'Son corps existe encore. . . . Elle n'existe plus' (*OR* 120). This invites the reader to identify the extinguished consciousness of Lucienne with the familiar spirit of

Rollebon so suddenly departed, and further to strengthen the feminine identification of the wounded flesh of the dead girl with the 'castrated' Roquentin. This hypothesis is supported by a previous attack of nausea brought on when Roquentin fears the death or disappearance of Monsieur Fasquelle. Fasquelle's predictable, paternal presence had guaranteed the stability of the micro-world of the Café Mably; when Roquentin believes he has died, this world undergoes a startling transformation and he is once again plunged into a castrated universe peopled by 'ces êtres instables' and 'ces choses affaiblies' (*OR* 92).

To summarise, the nausea of castration anxiety is connected not only to an anxiogenic figure of an engulfing mother, but also to the absence or disappearance of a paternal guarantor of masculine identity.

If, in this existence, it is above all emasculation that threatens Roquentin, is there another world, a 'masculine' world? The answer to this question is clearly 'yes', but salvation is otherworldly: it lies in the world of the imagination, outside the plenum of existence, in the melody, the work of art. Of course, Roquentin has already realised that art does not offer a permanent antidote to nauseous existence: he knows that one cannot stop oneself from existing, *and* that one must either 'vivre ou raconter'. The Negress and the Jew are saved only in the imagination. The fact nevertheless remains that respite is afforded by a series of parallel experiences: going to the cinema, reading Stendhal (and pornographic magazines!) and, above all, listening to the refrain of 'Some of these Days'.

The very unreality of the latter places it beyond the rising tide of nausea: in another world, thinks Roquentin, circles and musical melodies retain their 'lignes pures et rigides', but 'l'existence est un fléchissement' (*OR* 151) Here again the *real* opposition is between phallicity ('leurs lignes pures et rigides') and castration ('un fléchissement'). These phallic attributes of the work of art are particularly noticeable in the predicates associated with the melody: it is above all the predictable return of the refrain that pleases Roquentin, the way it thrusts itself forward 'comme une falaise contre la mer' (*OR* 28). Furthermore, the time of the melody is radically different from the time of existence; it is a negation, a refusal of human time, tearing into it with its 'sèches petites pointes' (*OR 28)*. It is worth recalling at this point the analysis of the Viscous in Chapter 1, where Sartre posited a masculine and a feminine temporality. The feminine pole was the 'indifferent', the 'continuous'; the masculine pole was the 'granular', the 'discontinuous'. This sexualisation of temporality is established here in *La Nausée* by the unmistakably granular nature of the time of the melody ('ses sèches petites pointes') over and against the indifferent flux of existence. These phallic notations prepare the way for Roquentin's projected *Meisterwerk*, which will, he hopes, be as beautiful and as hard as steel (*OR* 210). Roquentin's aesthetic conversion comes as no surprise, since it has been implicit in the dualistic imagery of the text all along. Very early in the novel he muses, 'quels sommets n'atteindrais-je point si ma *propre vie* faisait la matière de la mélodie?' (*OR* 48).

Quite clearly, writing is viewed as a protection against the collapse into emasculation (cf. *OR* 504). The phantasmatic subtext to this process could be unearthed in any number of Sartre's other writings; in *Baudelaire*, for example, and even more dramatically in *L'Idiot de la famille*. But I shall pursue this line of writing into *Les Mots*, which is, after all, presented as an account of how Sartre himself 'chose' his literary vocation.

The parental figures in *Les Mots* all have a double articulation. Jean-Baptiste, initially, seems to be simply absent, dismissed at a cavalier stroke of the pen. But Sartre has an ambivalent attitude towards this disappearance. In one breath he describes it as a deliverance (*Mots* 18), in the next it is seen as a tragedy which very nearly leads to the definitive feminisation of Poulou (*Mots* 97). Charles Schweitzer is at one moment the absurd buffoon, principal player in the 'comédie familiale', but in the next he is Karl, the stern, law-giving paterfamilias, Kronos who had devoured his own sons. Anne-Marie, too, is double. Most often she is the virgin mother, albeit a 'vierge avec tache'. She is constantly a 'jeune fille', in the sense of an *unmarried* young woman. The emphasis, then, is on her chastity, her virginity, those aspects which situate her as companion or friend but not as mother (*Mots* 21). She and Poulou appear to be locked into a sempiternal pre-Oedipal Eden whose harmony will never be destroyed by a brash Moses. There could be no clearer statement of this than the passage where Sartre explains, almost seriously, that he has no superego: 'ma mère était à moi, personne ne m'en contestait la tranquille possession' (*Mots* 25). But there is another side to this situation, and another face to

Anne-Marie. If there was no one to contest the child's absolute possession of the mother, then by the same token the mother enjoyed the total *possession* of the child. Mother and child are locked in the imaginary dyad. It is Eden before the Fall, or almost. This Garden of Eden has certain of the more disturbing features of the parks and gardens of *La Nausée*, where Roquentin peeps in to see the child and the exhibitionist 'rivés l'un à l'autre par la force obscure de leurs désirs' (*OR* 95). The dyad is cemented by *mutual* desire. Left to the mother's tender ministrations, the child runs the risk of becoming nothing more than the object of her desire; and, indeed, at several points in the text, the representation of Anne-Marie topples over into menace.

For Anne-Marie is also the potent phallic mother, the 'jeune géante'.[12] The threat that she embodies ranges from engulfment to castration and mutilation. The engulfment consists in Poulou's conversion into a doll for the pleasure of the grown-ups: 'je permets gentiment qu'on me mette mes souliers, des gouttes dans le nez, qu'on me brosse et qu'on me lave, qu'on m'habille et qu'on me déshabille, qu'on me bichonne et qu'on me bouchonne' (*Mots* 25). Lucien Fleurier, the black double (cf. *OR* 310),[13] and Poulou both start from the same position, but Lucien remains a 'Cindy Doll', whereas Poulou, Sartre would have us believe, turns himself into an 'Action Man'. The child's illnesses, felt to be desired by the adults, only exacerbate his status as passive object: 'sous ces regards inquisiteurs, je me sentais devenir un objet, une fleur en pot' (*Mots* 77).[14]

There are countless instances of the mutilatory desire of the mother in *Les Mots*. I shall look briefly at just two.

Sartre certainly appears to have experienced both his shortness and the ugliness of his strabism as mutilations. As for Anne-Marie, this 'grande et belle femme' apparently found Poulou's diminutive stature quite natural, even appealing: 'Elle aimait que je fusse, à huit ans, resté *portatif et d'un maniement aisé:* mon *format réduit* passait à ses yeux pour un premier âge prolongé' (*Mots* 115; emphasis added).[15] Elsewhere in Sartre's work the process whereby parents transform their progeny into 'monsters' in order to fulfil their own ignoble desires is exposed and dissected quite ferociously. I refer, principally, to *Saint Genet*, and in particular to the passages on the Bohemian custom of turning children into geeks for the financial profit of the family (cf. *SG* 29). Sartre was writing a first draft of *Les Mots* whilst working on *Saint Genet*, and we find more than one echo of this in *Les Mots:* 'j'étais un enfant, ce monstre que les adultes fabriquent avec leurs regrets' (*Mots* 72).

Admittedly, if Poulou is a monster, it is not entirely the doing of his mother: part of his 'monstrosity' derives from his being forced into the role of ham actor for the delighted audience provided by his grandfather. But the specific theme of mutilation points back more to the mother herself. And this emerges very forcefully on the occasion of the child's first hair-cut.[16]

This episode has to be seen in the context of weaning or *sevrage*. The English word emphasises the positive aspect, inasmuch as the child is accustomed to other more nourishing food; the French term has much stronger associations of severing, cutting-off, separation and deprivation. In his attempt to stress the harmonious unity of the mother–infant dyad, Sartre makes light of this initial separation: sickly and feverish, the infant does not even notice '*le dernier coup de ciseaux* qui tranche les liens de la mère et de l'enfant' (*Mots* 17; emphasis added). But this brutal cut of the scissors is not the last one: it recurs with the barber's 'coup de ciseaux' which deprives Poulou of his golden locks. It is important to note that Anne-Marie opposes the hair-cutting, because, perhaps, it forces her to relinquish a deep-seated phantasy. The child's specular ego is, literally, in the hands of his mother: 'on tire de moi cent photos *que ma mère retouche* avec des crayons de couleur. Sur l'une d'elles qui est restée, je suis rose at *blond, avec des boucles*' (*Mots* 26; emphasis added). The mother's desire appears sinister at this point: she loves her son, but not as a son, more as a daughter, a replacement for the daughter she never had. Sartre imagines that Anne-Marie, like the Caroline Flaubert of *L'Idiot*, had wished for a girl child in order to compensate for the affective deprivation that had marred her own childhood (*Mots* 89). [17]

Significantly enough, it is the grandfather who 'rescues' Poulou from his lingering androgyny. Suddenly, he takes on the guise of the absent father and lays down the law: 'c'est un garçon', he tells Anne-Marie; 'tu vas en faire une poule mouillée' (*Mots* 89). And to impose his will he takes Poulou clandestinely to the barber's. The result of this was what Sartre calls in *L'Idiot* a 'contre-sevrage': the mother's rejection of this little monster, this bald toad, when he returns from the barber's; far from rushing to embrace her little angel, Anne-Marie is horrified and locks herself in her room to cry out her disappointment: 'on avait troqué sa fillette contre un garçonnet' (*Mots* 90).[18] The importance of this event is only revealed 'après-coup', says the text, when Poulou is twelve years old: this could be a reference to his discovery of his ugliness in La Rochelle, but it could also point to the remarriage of the mother (when Sartre was eleven, in fact) and the third 'coup de ciseaux', delivered by Joseph Mancy.

The episode is somewhat ambiguous in itself. On the one hand, it is a mutilation by the grandfather (the 'structural father') which casts Poulou out of his Edenic relationship with the mother. On the other hand, it is a salutary setback for the mother's feminising designs on her son. But there is a third level which points to the mother as the agent of an originary mutilation. For the hair-cut reveals a mutilation that was already in place – that is to say, congenital: the atrocious squinting eye. It is the evidence of *her* own eyes (the ugliness of her son) that Anne-Marie is no longer able to deny. Her phantasy proves unresistant to the reality principle.

It is as if Poulou experienced his infirmity, since it is congenital, as a mutilation performed on him by the mother, similar to that performed by the Bohemian geek-makers. Support for this hypothesis comes from the *Carnets de la drôle de guerre*. Besides containing long autobiographical sketches which are embryonic versions of *Les Mots*, the *Carnets* also include an early 'existential analysis' of Kaiser Wilhelm, through the text of a work by Emil Ludwig.[19] In discussing the congenitally atrophied arm of the Kaiser, Sartre makes some interesting assumptions regarding the Kaiser's attitude towards his mother: 'cette mère le méprise et le hait tout d'abord parce qu'il est infirme' (*Car* 383). The mother despises him for a mutilation that she herself had inflicted! The extent to which Sartre is *identifying* with Wilhelm can be seen in his insistence that power bypasses the father and goes straight from grandfather to grandson (the same structure as in *Les Mots*); but also, explicitly, when he compares his own 'oeil éteint' with the withered arm of the Kaiser (*Car* 371).

The statement of the central problem in *Les Mots* comes in the following pivotal passage:

> L'enchaînement paraît clair: féminisé par la tendresse maternelle, affadi par l'absence du rude Moïse qui m'avait engendré, infatué par l'adoration de mon grand-père, j'étais voué par excellence au masochisme si seulement j'avais pu croire à la comédie familiale. Mais non . . . je pris en haine les pâmoisons heureuses,

l'abandon, ce corps trop caressé, trop bouchonné, je me trouvai en m'opposant.... (*Mots* 97)

The absence of the father leaves the child in the possession of the mother. The fate that threatens him – here summed up by 'féminisé' and 'affadi' – is engulfment, emasculation and mutilation. As we have just seen, the grandfather is capable of stepping into the shoes of the absent father, if only momentarily. But in the above passage Charles is included amongst the elements of a defacilitating environment. Significantly, the extract quoted above is silent as to *how*, exactly, the child managed to escape from this crippling entourage. We are told simply that 'je me trouvais en m'opposant'. Sartre goes on to direct the reader's interpretation of this 'escape': we should not see it as a revolt, a rebellion; one only rebels against an oppressor, and in this family there were only benefactors. But these were strange benefactors who would kill with kindness. The child *does* revolt, and it is a characteristic brand of revolt: a miraculous autogenesis, a rebirth that circumvents both mother's womb and father's seed.

It is at this point that we rejoin the central problematic of *La Nausée*, for it is through the invention of writing – and the invention of 'self' in writing – that this escape is made good in *Les Mots*.

This Edenic, yet crippling intimacy of the mother–child dyad is referred to, in Lacanian psychoanalysis, as 'le désir de la mère' – the desire *for* and *of* the mother. The invention of writing by Poulou could be seen as a late self-inscription into the Symbolic Order where the dyad becomes triad through the mediation of the name-of-the-dead-father – that is to say, 'language'. The child's progressive involvement with words – as indicated by the book's title – marks the stages on the way to a liberation, albeit ambiguous.

Poulou's fictions pass through numerous stages. There are the nocturnal phantasies, then the pantomimes, and finally, via infantile plagiarism, the 'novels'. It is only the latter that present genuine satisfaction. The earliest phantasies are fairly transparent. Despite Sartre's disingenuous disclaimer to the effect that 'Karlémami' were excluded from his phantasies (*Mots* 98), the latter are scenarios for three actors: the young girl ('ces frêles créatures' – *Mots* 98); the father of the girl, taking the various guises of margrave, magistrate, tsar and emperor – that is to say the Law; and the young hero himself, the subject of the phantasy. This is none other than Poulou himself with the added attributes of

Herculean strength and indomitable courage. The girl is in danger, the hero saves her and returns her to a grateful father; then he canters off, down the Boule' Saint-Michel, into the sunset. The phantasy of saving the young girl translates a fairly transparent desire, but the condition of representability (its certificate from the Board of Film Censors) is the non-fulfilment of this very desire: 'Héros toujours future, je languissais pour une consécration que je repoussais sans cesse' (*Mots* 111). This could be glossed in the following way: motivated by an original and inarticulate desire, the child is condemned to leave this desire in suspense, lacking the sexual knowledge as to what a consecration might entail, yet dimly aware of the dangers this consummation may represent.

The phantasy is repeated *mutatis mutandis* in what Sartre calls his 'pantomimes'. These spring from his encounter with the cinema. The visit to the cinema in *Les Mots* is illustrative of the extreme coherence of the dyad formed with the mother, but also of the *foretaste* of a possible mediation – a kind of 'mirror phase': '*ce n'était pas moi*, cette jeune veuve qui pleurait sur l'écran et pourtant, nous n'avions, elle et moi, qu'une seule âme: la marche funèbre de Chopin' (*Mots* 106; emphasis added). Difference is instituted by the screen image, identity through the melody. Back home, Poulou prevails upon Anne-Marie, that other 'young widow', to reproduce this cinematographic intimacy by playing the pieces that appeared to animate the soul of the screen heroine. Meanwhile, Poulou is temporarily beside himself – Other – as he acts out with his body the scenarios he had so often rehearsed alone in bed. Here again this consummation is deferred; 'je renvoyais aux calendes mon triomphe' (*Mots* 109). Because these are basically *mimetic* phantasies, they do not provide the child with the possibility of distancing himself from the representation of his truth. But if the function of these phantasies was to keep the idyll intact, they were also intended to neutralise the anxiety-provoking aspects of this intimacy. Sartre writes that the fiction merged into the truth (*Mots* 110). This may be so, if we take 'truth' to refer to one that is destined to remain unknown: the reality of the bonds of desire that held mother and son riveted to each other in their indissoluble couple.

What is missing is a mediating term – that is to say, the Father; or perhaps the creation of a mode of representation in which the same phantasies could be employed, but whose principal actor is designated as simultaneously Same and Other as the child. Such a creation would allow the squaring of the circle: the basic *indifference* of the idyll would remain intact at one level, but the anxiogenic aspects of this idyll would be neutralised by the creation of a subject of the representation who is radically Other than the author – a third-person narrator.

It is writing that furnishes Poulou with his deferred entry into the Symbolic Order. The crucial difference between 'writing' and 'pantomime' emerges very clearly from the following:

> L'année précédente, quand je 'faisais du cinéma', je jouais mon propre rôle, je me jetais *à corps perdu* dans l'imaginaire et j'ai pensé plus d'une fois m'y engouffrer tout entier. Auteur, le héros c'était encore moi, *je projetais en lui mes rêves épiques. Nous étions deux pourtant*: il ne portait pas mon nom et je ne parlais de lui qu'à la troisième personne . . . je me réjouis d'être *lui* sans qu'il fût tout à fait moi.   (*Mots* 125; emphasis added, other than for 'lui')

It is, however, not clear from this account why the child should have felt the need to distance himself from his epic dreams, unless of course these dreams were the symbolic representation of some desire dimly perceived to be illicit or dangerous.

At this level, the discovery of writing functions in much the same way as a classic compromise formation: desire is indulged and denied simultaneously. Something akin to the splitting of the ego, where the aspect of he ego to be disavowed is split off and projected into another person or object.

On the subject of the mirror-phase Lacan writes

> Cette forme [l'idéal du moi] situe l'instance du *moi*, dès avant sa détermination sociale, *dans une lignée de fiction*, à jamais irréductible pour le seul individu – ou plutôt, qui ne rejoindra qu'asymptotiquement le devenir du sujet, quel que soit le succès des synthèses dialectiques par quoi il doit résoudre en tant que *je*, sa discordance d'avec sa propre réalité.[20]

Whilst situated within the Imaginary, the mirror-phase prefigures the inscription of the subject into the Symbolic Order (the crucial aspect of this being the accession to communicative language capable of articulating need in the form of demand), in that here, for the first time, the *je* flows into a *Gestalt* which is both me and not me (the disparity between the perceived movement of the mirror-image, and the internal perception of motor inco-ordination.[21] In light of this, it is fascinating to see the literary metaphor of the mirror occurring in the context of differentiation and mediation in Les Mots. At one point Sartre finds the image of 'un palais de glaces désert' to describe the fundamental dependency of the child on the gaze of the adults. With writing, he is turned into a two-way mirror: 'Je suis né de l'écriture: avant elle il n'y avait qu'un *jeu* de miroirs; dès mon premier roman, je sus qu'un enfant s'était introduit dans le palais de glaces' (*Mots* 130; emphasis added). This could be taken literally: *je* is born of writing where previously there is only a '*je*(u) de miroirs'. There could be no more eloquent summary of the passage from mirror-phase to Symbolic Order, with all this entails in terms of loss and gain: a position from which to speak (*je*), but a position which casts the subject and his constitutive desires into an order governed by a law which forbids the unmediated expression of these desires.

The final mediation comes with the discovery of the role of the writer as socially valorised figure. This could be termed the entry into the 'Cultural Order'.

Sartre talks of homosexuality as the way-out that Genet invents at the moment of suffocation; one could see the invention of writing as a similar way-out discovered by Poulou. The discovery of writing is thus tantamount, in the case of Poulou, to the reinvention of the missing father.

But before we lose ourselves in rapturous admiration for this miraculous self-creation, it must be said that the very desire which this escape is intended to put at a safe distance insists powerfully in the images used to describe it. I shall look at two typical instances. The first passage describes the importance of Poulou's newfound *alter ego*: 'c'était ma poupée je le pliais à mes caprices, je pouvais le mettre à l'épreuve, lui percer le flanc d'un coup de lance . . . et puis le soigner comme me soignait ma mère, le guérir comme elle me guérissait' (*Mots* 125). The likening of the child to a doll is an image of feminisation, and signifies the position of the child as he is *manié* by his mother. Moreover, the double articulation of Anne-Marie persists in this passage. Throughout Les Mots it is the caring, affectionate image that serves as the 'official version'; the mutilating, phallic mother is repressed – she returns here in the form of this displaced 'coup de lance'. In this passage, the comforting intimacy of the mother–child couple is maintained, but the anxiogenic features are neutralised by appropriation: the child takes over the function and controls it himself.

On the eve of his discovery of the social function of the writer, Poulou avidly scours the pages of the *Grand Larousse* for some indication of how the signs of future greatness may be recognised. He is disappointed. But one engraving catches his eye and his imagination – the arrival of Dickens in New York: '[la foule] ouvre toutes ses bouches et brandit mille casquettes, si dense que les enfants étouffent, solitaire, pourtant, orpheline, veuve, dépeuplée par la seule absence de l'homme qu'elle attend' (*Mots* 143). It is not just that this crowd has the feminine attributes elsewhere associated with Sartrean crowds (for example, in *OR* 729–47); it is identified, through the terms 'orpheline' and 'veuve', with Anne-Marie herself. Importantly, this maternal throng is so dense, so engulfing, that it stifles the children cowering in their mothers' skirts. By a second association, one is forcibly reminded of another crowd in *Les Mots* depopulated by the one absence that could have made it whole: the party at the language institute where the vertiginous absence is that of Monsieur Simonnot. Dickens, Simonnot and, perhaps, Jean-Baptiste are conspicuous by their very absence – 'absent en chair et en os' (*Mots* 79), but whose flesh and blood? The above quotation seems to express the need to break away from the stifling desire of the mother – whilst maintaining her protection – by taking the place of the father. In other words, to play both ends to the middle: to *be* the (mother's) phallus, and to *have* the (father's) phallus.

One further extract makes this point quite forcefully. I have already alluded to a passage where Sartre talks of his mother's handling of him as expressing her desire to feminise, to emasculate. The terms he uses would apply better to a book: 'portatif et d'un maniement aisé', 'format réduit', and so on. All through *Les Mots*, books are likened to dolls or babies: they are expertly opened up at the right page by Karl, perused at leisure by Louise, and read aloud from by Anne-Marie. In Poulou's final metamorphosis he is transformed into nothing less than a leather-bound paper totem. The equation penis = doll = book is there for all to read: 'on me prend, on m'ouvre, on m'étale sur la table, on me lisse du plat de la main et parfois on me fait craquer. Je me laisse faire et puis tout à coup je fulgure, j'éblouis, je m'impose à distance. . . . Je suis un grand fétiche maniable et terrible' (*Mots* 164). Inasmuch as he is a 'grand fétiche maniable', he remains stalled in the Imaginary, as the mother's phallus – that which is phantasised to make her whole. Inasmuch as he is 'un grand fétiche terrible', he *has* the father's phallic power. But, precisely, this passage from Imaginary to Symbolic is not a passage from being to having: the identification is not, as is normal, with a *position*, but with an *entity* – the underlying phantasy centres on the appropriation of the phallus of the phallic mother, who has already acquired the phallus of the father.

In Sartre's account of his liberation, the role of the father is passed over in silence: he was simply absent and therefore had to be reinvented in the imaginary mode. But we have seen that the symbolic father (Karl) is very much present when he 'saves' Poulou by having him shorn. Similarly, although the discovery of writing is presented by Sartre as a miraculous self-creation, it is Karl who alerts Poulou to his calling: by the trouble he takes to divert him from becoming a professional writer, he precipitates him into this very profession (cf. *IF* 1598; *Mots* 138–9). Talking of the effect of the crushing paternal judgement on Flaubert, Sartre employs a favourite image from Kafka's 'In der Strafkolonie': 'la sentence est intériorisée, cousue sous la peau du condamné' (*IF* 844). It is precisely this image that Sartre uses to describe the atavistic judgement handed down by Karl. Like Roquentin, he is afraid to let go of his pen: 'on m'a cousu mes commandements sous la peau: si je reste un jour sans écrire, la cicatrice me brûle' (*Mots* 139).

The curtain is about to go up on the final act of the scenario. We have seen that a 'father' was absolutely necessary if Poulou was to escape from the engulfment and castration threatened, however obscurely, by his mother. Jean-Baptiste has opted for early retirement, but there is a ready-made patriarch to hand: Karl. Unfortunately, Karl is *not* a good father. The opening of *Les Mots* presents us with an ogre, a Kronos, a cannibal *devouring* his sons.[22] In Sartre's work, fathers are either not father enough (Jean-Baptiste), or father far too much! It is a problem of identification: the mode of identification that haunts Sartre's texts is alimentary.[23] Either the father swallows up the son, or the son swallows the father. In both cases anxiety results: the father is not digested; he persists within and gives rise to that most persistent of Sartrean nightmares – the perverted consciousness.

5

The Perverted Consciousness

L'aventure de Genet, c'est d'avoir été nommé.

Agir . . . écrire son nom.

Sartre's theorisation of desire does not permit of a concept of perversion. All sexual attitudes, from algolagnia to zoophilia, are ultimately reducible to variations on the essential aim of sexual desire: the 'perpetual attempt of an embodied consciousness to come to terms with the existence of others'.[1] In *L'Etre et le néant* this aim is stated to be impossible *a priori*. In later works such as the *Cahiers* a glimmer of hope appears on the horizon in the form of a Utopian society where conflict would no longer form the basis of human relations: 'the element of the same'.[2] But the present reality of alienation (economic, ontological, social, and so on) effectively extinguishes this ray of hope. Human relations continue to unfold under the sign of alterity; it is the presence of the Other – original and sempiternal – which ensures that the original purity of desire will be defiled, deviated and perverted.

But, whether or not the concept of perversion has a theoretical basis in Sartre's writings, this concept remains very active. In fact, it is more of an intuition, or even a dread, than a concept. This dread takes the form of a kind of 'anxiety of influence': the fear that the invisible Other has interwoven himself insidiously into the warp and weft of the conscious mind, deviating its intentions, possessing it from within. In the pages that follow I shall begin to trace this phantasy of possession through the adventures of an emblematic figure for Sartre: the male homosexual.

THE ORIGINAL POSSESSION

The only discussion of homosexuality in *L'Etre et le néant* is in the context of a discussion of bad faith and sincerity. Sartre asserts that a homosexual will frequently have an intolerable feeling of guilt, and his whole existence may be determined in relation to this feeling (*EN* 100). This man may recognise his homosexual penchant and recognise each individual 'misdemeanour' he has committed, but still refuse to consider himself as a homosexual: he is a special case, he was merely experimenting, he was a victim of circumstance, and so on. At this point Sartre has the homosexual's friend enter upon the scene; he is vexed by the homosexual's apparent duplicity, and demands in the name of sincerity that he come clean and admit that he *is* a homosexual: 'Qui est de mauvaise foi', wonders Sartre, 'l'homosexuel ou le champion de la sincérité?' (*EN* 100). If the homosexual understands the phrase 'I am not a homosexual' in the sense of 'I am not that which I am', then he is in good faith.[3] If, on the other hand, 'il déclare n'être pas pédéraste au sens où cette table *n'est pas* un encrier' (*EN* 100), then he is in bad faith. The homosexual's problem is that he is caught between two sets of contradictory values: 'L'homosexuel reconnaît ses fautes, mais il lutte de toutes ses forces contre l'écrasante perspective que ses erreurs lui constituent un *destin*' (*EN* 100). So the homosexual who declares that he is not a homosexual in the way that a table is not a chair is guilty of a kind of bad faith by overcompensation – he cannot risk admitting that he has behaved like a homosexual for fear of this image being taken over and frozen into a destiny by the crushing condemnation of the Others.

The symbolic importance of Jean Genet in Sartre's later work is, perhaps, prefigured here, in the shape of the passage from homosexual to existential hero. The homosexual is he who must most energetically dissociate himself from his accumulated past; to cease to flee would involve becoming a static target for the petrifying 'jugement de la collectivité'. Furthermore, in this champion of sincerity we have an early avatar of the crippling *justes* of *Saint Genet*. Homosexual desire is not perverted *per se*; it is pure in its origins: 'ne reconnaît-il pas, par lui-même, le caractère singulier et irréductible de la réalité humaine?' (*EN* 100). The would-be agent of perversion is, paradoxically, the *honnête homme*, the champion of sincerity. There is something vaguely sinister about the desire of this upright Other to force the homosexual to recognise his perversion in the name of sincerity: 'Qui ne voit, en effet, ce qu'il y a d'offensant pour autrui et de rassurant pour moi, dans une phrase comme: "Bah! c'est un pédéraste", qui raye d'un trait une inquiétante liberté et qui vise désormais à constituer tous les actes d'autrui comme des conséquences découlant rigoureusement de son essence' (*EN* 101). The implication of this passage is that the sincere man is electing a scapegoat: he is localising the Evil in the Other, in order to deny its presence in himself. This other freedom is worrying not because it is a pathological anomaly, but because it is a universal possibility for all. This pattern of original purity, rendered impure and illegitimate by the representative of societal Good, is perceptible in outline in these short extracts from *L'Etre et le néant*; it is fleshed out and made concrete in Sartre's brilliant study of Genet, *Saint Genet, comédien et martyr*.

Sartre's aim is to show how Genet becomes 'Genet'. All material is grist to the biographical mill – plays, novels, interviews, anecdotes, and so on. These elements are gathered into a coherent whole by the method of empathetic reconstruction which Sartre had employed, to lesser effect, in the study on Baudelaire. The facts of Genet's existence are not treated as isolated data, but woven into a 'text' by means of the unifying thread of the 'original choice'. In this way, Genet's homosexuality, his criminal activities, his writing, and so on, are assumed axiomatically to be united by this synthesising thread: they are not discrete unities with no communicating staircase between the various levels.

Freudian psychoanalysis is rejected in *Saint Genet* as 'deterministic': it risks missing the irreducible kernel of Genet's history, which is 'le travail d'une liberté acharnée à faire son salut' (*SG* 121). This emphasis on ontological freedom disqualifies any recourse to explanation by unconscious determinism; Genet's homosexuality is the function of a special choice of being, not of a psycho-biological given: 'On ne naît pas homosexuel ou normal: chacun devient l'un ou l'autre selon les accidents de son histoire et sa propre réaction à ces accidents' (*SG* 80). Inversion is not the result of a hormonal imbalance, nor is it the passively determined effect of complexes; it is rather, 'une issue qu'un enfant découvre au moment d'étouffer' (ibid.). In fact, Sartre could probably have integrated much of Freud's thought – as he was to do in *L'Idiot* more-or-less successfully – into his own framework, without falling into the trap of determinism. Freud, too, believed that the achievement of a 'normal' sexual orientation was far from self-evident; it had to be explained in just the same way as inversion. On this point, then, there is no disagreement. But Sartre's rejection of *biological* determinism appears extreme: few, if any, modern sexologists would entirely discount at least the influence of biological factors. Similarly, the rejection of 'complexes' seems to be based on a misconception. Sartre appears still to view complexes as entities or inhabitants of consciousness, whereas in fact they are nothing if not the 'accidents de son histoire et sa propre réaction à ces accidents'. The reference to complexes, in the plural, points more to a Jungian conception than a Freudian one – for Freud the *one* nuclear complex was the Oedipus complex, and its 'dark face' the castration complex.[4] By the time Sartre came to write *L'Idiot* his position on this key Freudian concept had become far less rigid, to the extent that he was able to *use* the notion quite freely.

Having raised these brief questions of method, I shall now look at the outline of Sartre's analysis of Genet's homosexuality.

As a foundling, Genet was an outsider from birth, never knowing the protective cocoon of a family, knowing only the antiseptic interiors of state orphanages. It is not, however, at this stage that Sartre situates the original crisis – although this original ejection from *Society* and therefore, Sartre claims, from *Nature* was to create a defacilitating environment. Genet was farmed out to peasants in the Morvan and it is there that the original crisis occurred. The child was discovered pilfering from his adoptive community. The scene, as imagined by Sartre,[5] has Genet pinned down from behind like a butterfly on a board, raped by a look, frozen by a vertiginous word, 'Voleur!': 'Genet, sexuellement, est d'abord un enfant violé. Ce premier viol, ce fut le regard de l'Autre, qui l'a surpris, pénétré, transformé pour toujours en objet' (*SG* 81). This is not, Sartre stresses, a figurative rape; it *is* a rape. This is the linchpin of the analysis. It is impossible to overstress the importance, both from Sartre's point of view, and from my own, of this primordial identification of the gaze of the Other with an anal rape. By the same token, it is worth pointing out at this early stage that the gaze–rape is further identified with the *nomination* (in this case 'Voleur'). Genet is, then, objectified by the gaze of the Other; and at the physical level this is experienced as a feminisation: 'une étreinte de fer l'a rendu femme' (*SG* 81). This last identification should give pause for thought: why a woman? There are two related strands in the answer to this question. The first is provided by Sartre himself. He claims he is taking 'woman' in the ontosociological sense, as defined by Simone de Beauvoir, who noted that 'la sexualité féminine tire ses principaux caractères de ce que la femme est objet pour l'Autre et objet pour elle-même avant d'être sujet' (*SG* 41). It is easy to see how this fits in with the objectifying gaze of the Other, but 'une étreinte de fer'? The second strand is less obvious. It is as if Sartre's deep model for gender identity lay in the sado-masochistic phantasy of the primal scene. In *L'Idiot* the primal scene appears several times. For example: 'être objet d'aggression, devenir proie, se pâmer sous des caresses brutales . . . être humecté, fécondé donc pénétré' (*IF* 685). Or, again: when Sartre imagines Gustave being devastated by the revelation that his 'virile half' 'se révélait *femme et proie* entre les bras de son père' (*IF* 697; emphasis added).

On the one hand, Genet is a 'woman' because women are defined socially as relative beings in the patriarchal society. On the other hand, Genet is a woman because 'woman' is first and foremost the mother who submits to a brutal rape at the hands of the father.[6] The first, sociological strand equates with the generalised principle of the objectifying look – the 'écrasante perspective', which we encountered in *L'Etre et le néant*, of having his past errors converted into a destiny. But through this highly charged epithet, 'écrasante', we are led away from general sociology and back into individual psychology. In *L'Idiot*, again, the two strands come together in the following version of the primal scene: 'le Bien l'avait prise et mise dans son lit, elle avait porté *cet ange écrasant*, elle s'était pâmée' (*IF* 89; emphasis added).

In short, the gaze that sodomises Genet is that of the father: both as representative of a social order, and as figure in an obscure phantasmatic. This crucial identification could be confirmed by an exploration of the notion of Good and Nature in *Saint Genet*.

The original crisis has such a devastating effect on Genet for two reasons. First, he is too young to liquidate, with a sneer, the paternal values by which he stands condemned. Second, he is originally outside Nature; those who are on the inside (the adults, the peasants, the *justes*) are by definition right. Genet feels in his closeness to nature ('douce confusion') the essential goodness of his 'nature', but he is incapable of realising the difference between the nature that is really there, and the socialised image of nature of which the *justes* are the jealous guardians. On this socialised Nature, Sartre writes that, when the *justes* seek Nature within their own hearts, they are seeking, in reality, the symbol of the legitimacy of their birth: 'L'ordre naturel qu'ils perçoivent au dehors et en eux-mêmes, c'est tout simplement l'ordre social' (*SG* 250). To recapitulate, the adults are necessarily *right* because Genet is fundamentally wrong: his appearance in the world is a scandal, accidental and illegitimate; his place in the social order was not sanctioned by the transmission of a patronym which would have marked his insertion into the patriarchal order.

Now, Sartre does not perhaps intend this father who is head of the social order to be identified with the symbolic father of psychoanalytical discourse. Indeed, the aim in *Saint Genet* is to de-Oedipalise these family relations: if the *justes* are father-figures it is due more to relations of production than to bonds of desire. The *justes* endow Nature (not significant in itself) with a projected social significance, and are concerned with maintaining the political, economic and social *status quo*; 'la forêt même parle des hommes: c'est la propriété d'un grand seigneur, c'est une réserve de bois de chauffage' (*SG* 250).

If the transmission of a legal patronym is the cornerstone of patriarchal society, Genet's illegitimacy is antagonistic to this order that it is in the interest of the father to protect. The analysis is convincing to a large degree, but it is only half of the story. By definition, the father in a patriarchal society is the Law, and the Law must be taken to include the totality of historically determined societal prescriptions and interdictions in force at that moment. Sartre, however, suppresses the properly Oedipal half of the equation. What is the source of the father's prestige? In reducing the 'patriarchal order' to 'bourgeois capitalist society', Sartre effectively ignores the desire for the mother which makes the patriarch what he is: the enforcer of the Law would be nothing were it not for the desire to transgress. We shall see that the Oedipal discourse which Sartre attempts to brush aside reappears and insists in the gaps in his own analysis.

So the *justes* have imposed an identity on Genet. Like the homosexual in *L'Etre et le néant*, he is caught between conflicting values: he *is* nothing more than what they condemn him to *be*, but this identity is an absolute only for them, and absolutely *evil*. Genet is an impossibility: 'Quant à sa propre existence, comme il ne l'atteint que par la médiation d'autrui . . . il n'en est pas plus assuré que de celle de Groenland ou du Masque de Fer' (*SG* 41).[7] It is in this sense that I entitled this chapter 'The Perverted Consciousness'. Genet is Other at the very heart of his subjectivity; his possession is so deep that it preconditions the concepts and reflections through which he seeks to grasp it. Genet, like Kean, is an actor who, even when he steps outside of his role, in order to question it, does not escape from it, since even departures from this role have been written into it.[8] His being is 'une personne au sens latin de *persona* – je veux dire un masque et un rôle, dont les conduites et les répliques sont déjà fixées. C'est l'Autre enfin, un "zar" qui le possède' (SG 65). We have rejoined here the phantasmatic father-figure of the *zar* that was encountered in Chapter 3. Genet is possessed by a ghostly paternal occupant – possessed from within, but also possessed from *behind*: the original possession is a phantasied anal rape at the hands of the father – the father 'enjoys' him. The fundamental human aim, for Sartre, is to 'jouir de soi', and this is precisely what Genet is incapable of doing so long as he is 'enjoyed' by the Other, so long as his *moi* is another.

THE REPOSSESSION

If this Other could be likened to a particularly tenacious squatter, then Genet must dispossess him in order to regain possession of his self. The first attempt at repossession takes the form of a sort of 'mirror-phase'. Is not Genet simply a narcissist as he stands contemplating his reflection? Yes, as long as we remember that Narcissus, too, was already bewitched; that his being had been stolen. For Genet, the mirror is also a weapon: 'Le miroir c'est les yeux des Autres et le rêve de Narcisse traduit la volonté secrète *d'arracher ces yeux pour se les greffer*' (SG 77; emphasis added). Genet attempts to see himself as he appears to the Other who constituted his culpable being; he attempts to appropriate the gaze of the Other in front of the mirror, but the mirror reflects his own gaze and the illusion of alterity is shattered. All of this is perfectly in line with the dialectic of the look as elaborated in *L'Etre et le néant*. However, the italicised phrase speaks of a different desire. The subtext is patently concerned with castration; the original possession, then, has a further determinant. It is an anal rape, and the desire to appropriate the organ of the rape (the eyes) is a desire to rape the rapist. But this tearing-off and grafting-on of the raping organ is also a reversal of castration: Genet has been raped by the Father and nothing short of a violent appropriation of the paternal phallus will remedy the original violence. Not surprisingly, Sartre suppresses this dimension of the text in *Saint Genet*, but in *L'Idiot* the self-same image occurs, this time recognised for what it is, albeit projected onto Gustave (cf. *IF* 460).[9]

In any case, the mirror proves inadequate, but the imperative remains. Genet must rid himself of the Other. A more effective strategy is to manoeuvre the Other into seeing him as he wishes to be seen, although the eyes of the Other are untrustworthy witnesses, as the protagonists of *Huis clos* discover: 'Ce que les lustres et les appliques et la psyché n'arrivaient pas à faire, une conscience aimante ne peut-elle réaliser?' (*SG* 77). But the young thugs of the correctional centre are too much loved themselves to be bothered to love Genet. The only role he can expect is that of lover – a role which appears ill-suited to his purpose since it seems to destine him to an eternally relative existence.

At this point Genet operates a telling reversal, a 'tourniquet': he will surmount his original sodomisation by allowing himself to be sodomised again, only this time he controls the act. All of this, it should be recalled, takes place in a realm of perversion that is characterised not by the nature of the act, but by its unreality. It is what Sartre later called an 'irréalisation portée au carré' (*IF* 694): the males and females in Genet's world are in reality 'tantes-mâles' and 'tantes-filles'. Yet the symbolism remains clear – the male of the homosexual relationship is none other than the reincarnation of the *justes*, the father, who had raped him as a child (*SG* 126). And Genet, in allowing himself to be sodomised, is reliving this original possession, with a difference. This time he will castrate his paternal assailant: '*le coït est une greffe*. Genet, mante religieuse, dévore son mâle' (*SG* 126). Once more, the phantasy underpinning Sartre's terms of analysis is the primal scene: the father's penis, in copulation *a tergo*, disappears, is devoured by the mother. The mother triumphs, for she has now appropriated (grafted on) this phallus: from primal scene to phallic mother! And once more the female of the partnership is phantasised not only to castrate, but also to *devour* the male.

So if Genet is possessed by a *zar* of dubious morals – the pederastic father – the way he finds to eject him is to elect the *Dur* as his living representative (thus re-exteriorising the internalised 'evil') and castrating him in the person of this homosexual lover. As Sartre points out, this curious act of love–hatred–exorcism is also a cathartic repetition of the original crisis:[10] 'mais cette fois la crise est provoquée, consentie et, comme dans un traitement psychanalytique, elle acquiert une valeur cathartique' (*SG* 109).[11]

It will be recalled that the original possession took the form not just of a rape but also of a nomination: Genet's being was reduced to a vertiginous word – 'Voleur'. Accordingly, Genet's revenge is carried out not only on the properly sexual plane, but also at the level of writing. A large part of *Saint Genet* is taken up with a fascinating account of how Genet turns the tables on the *justes* through his literary activities. The use that he makes of the first-person narrative, for example, is a way of inducing complicity on the part of his reader: to the extent that he is absorbed in his reading, the reader becomes the *je* of the narration, but – horror of horrors – he wakes up to find that the *je* to whom he has lent his body is a thief and a pederast. The 'honnête homme' is caught in an embarrassing dilemma: either he desires 'la chair d'un garçon qui est secrètement fille', or he desires 'le garçon en tant que son Je est un Autre secrètement pédéraste' (*SG* 463). The progression runs as follows: the *juste* possesses Genet and installs himself inside of him as a 'zar pédéraste'; Genet splits and creates a double of himself in the *je* of the narration which is endowed with the same powers as the *zar* that possesses him. He lies in wait, as soon as the book is opened; the possessor is possessed by his own demon: the evil has come home to roost and Genet is cleansed (cf. *Mots* 164).

So Genet has caused the father to kneel down before him – just as Roquentin dreamt, literally, of spanking Maurice Barrès (*OR* 72). But Sartre goes one step further than Genet himself. He suggests that the father would not need to create monsters such as Genet were it not for the fact that he himself is already perverted: 'cette paix qui règne en [les Justes], sais-je s'ils ne l'ont pas obtenue *en faisant leur soumission* à un protecteur étranger qui règne à leur place' (*SG* 85; emphasis added). Who possesses whom? Atavistic perspectives are opened up: perhaps Anchises, too, is condemned to ride Aeneas in order to unseat his own paternal jockey.[12]

The same theme recurs in *Les Mots*: 'le plus autoritaire commande au nom d'un autre, d'un *parasite sacré* – son père – transmet les abstraites violences qu'il subit' (*Mots* 20; emphasis added). There is no good father, which is to say, psychoanalytically, that all fathers are the bad father. Even, or especially, the *justes*, the *salauds*, the *Genitors* of this world are possessed by atavistic spirits, and their fate is to pass on this possession to their sons.

So, to resume, even as Genet is sodomised by his brutal father-surrogates, he is stealing their being as they had stolen his.

The anal sphincter is a knife-edged instrument of metaphysical castration and at the level of writing the same strategy is at play.

Throughout this brief analysis of *Saint Genet* I have indicated, by means of notes, points of repetition in *L'Idiot de la Famille*: the analysis is precisely the same when reduced to its basic actors and structural patterns. The father rapes the child and possesses him. The child has a choice: either bend down and submit to the father's pederastic designs, or revolt and cast off this paternal parasite by means of a vengeful castration. In many ways this is a prefabricated schema waiting for an application, a drama looking for a stage. There is a sense in which the object of the biographical project – to know everything that one can know about a man today – is secondary to the instrument employed in its pursuit. But, if this 'existential psychoanalysis' is rooted at one level in a very Sartrean phantasmatic, at another level it perhaps succeeds in transcending this. It is not necessary, even from a psychoanalytical perspective, to see the books on Genet and Flaubert as *nothing more than* the vicarious acting out of a neurotic phantasy; after all, these books seek to demonstrate how Genet and Flaubert, themselves, converted potential neurosis into praxis, a process repeated endlessly by Sartre himself. Furthermore, one should note the increased politicisation of Sartre's analyses. Already in *Saint Genet* Sartre is attempting to wrest the father-figures from the psychoanalytic domain and relocate them in a socio-political context: they are indeed figures of enormous symbolic importance within the child's world, but they are also representatives of a social class which has its own instruments of domination, its own means of perpetuating this domination. In *L'Idiot*, the violence practised by Achille-Cléophas is not only the – inevitable for Sartre – violence of a father toward his son; it is the violence of a whole class, or even the violence generated by the agonistic conflict between two classes: country landowners and professional bourgeoisie.

The situation surrounding Sartre's choice of analytical instrument is even more complex. The fact is that he denounces Freudian psychoanalysis in precisely the same way as he denounces the insidious possession by the pederastic Father.[13] This is why Genet is extolled as a kind of existential model: the vampires and ghouls that haunt his darkest night are cast out when the bright light of (Sartrean) freedom dawns. But what of the subject that Sartre liberates through his discourse? On the publication of *Saint Genet*, Genet himself was said to have been devastated, paralysed, turned inside out. By a final cruel twist Sartre has stepped into the shoes of the raping adult *vis-à-vis* his biographical son: he has appropriated the 'coup d'oeil chirurgical' of Achille-Cléophas and turned its penetrating glint onto his hapless object: the final liberation is Sartre's own.

I shall return to this suggestion later. But for the moment it is time to follow the patterns of this father–son relationship out of the biographies and into Sartre's fictions and plays.

To reconstitute the itinerary of Daniel in *Les Chemins* is almost to repeat the foregoing analysis: the guilt of the homosexual in *L'Etre et le néant*, the progressive liberation of Jean Genet, except that Daniel's liberation is a function of historical contingency rather than a conscious strategy of liberation.

'Tous les invertis sont honteux', remarks Daniel; 'c'est dans leur nature' (*OR* 726). This is the familiar play of sincerity and bad faith: to the extent that shame is connected with being *looked at*, Daniel is correct; for the homosexual, as we have seen in *Saint Genet*, is essentially 'celui qui se fait voir'. Daniel, too, senses that his homosexuality is not a substantial entity: 'je ne *suis* pas . . . on n'*est* jamais rien' (*OR* 485). One is not a homosexual in the way that a table is a table. His dream is to be born again, to leave Nature and destiny behind and erupt towards a brave new world: 'être sans odeur et sans ombre. Sans passé, n'être plus rien qu'un invisible arrachement à soi vers l'avenir' (*OR* 486).[14] To remain stationary is to expose himself to the crushing judgement of the collectivity. This is, once more, the original possession. Once more the equation is established between the gaze of the Absolute Subject and the sexual aggression at the hands of a strong male. As in *Saint Genet*, the threat clearly emanates from the solid citizens. And *normaux, justes*, and so on, are nothing more than names under which the father-figures unite: 'comme ils étaient durs, malgré leur abandon. Il suffirait d'un signal pour que ces hommes se jettent sur lui et le déchirent. Et . . . toute la Nature serait d'accord avec eux, comme toujours' (*OR* 541). Nature is a projection of the social order and the guardian of the social order is the father. Here one is reminded of that other possessed character, Hilbert, who entertains similar fearful phantasies of being torn apart by the representatives of 'normal' society and who, like Daniel, never knows a moment of relaxation. The bourgeois are *right* and *good* because they have made the rules by which such values are defined: they have monopolised the meaning of life (*OR* 271).

Daniel, then, is *le Mal*. He is a perverted soul, originally possessed, because even in that which is most his – his desire – the Other has set up home. He complains of never feeling at home, and this because he has a squatter – the 'parasite sacré'. Starting from this original possession, the operations by which he attempts to free himself follow precisely those described in *Saint Genet*, *Les Mots* and, later, *L'Idiot de la famille*.

First, he attempts to appropriate the raping gaze of the Other, but in vain: 'il avait beau faire, il n'y avait qu'un Daniel' (*OR* 484). Daniel's very self is a heart of darkness: 'Un Autre: moi. Moi – et l'horreur est au centre' (*OR* 849).

It is the experience of desire as desire of the Other that informs the episode in which Daniel tries to castrate himself. This could be read primarily as an attempt to castrate his ghostly indweller. It could only be described as self-punishment inasmuch as this self is Other. For Daniel experiences his penis as the emblem of his possessor. His erection is not *his*; it is the way in which the desire of the parasite manifests itself: 'il emporte la bête collée à son ventre, elle le suce, il la sent' (*OR* 693). It seems that Daniel's possession runs so deep that his own death is necessary in order to kill the parasite.[15]

So Daniel's attempt to appropriate the raping gaze of the Other fails: the gaze is woven into the very fabric of his being. The next stage is to attempt to coincide entirely with the object of that gaze, to be pure object for the surgical gaze of the Absolute Other. In other words, Daniel elects a real Other to be the representative of the phantom Other he carries within. If someone could *see* that he is a homosexual, perhaps then he would be able to coincide absolutely with this condemnation that he had felt hitherto to be both too strong and not strong enough, crushing but somehow abstract. But he chooses badly: Mathieu is far too much of a tolerant liberal to be able to incarnate the severe *justicier* he requires. He is just a man, so it is to God that Daniel turns next.

It is clear that Daniel's 'conversion' is a resignation. He had suffered from never being at the *rendez-vous* with himself; what he sought was self-coincidence: 'Etre ce que je suis, *être* un pédéraste, un méchant, un lâche. . . . Etre pédéraste comme le chêne est chêne' (*OR* 850). It will be objected that one does not need to rummage around in a hypothetical phantasy world in order to explain all of this; it is perfectly comprehensible within the terms of Sartre's own theory of consciousness and bad faith: unable to withstand the nagging non-coincidence that characterises the human condition, Daniel takes flight into a world of objective being; he aspires to *be* as an object *is*. As far as it goes this is quite true, but it is important to look closely at the moment when Daniel feels himself to be transpierced by the look of God. This instant is conveyed in highly resonant language: 'l'image: c'était une plaie béante, une bouche amère, elle saignait, c'est moi, je *suis* les deux lèvres écartées et le sang qui gargouille entre le lèvres' (OR 850). It is hard to imagine a more vaginal image than this. Moreover, these labia are covered in blood, as if they had been the object of an aggression by some huge phallus. Daniel does not merely desire to be the vagina penetrated by the father – he already is this. So his possession is not simultaneous with the pretence of his evocation of God; this is merely a reaffirmation of a prior possession. I take this to be a further figuration of the primal scene: the subject views the coitus *a tergo* between father and mother as a monstrous act of aggression, a wounding. But the phallus disappears and the aggressor is apparently punished for his temerity. The moment of quasi-orgasm which sees Daniel become a homosexual for all eternity is also described in typically sexual terms – 'ouvert, ouvert, la cosse éclate, ouvert comblé moi-même pour l'éternité, pédéraste, méchant, lâche' (OR 852)[16] – and is irresistibly reminiscent of Genet's sodomisation by/castration of the *durs* in *Saint Genet*: 'Empalé par l'Etre! . . . écrasée, comprimée, perforée, la conscience meurt pour que l'En-soi naisse' (SG 108). So, in Sartre's terms, Daniel is possessed by a human judgement. He cannot touch this judgement; he cannot appropriate it. He is 'evil', but he cannot *be* evil enough. So he invents a super-judge, a God to freeze him in his evil essence. But the secret side of this strategy consists in his creating God according to his own image: God is a pederast!

However, Daniel need not have bothered reinventing the father: this deity is soon to be shot from the skies. The Germans invade. As Daniel strolls through the deserted streets of the capital he is filled with elation: 'Un procès en cours depuis vingt ans, des espions jusque dans son lit; chaque passant, c'était un témoin à charge ou un juge ou les deux; tout ce qu'il disait pouvait être retenu contre lui. Et puis, d'un seul coup, la *débandade*' (OR 1218; emphasis added). The ancient law is no more: the society of judges has melted away (OR 1219). The judgement that had condemned

Daniel is suddenly nullified; the father may have been the guardian of the Law, but the Law is dead: the old gods have been supplanted by the pagan gods of the New Order. This 'débandade' takes on intriguing overtones when read against *Saint Genet*: '[le mâle] est l'archange effrayant dont l'épée de fer défend l'entrée du Paradis. L'épée flamboyante s'éteint et se ploie: c'était du fer blanc enduit de phosphore; *des yeux de juge se ferment*' (*SG* 126, emphasis added; cf. *IF* 1864). The penetrating, raping gaze of the father goes out like a light; a savage instrument of aggression, the paternal phallus? No, just a conjurer's party trick, a magic wand that droops forlornly in his hands!

All of Daniel's behaviour from this point onwards can be read as a reversal of what had been done to him: he had been possessed, now it is his turn to be the possessor; the father had ridden on his back, now he will slip into the saddle. The father is on all fours and the opportunity is too good to miss. The seduction of Philippe is prepared with sadistic forepleasure: 'je te possède à distance . . . je m'enfonce en toi et tu ne t'en doutes même pas' (*OR* 1266). This seduction has a savoury double irony. 'I know your story', he tells Philippe, and with good reason, since it is his own. Daniel had been possessed by a *zar* in every way identical to the stepfather he guesses to be the possessor of Philippe (*OR* 1272). The irony operates at a second level also. Daniel claims to be 'psychoanalysing' Philippe, ridding him of the fear of the father, liberating him. But he has posterior motives; once more, analysis will reveal itself to be anal-ysis. Just as psychoanalysis operates through the reliving of the trauma, so Daniel will re-enact in the flesh, as it were, the possession of Philippe by his 'parasite sacré'.

We see, then, in Daniel the re-enactment of the phantasmatic scenario which emerged from a reading of *Saint Genet*: the original possession; the choice between abject submission (translated as a perpetual anal rape that fuses father and son), and revolt. Interestingly enough, we never see the submission of the judges in *Les Chemins*; it remains at the level of a projection, a textual phantasy: 'tu verras ramper les pères de famille, tu les verras lécher les bottes et tendre leurs gros culs aux coups de pied' (*OR* 1272). A phantasy not dissimilar to the one that informs Poulou's early fictions in *Les Mots*: 'agenouiller les magistrats de force' (*Mots* 111).

It will be recalled that Genet's possession is physical *and* verbal.

Sartre wrote of Genet, 'son aventure, c'est d'avoir été nommé' (*SG* 48). The remainder of this chapter will be devoted to a brief account of how the phantasy of 'possession: submission/revolt' is rendered through the metaphor of self-inscription.

The first reaction is an attempt to 'jouir de son nom'. This amounts to a total identification with the father. In a society which identifies its members by the transmission of the patronym, the latter represents the continued presence of the father in the son. To accept the name of the father is to be *nominally* identified with him. We will see that this identification is viewed by Sartre as 'cannibalistic': to identify with is to eat or be eaten by.

The other attitude, by far the more common in Sartre's work, is to reject the name of the father and to try to 'make a name for oneself'. Closely related to this sometimes literal, sometimes figurative self-inscription in the Symbolic Order is the theme of the violent act: an act which at least humiliates and at most assassinates the father. Through it, the subject transforms the world, it will never be the same again. Genesis is recommenced, and the Word which was in the beginning is phantasised to be the (new) name of the destructive hero.

'L'Enfance d'un chef' is the history of a submission. In *Saint Genet* we saw Sartre speculate as to whether the *justes* who victimised his hero had not gained their authority through a prior submission to a paternal tyrant; in 'L'Enfance', Sartre had already shown this submission at work. This could be read as a story about the power of the name. Everyone is named, and not least Lucien. He is offered a bewildering variety of 'names' which he briefly adopts, occasionally rejects. He is 'une petite fille', 'un ange' (*OR* 314); 'Pierrot' (315); 'l'orphelin', 'Oliver Twist', 'un affamé' (317); 'Jeanne d'Arc', 'un missionaire' (319); 'un somnambule' (323) a 'piston' (336); 'Rimbaud' (348); 'un pédéraste' (355); 'Lucien Bonnières' (367); 'un Déraciné' (371); 'anti-semite' (374); 'Camelot du Roi' (379); and finally Lucien Fleurier, son of Monsieur Fleurier, and captain-of-industry to be.

The above list is far from exhaustive. For example, Lucien is perched in a, for him, typical position, on the toilet seat, when he chances to read a vertiginous inscription: 'Lucien Fleurié est une grande asperche' (*OR* 327). He feels looked at, ashamed, pierced to the heart of his being by this childish graffiti. He has been labelled with a name that imposes a destiny upon him. What needs to be understood in this episode is the extent to which Lucien feels himself to be suddenly inscribed into a *lineage*: the condemnation emanates, indirectly, from his father. He had previously read the inscription 'Barataud est une punaise', and reflected to himself, 'c'était vrai: Barataud était une punaise, il était minuscule et on disait qu'il grandirait un peu mais presque pas, *parce que son papa était tout petit, presque un nain*' (*OR* 326; emphasis added). This causes Lucien severe anxiety and prompts him to enquire of his father as to whether gigantism runs in the family. The reply is not very reassuring: the Fleuriers had always been big and strong, and Lucien would doubtless continue to grow (*OR* 327).[17] The child is inscribed by the father even before his birth, his destiny written under his skin.

The next occasion on which Lucien is riveted to the spot by a name is when he has been sodomised by Bergère. This scene – even down to the seductive misuse of psychoanalysis – is the precise counterpart of the later scene between Daniel and Philippe in *La Mort dans l'âme*. Lucien *becomes* the pederast. It is as if his being had suddenly crystallised around this hated name. He succeeds in shaking off this particular *zar*, but only at the price of replacing it with another, more durable one: Lucien's reaction is to seek escape from his homosexual identity through an identification with his father, whom nobody could suspect of such an ignoble penchant. Contemplating his father over the dinner table, Lucien feels closer to him closer to those cold metallic eyes of the leader, and concludes, 'je lui ressemble' (*OR* 359).

Now, it is true that, in Sartrean terms, Lucien had always been more object than subject: this is after all, the fate of the child in any family. But it is only now that this object status begins to work itself out in terms of a passive submission to the father, in the form of a complete identification with him. For previously there had been a telling moment when Lucien had come close to rejecting this identity–possession: 'Qui suis-je? . . . Je m'appelle Lucien Fleurier *mais ça n'était qu'un nom*' (*OR* 333; emphasis added). The realisation here is that the name does not somehow encapsulate the essence of the object; it is simply a mark traced on its surface, a conventional signifier. Lucien's demission involves forgetting this intuition, and becoming 'Lucien Fleurier', son of Monsieur Fleurier and leader to be.

He was 'made for' this role. In a passage strongly reminiscent of that where Poulou sits on Karl's knee and receives his mandate in one of those 'dialogues de sourds', Lucien has his destiny revealed to him. 'Will I too become a leader?' asks Lucien. 'Naturally', replies the father, 'c'est pour cela que je t'ai fait' (*OR* 325).

It is significant that Lucien's final transfiguration into a leader is preceded and prefigured by an episode of *literal* inscription. Lemordant of Action Française is preparing a petition against the Jews at the Ecole Normale Supérieure. Lucien signs, and his name, in print, suddenly becomes condensed and definitive (in every sense of the word): 'presque aussi étranger que ceux de Flèche et de Flipot' (*OR* 371). It is not surprising that his name seems foreign to him: it is the name of the Other. Lucien's apotheosis is not the carving-out of his own identity, but the miserable and submissive acceptance of a ready-made identity. He wonders whether his father would not perhaps die in the not too distant future, but this is no Oedipal death wish, it is more a desire to become the father's recycled effigy.

In a curious sequence of images at the end of 'L'Enfance', this identification with the father seems to take on the guise of an *ingestion*: 'Il se rappela que sa mère, quand il était petit, lui disait parfois d'un certain ton: "Papa travaille dans son bureau" . . . il marchait dans les couloirs sur la pointe des pieds, comme s'il avait été dans une cathédrale' (*OR* 385). But a few moments later, 'Il vit réapparaître un dos musculeux et bossué et puis, tout de suite après, une cathédrale. Il était dedans, il s'y promenait à pas de loup sous la lumière tamisée qui tombait des vitraux. "Seulement, ce coup-ci, c'est moi la cathédrale"' (*OR* 386). From intruder in the father's cathedral, he becomes the cathedral itself, having internalised the father, who will live within like a parasite. He has now become one of those 'âmes habitées' that Sartre denounces in *Saint Genet*.[18]

Twenty-five years on, *Les Séquestrés d'Altona* reads like a reworking of 'L'Enfance d'un chef', but this time without the savage irony and the humour. This is a far more pessimistic work; in a quarter of a century of rewriting of the same story, the father has lost none of his petrifying power – if anything, he has gained in prestige. Referred to simply, and archly, as 'Le Père', he has become a giant of this world. One aspect of the pessimism of *Les Séquestrés* consists in the fact that Werner is no longer a child: he is a man of mature years who has broken away from the Family and made a name for himself commensurate with his own merits. But it is as though all the years of freedom Werner had known were but a dream, and that he was sure to wake up one day to find himself swearing on the Bible to obey his father's will (*Séq* 98). Werner cannot do otherwise, no explanation is proffered, except 'C'est le Père!' (*Seq* 43). The father is a numinous entity who cannot be circumvented; the abasement of the son before the father appears to be a necessary corollary, for Sartre, of the 'lien de paternité'. The Father is dying of a parasitic growth, and it is as a parasite that he will pass himself on to his son.

After the scene in which the Father tells Werner that in order to command one must take oneself for Another (a familiar injunction by now!), the latter remarks, 'Je ne me prends pour personne', only to be corrected, 'attends que je meure: au bout d'une semaine tu te prendras pour moi' (*Séq* 31). In this exchange, the terms 'personne' and 'moi' are equated: the self is a *persona* through which the father perpetuates himself, and one which cannot be thrown off – an Iron Mask. This prediction is realised in the course of the play: Werner loses the assurance of the self-made man and gains the factitious bombast of the Father. His fate is sealed in the first act of the play and is never seriously in doubt. He tells the Father that he will swear anything the latter demands, and receives the reply, 'cela va de soi!' (*Séq* 28).

The man who is possessed by a *zar* finds that whatever he does will be what the Father desires: his actions, thoughts and words are already inscribed in an inner sanctum – like that of Kafka's 'Vor dem Gesetz' – which is designed for him alone, but to which he alone may never gain access.

So the first attitude towards the original possession consists in a submissive acceptance of the Father's name – a name that is not *mien* but *à moi*, where *moi* is Another.

The second attitude involves a rebellious rejection of this crippling nomination, and corresponds very often to a supremely violent act in which the subject phantasises his rebirth. The actions of Paul Hilbert and Mathieu are exemplary in this respect.

The violent act which Hilbert envisages is modelled on the *acte gratuit* outlined by Breton in his *Manifestes du Surréalisme*. But for Hilbert there is nothing gratuitous about this act; it is phantasied as a kind of self-christening. He knows what he wishes to do before he knows the name of the perpetrator of the archetypal act: Herostratus. Hilbert's ignorance notwithstanding, Herostratus was above all someone who made a name for himself: as Hilbert remarks to his colleagues, they have forgotten the name of the architect of the Temple of Diana – if it was ever known – but they have remembered the name of its destroyer (*OR* 269). This self-inscription is typically a rebirth: the world is exploded, and the sole surviver of Armageddon, rising Phoenix-like from the ashes, is Hilbert. The New Order commences with his name: 'Un crime, ça coupe en deux la vie de celui qui le commet . . . Je ne demandais qu'une heure pour jouir du mien, pour sentir *son poids écrasant*' (*OR* 273; emphasis added). This symbolic renaming expunges the past, obliterates the ghosts that inhabit it. The image of carrying a heavy weight on the shoulders or back is very common in Sartre's writings. At the level of Sartre's own theoretical discourse it denotes the weight of the past and the massiveness of inert being-in-itself, as opposed to the unbearable lightness of being-for-itself. But it also opens up, simultaneously, onto the complex of images centring on the pederastic father, riding on the back of his son. Its occurrence in this context surely denotes a desire to appropriate this role for oneself.[19]

But Hilbert's desire to write his own name in the annals of crime makes more sense when one recalls his intuition that his language is haunted, originally possessed by the Other (*OR* 271). He aims for nothing less than the re-creation of language and the new world that goes with it. In *Saint Genet* this original possession through language is experienced as a homosexual rape at the hands of the father: 'Empalé par l'Etre'. Hilbert dreams of reversing this violence – it is as though he were trying to become the prime signifier in relation to which all significations are organised and subordinated: the father's phallus. The revolver that he purchases is, of course, a fairly obvious phallic symbol, on condition that one regards this properly as a *phallus*, as opposed to a monstrous prosthesis or penis-substitute: the penis is subject to possible loss, whereas the phallus cannot be lost, since nobody, in reality, possesses it. But Hilbert's dream is to *be* that phallus: J'étais un être de l'espèce des revolvers, des pétards et des bombes . . .' (*OR* 269).

A large part of the ambiguity of 'Erostrate' derives from the fact that the object of Hilbert's hatred is doubly determined. On the one hand Sartre himself surely shared Hilbert's hatred of a bourgeois class that had monopolised the meaning of life through its ideological manipulations. But at the same time these bourgeois have all the characteristics of the hated *justes* of *Saint Genet*, and the 'Genitors' we encountered in Chapter 2. They are all re-editions of the father who forbids access to the gates of Paradise with his flaming phallic sword.

At the properly sexual level, Hilbert's transgression is primarily voyeuristic: he approaches the forbidden grove, peeps inside, but goes no further for fear of the retribution that awaits him. This voyeurism is constitutive of Hilbert's sadism within the terms of Sartre's own dialectic of the look. The revolver is integrated at this level of the text, since it symbolises power at a safe distance: the look which cannot be looked at, the caress which cannot be returned. Hilbert's scopophilic interlude with the prostitute is like a prefiguring of the Diana episode in *L'Etre et le néant*. The schema is repeated with the wife of the warrant officer whom Hilbert spies on from his window: 'Elle s'habillait la fenêtre ouverte, quand l'adjutant était parti, et j'étais resté souvent derrière mon rideau pour la surprendre' (*OR* 265). Hilbert is Actaeon pulling aside the foliage, and the wife of the officer is the new Diana. In all of this, the father remains the ultimate target.

At the level of the primal phantasy, Hilbert re-enacts the scopophilic role of the child surprising his parents in intercourse. He appropriates the father's penetrating role, but avoids the castrating consequences by 'penetrating at a safe distance': the look, the revolver. Hilbert's dream concerning the tsar (later the *zar*!) is further to this point. Hilbert is wont to repeat this dream in which he murders the father (*OR* 270). In Hilbert's case, the consummation is deferred, but the phantasy is completed by a similar dream ascribed to a quite different character – Philippe in *Les Chemins*: he charges forward, bayonette fixed, crying, '"Victoire, victoire, à la victoire", les douze tsars déguerpirent, *la tsarine était délivrée* . . .' (*OR* 898; emphasis added).

It will be pointed out that all of this could be interpreted as a function of Sartre's quite conscious desire to portray Hilbert as a pathological pervert.[20] To a degree this is true, except that one finds precisely the same phantasy, with the same actors and the same structure, being played out by a character who is surely not intended to be seen as such a type : Mathieu in *La Mort dans l'âme*. The connection between the writing of one's name and the killing of the father can be seen nowhere more clearly than in the case of Mathieu.

Already in *Le Sursis* Mathieu had suffered the effects of a damning nomination. The gaze of the war, simultaneously everywhere and nowhere, replaces that of God as absolute entelechy of Mathieu's acts. He is suddenly given a being-for-the-war in which the finality of all his acts becomes the war itself. As he gazes at the mobilisation notice, 'C'était comme si on avait écrit son nom à la craie sur le mur, avec des insultes et des menaces' (*OR* 805).[21] Mathieu's reaction to this insidious expropriation of his being follows two converging paths: the desire to write his *own* name, and the desire to commit a violent, anti-paternal act. These paths conjoin in Mathieu's belltower apotheosis. But self-inscription and murder are rendered equivalent at the level of the textual imagery even before this climactic episode: 'Mathieu tira son canif de sa poche et commença de *tailler l'écorce du marronnier*. Il avait envie d'*inscrire son nom* quelque part dans le monde' (*OR* 1238; emphasis added). Previously, this inscription had taken the form of a violent desire to penetrate: 's'enfoncer dans un acte inconnu comme dans une forêt' (*OR* 1213). This equation between inscription and violence obtains elsewhere in Sartre's work: Oreste, for example, imagines his violent act as leaving the *trace* of his passage on Earth (*Mou* 174). In a similar way, Frantz's act of torture with penknife and lighter represents an attempt to engrave the trace of his passage, not on a chestnut tree, but on the very flesh of his fellow men. Part of the dreadful pessimism of *Les Séquestrés* resides in Frantz's very inability to 'write his name': everything he has ever attempted has been recuperated and deviated from its goal by the Father's desire; he simply plays out the role inscribed under his skin and, needless to say, the Father is the arch-*scénariste*:

FRANTZ. Vous avez écrit votre nom.
PERE. Si tu savais comme je m'en fous!
FRANTZ. Vous mentez, Père: vous vouliez faire des bateaux et vous les avez faits.   (*Séq* 367)

The one act that might have placed Frantz outside the Father's sphere of influence is the ultimately unacceptable act of torture, again visualised in terms of *writing*:

JOHANNA. Agir, c'est tuer?
FRANTZ. C'est agir. Ecrire son nom.
KLAGES. Sur quoi?
FRANTZ. Sur ce qui se trouve là.   (*Séq* 368)

This act is the focus of some ambiguity. There is no doubt that, for Sartre, the commission of torture places Frantz definitively beyond the pale. Yet it is the ultimate failure of this act which signals his inability to escape from the Father; even this monstrous act has been turned to profit: 'Ton tourment a fini par te pousser au crime et jusque dans le crime elle t'annule: [l'Entreprise] *s'engraisse* de ta défaite' (*Séq* 369; emphasis added). The enterprise is not just the shipbuilding business; it functions here – as in *L'Idiot* – as a metaphor for the (bourgeois) Family. The italicised word signals the reappearance of the digestion motif: Frantz is swallowed, digested and converted into profitable substance by the Father inasmuch as the latter is head of the Family.

Both Oreste's acts of murder and Frantz's acts of torture can be seen, then, as (failed) revolts against the Law of the Father. And indeed, to return to *Les Chemins*, Mathieu envisages his act as a penetration of the father's domain, an act of transgression. He will gain access to the 'forêt du grand seigneur' of *Saint Genet* (*SG* 250) and poach the game in the 'forêt seigneuriale' of *Les Mouches* (*Mou* 231). In the belltower scene these phantasies merge in a striking image of a murder which is also a homosexual rape: 'Pendant des années, il avait tenté d'agir. En vain: on lui avait volé ses actes à mesure; il comptait pour du beurre.'[22] But this time nothing has been taken from him; he contemplates the dead German with the satisfaction of an author admiring his completed manuscript: '*Son* mort, *son* oeuvre, la trace de *son* passage sur la terre. Le désir lui vint d'en tuer d'autres: c'était amusant et facile . . .' (*OR* 1337). This passage becomes even more resonant when read in counterpoint to Daniel's adventures: the *homosexualisation* of Mathieu's act begins then to stand out. Daniel's desire is to possess, to penetrate at a distance: 'je t'épie, tu es nu dans le creux de mon regard, je te possède à distance, sans rien donner de moi' (*OR* 1266). And Mathieu repeats this desire, substituting the trajectory of the bullet for the direction of the gaze: 'il tenait un ennemi au bout du canon de son fusil et lui visait tranquillement les reins . . . . il *reluquait* son bonhomme, il avait tout son temps' (*OR* 1336; emphasis added).[23]

Doubtless, Mathieu's act can be seen as a kind of 'virilisation', but a strange one at that: the act of killing – more specifically the homosexualisation of that act – is seen to be more representative of the sexual act than this act itself.

This section of *La Mort dans l'âme* ends with the assertion of Mathieu's omnipotence and freedom (*OR* 1344). But has Mathieu purged himself, freed himself of his parasitic inhabitant? I would argue that he is no more free than is Lucien at the end of 'L'Enfance', or Oreste at the end of *Les Mouches*: his omnipotence remains a function of the Imaginary. For Mathieu had not killed the father with impunity. On the condition that we remember that we are dealing with the phantasmatic level of the *oeuvre*, this much can be seen to emerge from some previously unpublished fragments of *La Dernière Chance*, reproduced in the Pléiade edition of the *Oeuvres romanesques*. There is one particular scene in which we see Mathieu killing, or raping, Charlot with his gaze: 'Charlot soupira et Mathieu enfonça le couteau, sans haine, sans cruauté, avec amitié. Une manière de fair l'amour avec les hommes' (*OR* 1622). The shortest route to a man's heart is by the point of a sword. For Mathieu, this scene, infinitely repeated, is not a game but a reconstitution (*OR* 1622) – a repetition or a rehearsal in which Sartre too becomes caught up, since he made at least four attempts to write this scene, each time with slight variations. Far from being free, Mathieu seems to be wholly possessed: 'Les Allemands morts s'étaient installés en lui comme des ancêtres; ils lui conféraient des droits et des devoirs obscurs' (*OR* 1627). Re-enter the *zar*! According to Leiris, this figure is also associated with certain *cannibalistic* practices: as with Mathieu, the warrior who has slain an enemy eats him in order to incorporate the power of the enemy's spirit. It seems that the conclusion to be drawn from the oscillation between passive submission to the father (Lucien, Werner), and violent revolt (Hilbert, Mathieu) is that they *both* lead back to the original possession. The subject either eats the father or is eaten by him; in either case the hapless son remains possessed, at a gut level, as it were.

This strange dialectic wherein the identification is conceived of in *oral* terms is also prevalent in *Les Mots*. The Karl Schweitzer presented in the opening pages of that work is the paternal cannibal, Kronos devouring his progeny.[24] Sartre insists that the respective ages of Karl and Poulou prevented the former from practising this paternal tyranny on his grandson, yet there are several points in the text where Poulou is seen to be devoured by this cannibalistic father. One of these occurs in the old man's library, which is uncannily similar to the sacred shrine of Monsieur Fleurier in 'L'Enfance': 'A peine avais-je poussé la porte de la bibliothèque, je me retrouvais dans le ventre d'un vieillard inerte . . ., c'était Karl en personne: réifié' (*Mots* 61; cf. *IF* 1663).

On this occasion it is Poulou who is swallowed up by the old man – like Jonah in the stomach of the whale, or the pebble in the stomach of the ostrich. Elsewhere the terms of the phantasy are reversed, notably in the scene where Poulou receives his mandate from Karl-become-father, in one of those 'dialogues de sourds [cf. *IF* 1883] dont chaque mot me marquait' (*Mots* 138). Poulou *swallows* Karl's every word. The bizarre play of identification and incorporation is rendered very well by the English idiom 'to take in': Poulou takes in (swallows) the noxious ideology peddled by his grandfather, and is simultaneously, in his naïveté, taken in (fooled) by the grandfather. Moreover, these scenes perhaps mark the resurgence of the phantasy of the 'combined parents': the above scene is, structurally, a repetition of the scene in which Anne-Marie reads Poulou fairy-tales; it is as if Karl had taken on the role and attributes of Anne-Marie, and that the two roles were now combined.

In psychoanalytic terms, these passages speak of a *failure of identification*, in the proper sense of the term. The identifications which precipitate and resolve the Oedipus complex are of a structural nature: it is the various types of relationships obtaining between the three points in the Oedipal triangle that are internalised and form the matrix for the future identifications constitutive of the 'personality'. But there is nothing structural about the modes of identification which are seen to emerge from Sartre's texts. It is as if a very primitive mode of identification, characteristic of the oral phase, had insisted to the detriment of 'normal' identifications: 'Incorporation and introjection are prototypes of identification – or at any rate of certain modes of identification where the mental process is experienced and symbolised as a bodily one (ingesting, devouring, keeping something inside oneself, etc.).'[25]

There is a certain paradox in all of this which could lead us into the heart of the interrelation between conscious and unconscious determinations in Sartre's work. It could be summed up in this way: whilst the *phantasmatic* structures I have outlined in this book persist throughout all of Sartre's work, there nevertheless appears to have been a genuine 'prise de conscience', noticeable from about the mid 1950s onwards. This insistence of unconscious structures doubled with an intellectual awareness is mirrored in Sartre's very attitude towards the unconscious as a theoretical postulate: a practical acceptance of its existence, coupled with an explicit denial of the same. A kind of *Verleugnung*.

In the *Scénario Freud*, Sartre shows quite convincingly how Freud managed to free himself, precisely, from the oscillation between the two images of the father that pervade his own texts: one who was too weak (an object of pity and contempt), and the other too strong (a cause for fear and trembling). The end of the *Scénario Freud* synopsis demonstrates a clear grasp of the problematic: 'J'avais quarante-et-un ans', says Freud; 'c'était à mon tour de jouer le rôle du père' (*SF* 570). This reference to the *role* of father shows that Sartre has grasped the distinction between the omnipotent father of the Imaginary and the father imago of the Symbolic: the latter resembles more a positional function than a numinous entity; he too is subject to the Law.

Even earlier, in *Kean*,[26] not to mention *Le Diable et le bon Dieu*, Sartre had demonstrated a similar 'prise de conscience'. Kean is possessed: by his audiences, by the authors, in particular Shakespeare ('le vieux vampire'), whose plays he is condemned to bring back to life; and especially by the Prince of Wales, who, like the Father of *Les Séquestrés* converts all of Kean's actions into mere gestures. All the familiar obsessions are present, yet *Kean* is both a funny and a liberating play. As in the *Scénario Freud*, the great discovery is that the Prince is also acting a role; he too is a 'cabotin'. If it is true that Eléna was desirable for Kean because the Prince desired her, it is equally true that the fact that Kean desired her made her desirable in the eyes of the Prince. A deliciously Oedipal reversal! It is the Prince who requires 'black rites' (cf. *Séq* 268) to desire Eléna at the end of the play, not Kean. It is the Prince who fails to break free from the Imaginary.

Moreover, there is an element present in *Kean* which removes the conflict from the purely familial sphere of the Oedipal conflict: the dependency of Kean on the Prince is fundamentally economic and legal – that is to say, absolutely *real*. Of course, this element is intended to be foregrounded also in *Les Séquestrés*, but, in keeping with the oddly anachronistic pessimism of this play, this dimension remains unconvincing: one feels that, whatever Sartre might say in the *Critique*, the operative conflict is transhistorical, and it concerns the pure 'lien de paternité'.[27]

By the time Sartre came to write *L'Idiot de la famille*, economic, social and political factors were very heavily foregrounded; both psychoanalysis and Marxism are enlisted in the attempt to analyse the relationship between Gustave and Achille-Cléophas. At times Flaubert himself almost disappears from sight: the book takes on the guise of a summation, a vast compendium, a *tout compte fait* of all Sartre's phantasies and obsessions with regard to the familial trinity. But, for all the brilliant, if sometimes arcane, analysis, Flaubert remains, in Sartre's text, trapped in the dilemma indicated by François George:

> Sartre néanmoins oscillera toujours entre deux thèses, l'une officielle: le père n'est qu'une image qu'il soutient à l'être, l'autre secrète et plus opérante, suivant laquelle il n'est qu'une image dans le cerveau du père, une apparence inconsistante qui traverse le rêve de l'Autre.[28]

Gustave is condemned to toss a coin endlessly with his father; the coin arches upwards, catching the light; it falls to the ground. But the call has already been made once and for all by the father: 'Heads I win, tails you lose.' Or, as George puts it, 'qui père gagne'. Gustave is trapped through his conditioning – and it should be remembered, although Sartre himself forgets it on occasion, that this is due also, even mainly, to the mother; his conditioning condemns him to revolt only ever in the Imaginary: the father has appropriated once and for all the domain of the Real.

The principal instrument of Gustave's revolt is his writing – although his 'neurosis', Sartre claims, can also be read as an aspect of this revolt. This resolution through the Imaginary is recognised by Sartre to be deeply neurotic or even perverse, yet the Imaginary is the only tool at Gustave's disposal.

At the end of *L'Idiot*, Sartre announces a third volume: 'D'autre part la maladie de Gustave exprime dans sa plénitude ce qu'il faut bien appeler sa liberté: ce que cela veut dire, nous ne pouvons l'entendre qu'à la fin de cet ouvrage, après avoir relu *Madame Bovary*' (*IF* 2136). This liberty and liberation would have consisted perhaps in the passage from neurosis to praxis. Sartre never wrote this volume. Or perhaps he wrote nothing but.

Concluding Remarks

It is customary, in 'conclusions' to works of 'criticism', to attempt to tie together the loose ends of the thesis, to present some kind of unified meaning. I have arrived at a series of conclusions in the course of the preceding text; more often than not these conclusions complement each other, while at other times they supplement or modify what has gone before. No doubt, if I were to conclude traditionally, the result would resemble very closely the 'findings' presented in Josette Pacaly's *Sartre au miroir*:[1] the Sartrean *oeuvre* is structured through and through by a phantasmatic which is the dramatisation of castration anxiety; inability to confront and surmount the Oedipal moment, leading to a reversion on to archaic positions; identification with the mother, resentful submission to an omnipotent Imaginary father, inability to conceive of a 'relativised' father-figure, stereotypical resurrection of the primal scene from which the mother emerges as endowed with the paternal phallus – a renewed source of castration anxiety; and so on and so forth. All of this is summed up and conveyed by a small number of images which present themselves as propositions, such as 'The doll/child is being handled by the mother' or 'The father is riding on the back of his son.' But the problem resides in sorting out the status of these insights.

When he was working on the Freud screenplay, Sartre read Ernest Jones's biography of Freud, newly translated into French. Pontalis reports, in the introduction to the *Scénario*, that Sartre looked up from his reading and remarked, 'Mais, dites-moi, votre Freud, il était névrosé jusqu'a la moelle' (*SF* 16). Should one reach a similar conclusion regarding Sartre himself? And, even if one did, would not this conclusion be ultimately banal – in psychoanalytic terms? Who is not, to a greater or lesser extent, neurotic? Perhaps one of the triumphs of psychoanalysis consists in the way it has forced us to rethink previously unproblematical categories such as 'normality' and 'sanity'. Freud never claimed that psychoanalysis would turn sociopaths into excellent, well-adjusted citizens, and Lacan in particular fulminated against the American perversion of

Freudianism, which has become an insidious method of social normalisation: from the interpretation of dreams to the American Dream. In a moment of grim humour, Freud remarked that all psychoanalysis could hope to achieve was the substitution of ordinary depression for neurotic depression. Of course, the debate should not really be centred, in any case, on whatever psychological problems Sartre may or may not have had (this is destined, anyway, to remain hypothetical): he did after all succeed in producing one of the most wide-ranging, distinctive *oeuvres* in all of French literature, as well as turning himself into a figure who, for several decades exerted a real moral influence – 'I should have "problems" like that!' as Freud might have said. I suggested in my prefatory remarks to this work that psychoanalytic criticism should properly concern itself with the *interplay* of conscious and unconscious determinants, since this concern is most central to psychoanalysis itself. My final remarks will be on this subject.

It will have been noticed that, in the course of my analysis, I have spoken a great deal about the 'bad fathers' that haunt Sartre's fictional universe: most typically the bourgeois *salauds*, the Genitors riding on the back of their sons. I have not said very much about the many other characters who, at the representational level, could be said to form groups just as distinctive and coherent: the 'men of action', for example, such as Brunet, Schneider, Gomez, Hoederer, even Goetz after the 'conversion'. Could it be that these characters would have been damaging to my argument in that they indicate the extent to which Sartre's work is turned outward towards the world of concrete, political action, rather than inward towards a core of neurotic concerns? Not at all. First, it would be relatively easy to demonstrate that the representational traits that constitute these characters have uncanny similarities with the representations of other characters who are certainly not intended to be seen as political role models. At this level, there is little difference between the solid, massively impassive indifference of the Brunet of *L'Age de raison*, and the similarly massive proto-fascist of 'L'Enfance d'un chef', Lemordant. No doubt a critic such as Pacaly would feel justified in arguing that they are both figurations of the anal phallus. Second, Sartre's most 'committed' representations of the proletariat are *also* phantasy creations: Slick and Georges, in *Les Mains sales*, with their committedly bulging biceps and heroic barrel chests come straight from the pages of the comic books that regaled Sartre's childhood. From the bobbing top-hats,

Concluding Remarks 131

rising above the proletariat crowd, that comfort Poulou in his visits to the cinema, to the burly shoulders of Maurice and the cloth-caps that stand out from the 'feminine' crowd in *Le Sursis*, there is a direct, if involuted, line of descent. Sartre's proletariat inhabits a world which has little to do with that of the real workers of the real Billancourt: a world governed by need, and from which desire is banished; a world whose motto is 'baiser, bouffer, boire', where the three terms are comfortingly equivalent. It could be argued with some justification that Sartre came to fetishise need (in the *Critique* for example) in much the same way as Flaubert, in Sartre's view, fetishised desire.

Whilst all this may be very interesting, it is not quite central to the debate. Even if it could be *proved* – and it can't – that the figures through whom Sartre attempted to show the search for a reasoned political commitment were fundamentally determined by *psychological* conflicts inherent to the author, it would in no way alter the efficacy of this attempt in the real world, inhabited by real people. One right-wing critic thought that Sartre's vociferous opposition to the return of de Gaulle in 1958 could be neutralised by pointing out that Sartre had a 'father complex'. Now, if one understands this last phrase to mean that Sartre's failure to surmount the castration complex involved him in a lifelong and almost pathological hatred of authority, a refusal to submit to figures of authority, then that critic could well be correct. Where he was wrong was in thinking that this was sufficient reason to dismiss whatever political position Sartre may have taken up *vis-à-vis* de Gaulle. If the latter appeared as a figure of paternal authority to Sartre, it is hardly surprising: he shared this perception with 40 million other Frenchmen and women.

There is a sense in which these comments rejoin my earlier remarks about the banality of concluding that Sartre was in some way neurotic. If psychoanalysis has any claim to universality, this must surely consist in its demonstration of how *all* human beings make choices, adopt courses of action, entertain attitudes (towards authority, for example) that arise *against a background of* infantile experiences and conflicts. But where psychoanalysis could go astray is in the confident assumption that these experiences provide the *ultimate* determinant of any given choice made by an individual subject. In this case, the 'choice' would be a mere illusion. This kind of reductivism does not do justice to Freud's own thought: neurotic behaviour, for Freud, was not *only* the symbolic revivification of infantile conflicts; it was also a response to a real situation confronting the patient, a situation that was too difficult or painful to be confronted directly. Where psychoanalytic textual analysis is concerned, the automatic privileging of unconscious phantasy structures – as ultimate determinants of meaning – also has the effect of reducing the myriad other 'readable' meanings to the status of illusion. But any reading that does this is guilty of forgetting the best insights of psychoanalysis: those which concern the interplay between conscious and unconscious. Of course, this basic problematic is also fundamental to the theoretical works of Sartre. One of his abiding concerns was to theorise the process whereby any particular human action could be viewed, simultaneously, as singular and universal: the process whereby an individual becomes 'Tout un homme, fait de tous les hommes et qui les vaut tous et que vaut n'importe qui.'

What I have attempted to show in this book is something of the tension that exists in Sartre's work between the conscious orientation of his texts and the structuring forces of the unconscious. Perhaps these two levels of structure 'deconstruct' each other; I prefer to believe that the process is also one of mutual construction. The interplay in Sartre's texts between the *working-out* of a philosophy of freedom and action, and the *acting-out* of a phantasmatic scenario, comes increasingly to resemble the dialogue, in these same works, between an existential analytic position and Freudian psychoanalysis. The ultimate commingling of these levels doubtless occurs in *L'Idiot de la famille*. I would not be the first to point out[2] that any attempt to trace this interplay is complicated by two factors. First, Freud himself came to occupy, for Sartre, both consciously and unconsciously, the position of the father. I pointed out in Chapter 5 the identification of Freud with the figure of the bad father in *Saint Genet, L'Idiot de la famille*, and elsewhere. Second, the very clinical method of the psychoanalytic cure (which, admittedly, Sartre did not experience at first hand) came to serve as a kind of 'primal scene'. It came somehow to serve as the paradigm for the relationship between father and son: the son submissively prostrate before the erect father, who 'takes him from behind', opening him up, laying bare his soul, stripping away the defences, penetrating him.

Josette Pacaly concludes from this that Sartre's long 'dialogue de sourds' with the dead 'father of psychoanalysis' was, by and large, a bad thing. Poor Sartre, it seems, was caught in a no-win situation in which he had to placate both his own resentment of authority figures, *and* the need to stay abreast of intellectual developments in an age when the ultimate figure of intellectual authority was none other than Freud himself. She writes, 'il n'a pas eu assez de modestie pour *se soumettre*, dans sa vie, à une méthode élaborée par d'autres, ni assez de force, dans son oeuvre, pour ignorer Freud à partir du moment où ce dernier devenait, avec Marx, une des idoles du demi-siècle'.[3] Apparently, Sartre was never further from Freud than when he tried to draw closer. A little (intellectual) knowledge (of psychoanalysis) is a bad thing, and especially for Sartre's readers. Pacaly thinks it fortunate that *La Nausée*, at least, is not tainted by Sartre's 'lourde machine à digérer les pensées prestigieuses'.[4] The assumption behind all of this is that Sartre's unconscious attitude towards the father-figure prevented him from arriving at a 'real' understanding of Freud. This is precisely the same assumption as informs the view, mentioned earlier, according to which Sartre failed to grasp the real nature of de Gaulle's political ambitions because de Gaulle was, for him, the bad father.

But what if Sartre were, at least partially, correct? I am sure that Sartre did misunderstand the nature of the unconscious as theorised by Freud; sure also that this was due in part to the fact that this intellectual 'material' became sucked into the Sartrean phantasmatic surrounding the relation to the father. But it is far from certain that Sartre misapprehended the fundamental nature of the analytic relationship. The italicised words in the above quotation from Pacaly are very revealing. Why should the relationship between analyst and analysand always and necessarily be reduced to one of *submission*?[5] Unconditional submission is precisely what characterises the relationship to the bad father. It will be pointed out that this is necessary, precisely, for the cure to take its course: that a transference must be established in which the analyst replaces the father as authority figure, so that, in a second movement, the analyst can help the analysand towards confident subjecthood (thus becoming a good father), rather than abandon him as the bad father is phantasised to have done.

So has Sartre misunderstood again? Yes and no. The question must at least be allowed to remain open. The whole problematic of the psychoanalytic relationship (and I take this to include the relationship between psychoanalytic critic and text) is brought into closer focus by the notorious episode of 'L'Homme au magnétophone'. This text is an account of an agonistic encounter between analyst and lapsed patient, which ended with the analyst calling upon the forces of law and order to eject the unruly patient from the sanctum of his consulting-room. When the tape came to *Les Temps modernes*, there was heated discussion as to whether or not to publish it. Sartre wished to publish. Pontalis, the psychoanalyst, was against publication. It was agreed that the text would be published with appended texts by Sartre, Pontalis and Pingaud in which each would state his reasons for wishing to publish or not publish the text. Sartre's piece broadens out into the question of anti-psychiatry – as practised by Laing, Cooper, Balint, Basaglia, and so on – and the founding of an analytic *practice* which would not be grounded in violence: a reciprocal dialogue between one free subject and another. It is perhaps significant that Pontalis finally eschews this dialogue and, it could be argued, resorts to violence: rather than argue with Sartre as an equal, he slips into the role of the analyst *vis-à-vis* the patient by claiming that what is really interesting in the whole affair – and what should be *analysed* – is Sartre's ambivalent attitude towards psychoanalysis itself. In other words, the psychoanalytic discourse has closed itself to any thought of the subject ('pensée du sujet') by turning its guns on those who would throw into question its position of mastery: a further objectification.[6]

I stated earlier that I have sought to bring out in this book something of the tension in Sartre's work between the conscious orientation of Sartre's work (a subject trying to 'make itself'), and the structuring forces of the unconscious. Any reading that attempts to resolve this tension by the suppression of one of its terms will perpetuate a fallacy – either intentional or unintentional – since it is this tension that constitutes the very *texture* of the Sartrean text.

Notes

The place of publication for books in English is London unless otherwise stated; and, for books in French, Paris.

PREFATORY REMARKS

1. Elizabeth Wright, *Psychoanalytic Criticism: Theory in Practice* (Methuen, 1984) p. 5.
2. One of the most recent, and best balanced, accounts is to be found in Wright's *Psychoanalytic Criticism*.
3. Josette Pacaly, *Sartre au miroir. Une lecture psychanalytique de ses écrits biographiques* (Klincksieck, 1980) p. 451. This book is the one work which falls most squarely across the purview of the present study, even though it presents itself as a study only of the biographical works. It was reviewed late and not very widely in Britain, and in consequence I did not read it until my own book (originally a doctoral thesis) was more than half completed. My initial reaction was mixed: dismay that so many passages which I had singled out for analysis also received critical attention in Pacaly's book; pleasure when these analyses coincided; a certain relief when they did not! *Sartre au miroir* is an extremely dense and thorough study, and is *essential* reading both for Sartre scholars, and for those interested in a more general way in the applications of psychoanalytic criticism. Anyone working on Sartre within a psychoanalytic perspective must take this study into account, and the present work is no exception in this respect. My reservations about *Sartre au miroir* are voiced mainly in the Prefatory and Concluding Remarks to this book. These objections are of the same order as those made by André Gorz in his article 'Sartre malgré lui?', *Le Nouvel Observateur*, 6 Dec 1976, on François George's book *Deux essais sur Sartre* (Christian Bourgois, 1976).
4. Pacaly, *Sartre au miroir*, p. 20.

CHAPTER 1   THEORISING THE DIFFERENCE

1. Sigmund Freud, 'Infantile Sexuality', *Three Essays on the Theory of Sexuality*, Pelican Freud Library, vol. 7 (Harmondsworth: Penguin, 1977) p. 117.
2. Ibid., p. 312.
3. If I insist on this point here, it is because I shall be arguing later that

Sartre's texts bear witness to a failure of identification: what should be experienced as identification with a *position* comes to be experienced as a physical process of incorporation of, or by, a real person.
4. See Freud, *On Sexuality*, p. 127.
5. There have, naturally, been developments in endocrinology, ethology, and neuro-physiology since Freud's day. For the broad implications of this more recent research for Freud's theories, see for example Robert J. Stoller, *Perversion: The Erotic Form of Hatred* (New York: Aronson, 1968).
6. In this way, Daniel, in *La Mort dans l'âme*, experiences societal condemnation as the gaze of a thousand pairs of unseen eyes.
7. In *L'Idiot de la famille* Sartre uses the category of *activité passive* to describe a similar conduct on the part of Gustave Flaubert.
8. Sartre points out that between these two poles there is an infinite number of possible projects, just as there is an infinite number of possible men (*EN* 624). This statement is analogous to Freud's nuancing of the positions that separate the 'negative' and 'positive' outcomes of the Oedipus complex.
9. Doubtless, many would see the notorious affair of 'L'Homme au magnétophone' as Sartre's quintessential statement in this debate! See Concluding Remarks, below.
10. Sartre, amusingly, imagines Achille-Cléophas saying to his wife in their nuptial bed, 'viens là que je te fasse un médecin'.
11. See the Prefatory Remarks for a fuller explanation of this term.
12. This image of 'taming' or 'mastering' recurs below in the context of the skier's attempt to subjugate the *piste*.
13. Interestingly enough, Sartre does talk of digestion, whilst underlining the difference in his approach to that of the idealist 'philosophies alimentaires': 'On remarquera l'importance dans les imaginations naïves du symbole du *digéré-indigeste*, le caillou dans l'estomac de l'autruche, Jonas dans l'estomac de la baleine, il marque un rêve d'assimilation non-destructive' (*EN* 639). The debasement of the virginal object is replaced here by its ingestion, and the restoration of this Venus to her pedestal is captured by the phantasy of non-digestion. I shall suggest one determinant for this phantasy towards the end of this chapter.
14. It is worth recalling the aloof indifference that Sartre ascribes to Caroline Flaubert in *L'Idiot*, where this indifference is given in its specifically sexual form.
15. Hilbert, the Sartrean sadist in 'Erostrate', keeps himself literally buttoned up in his encounter with the prostitute. See *OR* 265–8.
16. Cf. the passage quoted above where the root has fallen into the trap avoided by the skier. In order to *use* the earth (masculine attitude), the root has to become part of it (feminine assimilation).
17. It is immediately striking how lyrical Sartre becomes – albeit in pseudo-parodic mode – in his descriptions of the anus: 'Et certes le trou de cul est le plus vivant des trous, un trou lyrique, qui se fronce comme un sourcil, qui se resserre comme une bête blessée se contracte, qui bée enfin, vaincu et près de livrer ses secrets . . .' (*Car* 187).

18. This insight is fully developed in Sartre's analysis of the mother–infant dyad in *L'Idiot de la famille*.
19. Freud insisted throughout on the necessity of seeing castration as linked to organ loss. Other analysts, both contemporaries of Freud and post-Freudians, have extended 'castration' to include loss of individuation, engulfment, and so on. Yet others have pushed back the prefiguring of this anxiety to weaning or to the separation from the mother's body at birth. See the entry for 'Castration complex' in J. Laplanche and J. B. Pontalis, *The Language of Psychoanalysis*, tr. Donald Nicholson-Smith (Hogarth Press, 1985) pp. 56–9.

CHAPTER 2 REPRESENTATIONS

1. I borrow these very apt terms from Suzanne Lilar's *A propos de Sartre et de l'amour* (Grasset, 1967). The present chapter is particularly endebted to Lilar's excellent chapter entitled 'La femme et l'amour dans la fiction sartrienne' (pp. 173–226)
2. See Chapter 4 below, where this passage is examined at greater length.
3. The male genital organ is often described as a flower – but only when it is detumescent and/or its owner is ashamed of it: Mathieu on learning of Marcelle's pregnancy; Daniel trying to castrate himself; and occasions too numerous to mention in *Saint Genet*.
4. As far as I am aware this transitive use of *exister*, and *être* ('est été') is peculiar to Sartre.
5. Lulu in 'Intimité' is a different case. She experiences her body as disgust because it provides the lever by means of which a dominating Other may act upon her freedom (cf. the English slang for 'name' – 'handle'). Her 'frigidity' is intended to be seen as willed more than suffered.
6. Cf. Lilar, *A propos de Sartre*, ch. 4.
7. In fact, she *pretends* to be horrified by her sticky mint syrup. Perhaps this episode foreshadows the revelation of her duplicity, which only becomes fully apparent when she *falls* into pregnancy.
8. The already strange intertextual relationship between Sartre's writings and de Beauvoir's *Le Deuxième Sexe* (Gallimard, 1947) receives a further twist at this point. The latter writes that woman 'guette comme la plante carnivore, le marécage où insectes et enfants[!] s'enlisent; elle est succion, ventouse, humeuse, elle est poix et glu, un appel immobile insinuant et visqueux: du moins est-ce ainsi que sourdement elle se sent' (148).
9. I would recall at this point the rhetorical question – left unanswered – with which I concluded Chapter 1.
10. Cf. *OR* 683, where Mathieu's dilemma is succinctly expressed.
11. It is somewhat ironic that, in a work that has been taxed with 'sordid realism', Ivich is virtually the only character who is seen to *eat* anything: an apple!
12. As far as the 'jeune femme lourde' of the present of the narration is concerned, the 'fall' has already taken place.

13. Except briefly in *Le Sursis*, where the 'inside' too is seen to be opaque!
14. In *Saint Genet* this is the active 'male' homosexual who subjugates the passive *tante-fille* to his pleasure.
15. It is surely not necessary to insist on the sexual connotations of this term: *faire une pipe* = 'to give head'.
16. Michel Contat speculates that this particular cut was made in order to avoid upsetting unnecessarily Sartre's stepfather, Joseph Mancy, who would doubtless have felt himself to be the target in this passage. This is almost certainly true, but the 'repressed' that 'returns' in this passage also has more archaic origins.
17. See also the description of Monsieur Fleurier in 'L'Enfance' (*OR* 359).
18. Pacaly makes an interesting connection between this figure and Poulou's Uncle Emile in *Les Mots*. See *Sartre au miroir*, pp. 105–6.
19. The word 'châtiés' is disturbingly close to 'châtrés' ('castrated').
20. I shall argue later that it is precisely this position that the subject in Sartre's phantasmatic scenarios is unable to occupy. The reasons for this will also emerge later.
21. The relationship between Charles and Louise Schweitzer appears to have provided Sartre with the model for the fictional Darbédat couple. Cf. *Mots* 13–14 and *OR* 235–40.
22. We saw in *Baudelaire* that Sartre equates the father with *le Bien* – that is to say, the bourgeois ideological notion of societal good. In this respect, *Les Séquestrés* could represent a *prise de conscience* on Sartre's part inasmuch as the deep conflict – that between father and son in the Oedipal context – comes squarely to the forefront.
23. Freud would argue, of course, that the very permanency of these figures reflects the relatively ahistorical universality of 'psychical reality'.
24. Laplanche and Pontalis, *The Language of Psychoanalysis*, pp. 317–18.
25. I shall leave aside for the moment the movement by which the phantasy structure constantly draws in new material. This implies a permanence of structure coupled with variability of means of representation.
26. I shall have more to say about Sartre's use and misuse of the notion of castration, this time in *L'Idiot de la famille*, in subsequent chapters.
27. Pinette's name ('little prick') points to the phantasy that underlies this exchange.
28. Pacaly argues that the re-emergent castration anxiety in this passage is probably associated with the repression that falls on infantile masturbation, Cf. Pacaly, *Sartre au miroir*, pp. 162–3.
29. The fact that we are dealing specifically with the Genitor, and not just with the symbolic head of a social class, is something that Roquentin's *own* obsessive insistence on this point does not allow us to forget. See, for example, *OR* 99.
30. In fact this abandonment is more longstanding than Oreste suggests. Already at the beginning of the play Oreste envies those who belong because they, at least, have a *master*: 'Un chien a plus de mémoire que moi: c'est son maître qu'il reconnaît' (*Mou* 120). Oreste's ambivalence regarding the question of belonging is reminiscent of the ambivalence

with which Sartre talks, in *Les Mots*, of the absent father: on the one hand he might have *saved* him; on the other he would certainly have *crushed* him, like Anchises riding on the back of Aeneas.
31. The marginality of Roquentin relative to the world of the bourgeois *salauds* hardly needs stressing. What is less clear is this notion of abandonment. But we shall see in Chapter 4 that this element is indeed present: in the *reversal* of his abandonment of the Rollebon project, for example.
32. See Michael Scriven, *Sartre's Existential Biographies* (Macmillan, 1984) pp. 99–100.
33. Michel Contat, *Explication des Séquestrés d'Altona de Jean-Paul Sartre* (Lettres Modernes, 1968) p. 23.
34. Unfortunately, Josette Pacaly goes so far in this direction that Sartre's conscious theoretical intentions in his biographies are regarded as a complete irrelevance: the biographies then become nothing more than a direct hotline to the author's teeming unconscious!
35. I shall reserve my discussion of Sartre's controversial use of psychoanalysis in *L'Idiot* for a later chapter. I would simply note at this stage that Sartre was to become infinitely more flexible in his attitude towards psychoanalysis than he had been in *Baudelaire*, *Saint Genet* or *Mallarmé*.
36. A term much used in *L'Idiot*, but originating perhaps in Gide's account of his childhood, *Si le Grain ne meurt*.
37. But there is one final twist in the irony: Freud emerges as less of a Freudian hero than a Sartrean one. One of the alternative endings has Freud departing thus: 'Je suis seul et le ciel s'est vidé. Je travaillerai seul, je serai mon seul juge et mon seul témoin' (*SF* 403). As Goetz had remarked, 'il y a cette guerre à faire et je la ferai!' (*DBD* 252).
38. 'Ein anderer Schauplatz': Freud's term for the locus of unconscious activity.

CHAPTER 3   THEORISING DESIRE

1. See Sigmund Freud, *The Psychopathology of Everyday Life*, Pelican Freud Library, vol. 5 (Harmondsworth: Penguin, 1975) pp. 34–44.
2. This Sartrean ego has marked similarities with the Lacanian conception of the ego, as constructed self, first adumbrated in 'Le Stade du miroir comme formateur du Je . . .'. This paper dates from 1936, but it was the 1949 version that was widely read and discussed.
3. Sartre does not seem aware, at this point, that the complex he imagines seeking to express itself is *already* the product of conflicts. He appears to view the 'complex' as a ready-made entity, whereas psychoanalysis actually sees the complex as a highly ramified nexus of *relationships*: it is desire that seeks expression, not the 'complex' itself.
4. This point throws into relief the differences between the approaches of Sartre and Freud. The latter – even to a certain degree in his

metapsychological writings – was concerned with operative concepts which could illuminate and inform the clinical practice. Sartre remains on a purely theoretical, therefore verbal, level.

5. Libido had the status of working hypothesis for Freud. More recent work, in endocrinology for example, has tended to disprove some of Freud's speculations, whilst being weakly supportive of others.

6. 'Instinct' is the standard translation of German *Trieb*, but the trend nowadays is to use the term 'drive' (cf. Fr. *pulsions*) in order to distinguish between human and animal sexuality. 'Instinct' should generally, then, be reserved for the latter. In his *Introduction to the Psychoanalytic Theory of the Libido* (New York: Robert Brunner, 1968) p. vi, Richard Sterba makes clear the distinction between the two: 'The term "instinct" should be reserved for the instinctual reactions of animals, their innately given responses to specific stimuli coming from the surroundings. Animals' instincts guarantee survival under the average conditions of the biological niche in which the animals belong', whereas 'the drives of the human being are characterised by their plasticity which enables them to some extent to be satisfied by substitute aims and objects. One of their essential features is transformability.' Characteristically, Sartre tends to ignore the plasticity implied in the Freudian notion of *Trieb*, preferring to see it as a mechanical process.

7. Sartre conveniently overlooks the problem that 'chemical castration' could cause for his theory: it is demonstrably possible to control, to the point of shutting down, a person's sexual drive through purely chemical means.

8. Without entering into any great detail, it is worth pointing out that the Lacanian conception of desire holds that the latter is also, ultimately, founded on a certain 'manque à être' which makes it unsatisfiable by nature.

9. Note the concrete *reality* of this object of desire. This position is very much at odds with the Freudian conception, which insists on the ultimately phantasmatic nature of our obscure objects of desire.

10. I shall show later that the *rapprochement* with psychoanalytic theory in *L'Idiot* involves an explicit, if partial, espousal of some of Lacan's ideas in his linguistic rethinking of Freud. But it is important to bear in mind that the question of *priority* is a very complex one: many of the ideas elaborated in *L'Idiot* (such as the ego as constructed self, desire as desire of the Other, human intercourse as an exchange of signs, and so on) were already present in Sartre's earliest work, long before any familiarity with the work of Lacan. This problem is further complicated by the common influence of Hegel (initially via Kojève) on both thinkers.

11. Thomas Nagel considers this account to be 'the best discussion of these matters that I have seen' – 'Sexual Perversion', *Mortal Questions* (Cambridge: Cambridge University Press, 1979) p. 43.

12. Sartre is not entirely consistent in his recourse to the 'evidence' of common usage. In 'L'Intentionnalité: une idée fondamentale de la phénoménologie de Husserl' he pours scorn on such a recourse by

showing that the expression 'manger quelqu'un des yeux' bears witness to a vulgar misapprehension of the (phenomenological) truth.
13. This virilisation of hunger (hard and dry) and feminisation of desire (moist and clammy) is quite typical and in fact becomes accentuated with time. Sartre later builds up *need* into a kind of privileged domain (occupied by 'scarcity', and hungry but rocklike proletarians), whilst disparaging desire as a supreme bourgeois anti-value.
14. The Oedipal moment in Lacan is also the passage from being to having: from being the maternal phallus (that which would satisfy the mother, make her whole), to having the paternal phallus, albeit in a deferred mode.
15. See for example J. Culler, *The Pursuit of Signs: Semiotics, Literature, Deconstruction* (Routledge and Kegan Paul, 1981) pp. 224–6.
16. We shall see that Sartre modifies his position on 'conditioning' and 'determinism' considerably in *L'Idiot*. But, once, again, it would be misleading to suggest that *L'Idiot* represents a deliberate break with the philosophy of freedom established in *L'Etre et le néant*: the key notion of *stress* in *L'Idiot* is little more than a long-winded reformulation of the relationship between 'milieu' and 'sujet' encapsulated in this quotation.
17. Etienne Barilier quotes in amazement a phrase from the *Morale* which he sees as typical of Sartre's 'magical' or 'incantatory' use of language in order to sidestep a genuine philosophical problem: 'il n'y a pas choix de désir, mais le désir est choix de désirer' (*Cah* 37). See E. Barilier, *Les Petits Camarades* (Julliard/L'Age d'Homme, 1987) p. 42.
18. This word 'illégitime' could appear puzzling in this context. It is however wholly explicable if we recall the Oedipal dimension of Sartre's analysis: desire is rendered illegitimate precisely when it is 'criminalised' by the paternal Law – here the quasi-original intervention of the Other.
19. This figure of the *zar* was to take on great significance in Sartre's theoretical discourse, but this practical significance is also mirrored at the level of the phantasmatic structure: it will be recalled that one feature of the phantasmatic is its ability to take in and integrate new material. The *zar* was able to become such a powerful theoretical tool because it struck a resonant chord in the Sartrean unconscious.
20. *Explication* is viewed negatively by Sartre: it is a deterministic method of explanation by causality. It is contrasted with *compréhension*, which embraces dialectically the subject's relations to his past and to the world.
21. This image of being 'taken from behind' will lead us later into another region of the phantasmatic.
22. *Saint Genet* was perhaps the first work to profit from this realisation. The treatment of childhood in *Baudelaire* was, by Sartre's own admission, at best schematic.
23. See C. Howells, 'Sartre and Freud', *French Studies*, XXXIII (1979) 165–7.
24. 'Foreclosure' is actually held to be at the origin of psychotic – not neurotic, as in *L'Idiot* – phenomena. Laplanche and Pontalis note that it consists in 'a primordial expulsion of a fundamental signifier (e.g.

the phallus as signifier of the castration complex) from the subject's symbolic universe' (*The Language of Psychoanalysis*, p. 166).
25. Cf. *IF* 434, where Sartre explicitly discusses the Lacanian position.
26. In a strangely vitriolic passage, reminiscent of passages in the *Cahiers* that I have already quoted, Sartre denounces in Flaubert the high priest, *avant la lettre*, of a Freudianism that appears in a very negative light: 'dolorisme, vocation de l'homme pour le martyre, prédominance éthique de affectivité sur la volonté, de l'instinct sur l'intelligence, supériorité reconnue de l'idée qui s'impose et qui obsède sur celles qu'on invente, de l'obscurité sur la transparence . . . les mots manquent encore mais ce qu'il prône, seul à son époque, c'est la décentration du sujet, le refus de la méditation consciente, l'abandon à la spontanéité conçue et ressentie comme *autre*, c'est-à-dire à l'inconscient' (*IF* 1696). Sartre's vitriol is directed as much against his own psychoanalytical contemporaries as it is against Flaubert. Indeed, the tone of the passage, the accumulations, the opposition of terms, and so on, are uncannily reminiscent of Lacan's attack on Sartre at the end of his 'Stade du miroir' (1949 version). Cf. Jacques Lacan, *Ecrits*, I (Seuil, 1966) 96.
27. Sartre's ambivalence towards Freud means that there are *two* Freuds in the *Scénario Freud*. There is doubtless Freud as bad father, but there is also a Freud with whom Sartre could certainly identify. Annette Lavers puts it this way: 'Here, for Sartre, was no longer a patriarch of dubious philosophical competence, but a brother-in-arms, an adventurer struggling against a hostile establishment and "thinking against himself", plagued by guilt and dependency, but driven by a burning desire for recognition and a sense of destiny' – 'Sartre and Freud', *French Studies*, XLI (1987) 298–317.

CHAPTER 4   THE STAGING OF DESIRE

1. Cf. François Le Lionnais, 'Le Théâtre Bouléen', in Oulipo, *La Littérature potentielle* (Gallimard, 1973) p. 268: 'Deux pièces complètement indépendantes et complètement différentes sont jouées en même temps et au même endroit. La plupart du temps des acteurs de la pièce A sont donc amenés à parler en même temps que parlent des acteurs de la pièce B, les uns et les autres s'ignorant complètement, le jeu des uns se déroulant comme si les autres n'existaient pas. . . . Sur cette base on peut imaginer un grand nombre de combinaisons: une pièce comique en même temps qu'une pièce tragique, des pièces complémentaires ou parallèles, etc.; et, éventuellement, une intersection de deux pièces dans la dernière minute.'
2. Maurice Cranston for example: 'Sexual congress is invariably depicted in his books as a charmless exercise; and his female characters are all repulsive' – 'Jean-Paul Sartre', *Encounter*, no. 103 (Apr 1962) 44. Quoted in Lilar, *A propos de Sartre*, p. 173n.
3. This same metaphor is used when Lucien sees his name in print – on the petition – and is struck by its strange otherness. See *OR* 371.

4. This melting varnish has already been encountered in the art-gallery scene in *La Nausée*. See Chapter 2 above.
5. This threatened destruction of the Cartesian clear and distinct idea, can be compared to the Rimbaudian revelation with which Bergère threatens/entices Lucien in 'L'Enfance': 'C'est sur moi que tu comptes pour les dérégler, tes petits sens' (*OR* 353).
6. Cf. Marcelle, who was 'passive et gourmande', and Nature in *La Nausée*, whose submission was mere 'paresse'.
7. 'L'Enfance' is also the *productive* meeting-point of conscious and unconscious determinants. Lucien passes through a series of debased objects before arriving, albeit in imagination, at the virginal 'jeune fille en fleur'. I have already pointed to the psychoanalytical implications of this series of object choices. Whilst in this respect the text looks inwards, in other respects it is consciously directed outwards in the form of a social critique. Wilhelm Reich shows that the choice of a debased, or virginal, love object is also intimately linked with the class structure of capitalist society. The gratification of sensual urges with women from a lower social class has the function of safeguarding the (economic) integrity of the dominant class. See Wilhelm Reich, *The Sexual Revolution* (New York: Vision Press, 1972) pp. 146–7.
8. See for example Rhiannon Goldthorpe, 'The Presentation of Consciousness in Sartre's *La Nausée* and its Theoretical Basis', *French Studies*, XXII (1968), XXV (1971). In *Sartre: Literature and Theory* (Cambridge University Press, 1984) Goldthorpe turns the tables on the approach she had adopted in these two articles. She now argues that Sartre's texts, when properly 'read', subvert the very oppositions and hierarchies that they, themselves, set up.
9. A term used in *Les Mots* to describe the dead father.
10. See George, *Deux études sur Sartre*. Chapters 1 and 2 of part II are especially good in demonstrating the aporia which haunts Sartre's vision of the father–son relationship. Any psychoanalytical study of Sartre's *oeuvre* would have to pass through George's seminal study, and the present work is no exception. For a 'Sartrean' critique of the *Deux études*, see André Gorz, 'Sartre malgré lui?', *Le Nouvel Observateur*, 6 Dec 1976.
11. The same image recurs in *Kean* (see Chapter 5 below). If we follow it further, into *L'Idiot*, it leads back explicitly to the father–son relationship. In the latter work Sartre uses the example of Kean to typify the relationship in which the son is the ham actor called upon to *représent* the father's desire: 'Ainsi, pour l'acteur véritable, chaque personnage nouveau devient une *imago* provisoire, un *parasite* qui, même en dehors des représentations, *vit en symbiose* avec lui, et, parfois, à la ville, au cours de ses activité quotidiennes, l'irréalise *en lui dictant ses attitudes*' (*IF* 664; emphasis added).
12. This is a reference to Baudelaire's poem 'La Géante' in *Les Fleurs du mal* (Gallimard, 1972) p. 50. It also functions, of course, as a self-reference to Sartre's own *Baudelaire*.
13. As will become apparent, the feminisation at the hands of the mother is coupled with a phantasised anal rape by the father. Lucien reverts

to the status of *poupée* as he is being sodomised by Bergère.
14. Is it necessary to point out the similarities between this account and the childhood that Sartre imagines for Flaubert? The latter, too, is 'manié' by his mother and becomes the passive object for these 'regards inquisiteurs', except in Flaubert's case the owner of this prying gaze is explicitly identified as the father: Achille-Cléophas.
15. The tall, beautiful mother, and the small, ugly child – the other italicised words are associated more with books than with humans. The significance of this will emerge later.
16. It is curious how important this event seems to be: there can scarcely be a family which does not have as part of its lore this ritual occasion of the first hair-cut. It seems also to be more significant for boy children than for girls.
17. The opening of 'L'Enfance' is a version of this feminising scenario. The difference is that Lucien has a convenient paternal imago to help him break out of his androgyny. But, as we shall see in Chapter 5, this 'escape' is viewed with extreme ambivalence by Sartre. Cf. also *IF* 90.
18. Sartre's 'psychoanalytic' reconstruction of Flaubert's childhood reads, in the light of this, more like a *projection* of his own: 'On connaît les effets du sevrage sur le nourrisson; je crois qu'on peut, à l'âge ingrat de l'enfance, parler d'un contre-sevrage de la mère: à cette époque déjà tardive, elle découvre l'altérité radicale de ce qu'elle prenait pour son reflect: un fil est rompu' (*IF* 365).
19. See Lavers, 'Sartre and Freud', *French Studies*, XLI, p. 315n.
20. Jacques Lacan, 'Le Stade du miroir comme formateur de la fonction du Je', *Ecrits*, I, 91.
21. In order better to analyse the Sartre–Lacan relationship, it would be necessary to analyse in detail, at the very least, the whole of the long section in *L'Idiot* on 'le miroir et le fétiche'. Sartre says, for example, that any 'Egologie véritable' would have to take into account the fact that *je* and *moi* are, in the first instance, *parts of speech* (*IF* 1294).
22. In *L'Idiot* Sartre talks with scarcely veiled hatred of the 'ogres rouennais si cupides de manger leurs progénitures' (*IF* 1338).
23. In psychoanalytic theory this identificatory mode is held to be characteristic of the oral or 'cannibalistic' stage.

CHAPTER 5 THE PERVERTED CONSCIOUSNESS

1. Thomas Nagel, 'Sexual Perversion', *Mortal Questions*, p. 44.
2. Sartre sometimes appears to forget in the *Cahiers* that, according to his own ontological analysis, conflict is not in itself a historically variable moment of interpersonal relationships, but a sempiternal ontological *datum*.
3. It is worth recalling that human reality, for Sartre, is defined as not *being* that which it *is*, in the way that a rock, for example, simply *is* what it *is*.
4. On this point see Howells, 'Sartre and Freud', *French Studies*, XXXIII.

5. As Sartre makes abundantly clear, the *historical reality* of this scene is neither here nor there.
6. The primal scene is often phantasised as copulation *a tergo*, which would go some way towards explaining why this possession is viewed as an *anal* rape.
7. Cf. *Mots* 20, where Sartre talks of his own father in similar terms: 'je le connais par ouï-dire, comme le Masque de Fer ou le Chevalier d'Eon[!]'.
8. Like Gustave too, it seems: 'Ainsi le sujet qui l'habite n'est point lui-même mais un être clos, impénétrable, *absent* qui prend consistance à travers ses gestes sans cesser pour autant de lui être étranger, tel Hamlet pour Kean' (*IF* 728). Cf. also *Mots* 134.
9. Flaubert too, it seems, wishes to reappropriate the 'coup d'oeil chirurgical' which had transpierced him.
10. Of course, this functions also at another level in Sartre's texts: as a cathartic repetition of a different primal scene.
11. In *L'Idiot* Flaubert practises an entirely analogous repossession *vis-à-vis* the father. He too is originally possessed, he too provokes the repetition of the crisis in the fall at Pont l'Evêque, and in a series of 'crises référentielles'. See *IF* 1784 and *passim*.
12. This analysis is repeated *mutatis mutandis* in *L'Idiot*, where Achille's accession to the status of paterfamilias is given as a simple rehearsal of the role, or *persona*, of Achille-Cléophas: the identification between father and first-born son is so perfect as to leave no gap into which the 'anxiety of influence' that afflicts Gustave could insinuate itself.
13. Cf. *SG* 65: 'C'est l'Autre enfin, un "zar" qui le possède, un inconscient qui, *comme celui des psychanalystes*, propose, impose, ruse et déjoue les précautions qu'on prend contre lui.' But Sartre rejects this psychoanalytical unconscious. There is doubtless a sense in which Sartre would see the analyst as anal-ist.
14. Cf. *La Nausée*: 'N'avoir ni sang, ni lymphe, ni chair. Couler dans ce long canal vers cette pâleur là-bas. N'être que du froid' (*OR* 34). The syntactic similarity is also quite striking.
15. The suicide, which is also a murder of the father, is another recurrent theme in Sartre: Hugo, Frantz, for example, and the reversal of this pattern in Sartre's description of the operation by which Achille-Cléophas 'commits suicide' by the hand of his eldest son.
16. This relates quite clearly to the experiences of Charles, the invalid, in *Le Sursis*: a passive object, he is masturbated, like a doll, by his nurse – 'la cosse allait éclater, un fruit tout droit vers le ciel, un fruit juteux' (*OR* 791).
17. The correlative of Sartre's strenuous *theoretical* denial of any genetic influence on the development of the individual is a *horror* of just such a transmission of characteristics. See for example *OR* 841.
18. See also the editor's comments on this in the Pléiade edition (*OR* 1859).
19. Genet achieves this reversal through his writing practice; the image used by Sartre to describe Genet's achievement is interesting when taken literally: 'on se *surmonte*' (*SG* 197).
20. Hardly 'pathological' in fact: Sartre rejects the pathology of perversion.

21. The similarities with the 'grande asperche' scene in 'L'Enfance' are obvious enough not to require further comment.
22. Ten years before the writing of *Les Séquestrés*, this is a strikingly accurate summation of Frantz's problem *vis-à-vis* his father!
23. *Reluquer* is always used in French to convey covetousness or sexual desire, as in to 'ogle' or 'eye up' in English.
24. The *vampire* is also implicit in this image. In *Kean*, the actor's paternal possessors are referred to as vampires, as are the various paternal imagos in *L'Idiot* who suck the life-blood of their progeny.
25. Laplanche and Pontalis, *The Language of Psychoanalysis*, p. 207.
26. Kean is also a crucial figure in *L'Idiot*: he enables Sartre to demonstrate how Gustave is defined as 'cabotin' in relation to the supreme audience constituted by his father.
27. As Annette Lavers remarks in her 'Sartre and Freud' (*French Studies*, XLI), this father is unique in Sartre's work in that he is not subject to the strategy of deflation that I outlined in Chapter 2. She also suggests that the anachronistic pessimism of *Les Séquestrés* could be due in part to external factors, not least the return in 1958 of the ultimate Sartrean 'bad father': de Gaulle.
28. George, *Deux études sur Sartre*, p. 211.

CONCLUDING REMARKS

1. Pacaly's conclusion reads, in fact, rather like the summing-up of a case history: the subject – Sartre – has been neatly tied up and packaged, totally mastered by the psychoanalytic discourse; no longer subject, he is transformed into object for the 'surgical gaze' of this omniscient author/Other. The irony of this conclusion lies in the reversal that has occurred, which could be termed 'transferential'. It never seems to occur to the author that her own extremely substantial text could be seen, in its denseness, impenetrability, closedness, as the symbolic equivalent of the anal phallus which she devotes so much energy and ingenuity to tracking down in Sartre's texts. Sartre's texts are shot through with dreams of narcissistic omnipotence, but what kind of dreams are we to ascribe to Pacaly's text, which represents a 450-page attempt to 'master' Sartre?
2. Pacaly makes this point with some vigour in *Sartre au miroir*.
3. Ibid., p. 452.
4. Ibid.
5. The question of submission is one of the axes of Annette Lavers's analysis in her 'Sartre and Freud', *French Studies*, XLI.
6. The text of 'L'Homme au magnétophone' first appeared in *Les Temps modernes*, no. 274 (Apr 1969), with appended texts by Sartre, Pontalis and Pingaud, and is republished in *Sit* IX. The whole episode could be read as an enactment, in the flesh, of the (unwelcome) return of the (unsuccessfully) repressed – and of its re-repression!

Bibliography

The following bibliography lists all works referred to in the preceding text as well as a selection of other works consulted. The place of publication for books in English is London unless otherwise stated; and, for books in French, Paris.

A. WORKS BY SARTRE

L'Imagination (Librairie Félix Alcan, 1936).
La Transcendance de l'ego, esquisse d'une description phénoménologique (Vrin, 1965; originally published in *Recherches Philosophiques*, no. 6, 1936).
Esquisse d'une théorie phénoménologique des émotions (Hermann, 1939; republ. 1960).
L'Imaginaire (Gallimard, 1940).
L'Etre et le néant, essai d'ontologie phénoménologique (Gallimard, 1943; republ. 1976).
Les Mouches (Gallimard, 1943; republ. in *Huis Clos* suivi de *Les Mouches*, Gallimard, 1964).
Huis Clos (Gallimard, 1945; republ. in *Huis Clos* suivi de *Les Mouches*, Gallimard, 1964).
L'Existentialisme est un humanisme (Nagel, 1946).
Morts sans sépulture (Lausanne: Marguerat, 1946; republ. in *La P... respectueuse* suivi de *Morts sans sépulture*, Gallimard, 1954).
La Putain respectueuse (Nagel, 1946; republ. in *La P . . . respectueuse* suivi de *Morts sans sépulture*, Gallimard, 1954).
Réflexions sur la question juive (Paul Morihen, 1946; republ. in Gallimard, 'Idées', 1961).
Baudelaire (Gallimard, 1947).
Les Jeux sont faits (Nagel, 1947; republ. New York: Appleton–Century–Crofts, 1952).
Situations I (Gallimard, 1947).
Qu'est-ce que la Littérature? (Gallimard 'Idées', 1964).
Les Mains sales (Gallimard, 1948).
Situations III (Gallimard, 1949).
Le Diable et le bon Dieu (Gallimard, 1951).
Saint Genet, comédien et martyr (Gallimard, 1952).
Kean (Gallimard, 1954; republ. London: Oxford University Press, 1973).
Nekrassov (Gallimard, 1956).
Questions de méthode, in *Les Temps modernes*, nos 139–40 (1957; republ. in volume form in Gallimard 'Idées', 1967).

Les Séquestrés d'Altona (Gallimard, 1959).
Critique de la raison dialectique, I (Gallimard, 1960); II (Gallimard, 1985).
Les Mots, in *Les Temps modernes*, nos 209–10 (Nov 1963; republ. in volume form, Gallimard, 1964).
Situations IV (Gallimard, 1964).
Situations V (Gallimard, 1964).
Situations VI (Gallimard, 1964).
L'Idiot de la famille, I and II (Gallimard, 1971); III (Gallimard, 1972).
Situations IX (Gallimard, 1972).
Un Théâtre de situations (Gallimard, 1973).
Situations X (Gallimard, 1976).
Oeuvres romanesques (Gallimard, 'Bibliothèque de la Pléiade', 1981).
Les Carnets de la drôle de guerre (Gallimard, 1983).
Lettres au Castor et à quelques autres (Gallimard, 1983).
Cahiers pour une morale (Gallimard, 1983).
Le Scénario Freud (Gallimard, 'Connaissance de l'Inconscient', 1984).
Mallarmé, la lucidité et sa face d'ombre (Gallimard, 1986).

More complete biographical details may be obtained from the following sources.

Michel Contat and Michel Rybalka, *Les Ecrits de Sartre* (Gallimard, 1970). Supplements to this bibliography are to be found in *Le Magazine littéraire*, nos 55–6 (Sep 1971) and in *Obliques*, nos 18–19 (1979). A completely new and revised edition is expected in 1990.
Robert Wilcocks, *Jean-Paul Sartre: A Bibliography of International Criticism* (Edmonton: University of Alberta Press, 1975). See also the supplement in *Obliques*, nos 18–19 (1979).
François H. Lapointe, *Jean-Paul Sartre and his Critics: An International Bibliography (1938–1980)* (Bowling Green, Ohio: Bowling Green State University, 1981).
The *Bulletin d'Information du Groupe d'Etudes Sartriennes* publishes an invaluable yearly update of primary and secondary material (enquiries to Geneviève Idt, 89, bd Auguste-Blanqui, 75013 Paris).

B. PSYCHOANALYSIS AND RELATED DISCIPLINES

Works by Freud in the Pelican Freud Library (Harmondsworth: Penguin) are listed by title, followed by 'PFL' and vol. no. Dates of publication of individual volumes cited are as follows: vol. 1, 1973; vol. 4, 1976; vol. 5, 1975; vol. 6, 1976; vol. 7, 1977; vol. 9, 1979; vol. 14, 1985.

Chasseguet-Smirgel, J., *Pour une psychanalyse de l'art et de la créativité* (Payot, 1977).
——, *La Sexualité féminine, recherches psychanalytiques nouvelles* (Payot, 1982).
Deleuze, G., and Guattari, F., *Capitalisme et schizophrénie, l'anti-Oedipe* (Minuit, 1973).

Bibliography

Freud, S., *The Interpretation of Dreams*, PFL 4.
———, *The Psychopathology of Everyday Life*, PFL 5.
———, *Jokes and their Relation to the Unconscious*, PFL 6.
———, *Three Essays on the Theory of Sexuality*, PFL 7.
———, 'The Sexual Enlightenment of Children', PFL 7.
———, 'On the Sexual Theories of Children', PFL 7.
———, 'Leonardo da Vinci and a Memory of his Childhood', PFL 14.
———, 'Notes upon a Case of Obsessional Neurosis', PFL 9.
———, 'Family Romances', PFL 7.
———, 'Character and Anal Eroticism', PFL 7.
———, 'A Special Type of Choice of Object Made by Men', PFL 7.
———, 'On the Universal Tendency to Debasement in the Sphere of Love', PFL 7.
———, 'The Taboo of Virginity', PFL 7.
———, 'Two Lies told by Children', PFL 7.
———, 'On Transformations of Instinct as Exemplified by Anal Eroticism', PFL 7.
———, 'The Infantile Genital Organisation', PFL 7.
———, 'The Dissolution of the Oedipus Complex', PFL 7.
———, 'Some Psychical Consequences of the Anatomical Distinction between the Sexes', PFL 7.
———, 'Fetishism', PFL 7.
———, 'Libidinal Types', PFL 7.
———, 'Female Sexuality', PFL 7.
———, *Two Short Accounts of Psycho-Analysis (Five Lectures on Psycho-Analysis and the Question of Lay Analysis)* (Harmondsworth: Penguin, 1962).
———, 'Psychoanalytic Notes on an Autobiographical Account of Case of Paranoia (Dementia paranoides)', PFL 9.
———, *Totem and Tabou* (Routledge and Kegan Paul, 1960).
———, *Introductory Lectures on Psychoanalysis*, PFL 1.
———, 'From the History of an Infantile Neurosis', PFL 9.
———, 'The Psychogenesis of a Case of Homosexuality in a Woman', PFL 9.
———, *Beyond the Pleasure Principle* (Hogarth Press and Institute of Psycho-analysis, 1974).
———, *The Ego and the Id* (Hogarth Press and Institute of Psycho-analysis, 1974).
———, *Civilisation and its Discontents* (Hogarth Press and Institute of Psycho-analysis, 1974).
———, *New Introductory Lectures on Psychoanalysis* (Hogarth Press and Institute of Psycho-analysis, 1974).
———, *Moses and Monotheism* (Hogarth Press and Institute of Psycho-analysis 1974).
Horney, K., *Feminine Psychology* (New York: Norton, 1973).
Jones, E., *Papers on Psychoanalysis* (London: H. Karnac, 1977).
Klein, M., *Love, Guilt and Reparation and Other Papers* (Hogarth Press, 1975).
———, *Envy and Gratitude and Other Papers* (Hogarth Press, 1975).
Lacan, J., *Ecrits*, I (Seuil, 1966).
———, *Ecrits*, II (Seuil, 1971).
———, *Les Quatre Concepts fondamentaux de la psychanalyse* (Seuil, 1973).

Laing, R. D., *The Divided Self: An Existential Study in Sanity and Madness* (Harmondsworth: Penguin, 1965).
——, *The Politics of the Family and Other Essays* (Harmondsworth: Penguin, 1971).
Laing, R. D., and Cooper, D., *Reason and Violence: A Decade of Sartre's Philosophy 1950–1960* (Tavistock, 1964).
Laing, R. D., and Esterson, A., *Sanity, Madness and the Family* (Harmondsworth: Penguin, 1970).
Laplanche, J., and Pontalis, J.-B., *The Language of Psychoanalysis*, tr. Donald Nicholson-Smith (Hogarth Press, 1985).
Leclaire, S., *Psychanalyser* (Seuil, 1968).
Reich, W., *Sex-Pol: Essays, 1929–1934* (New York: Vintage, 1972).
——, *The Sexual Revolution* (New York: Vision Press, 1972).
Rycroft, C., *A Critical Dictionary of Psychoanalysis* (Harmondsworth: Penguin, 1972).
Safouan, M., *Le Structuralisme en psychanalyse* (Seuil, 1968).
Segal, H., *Introduction to the Works of Melanie Klein* (Hogarth Press, 1978).
Sterba, R. F., *Introduction to the Psychoanalytic Theory of the Libido* (New York: Robert Brunner, 1968).
Stoller, R. J., *Sex and Gender: On the Development of Masculinity and Femininity* (New York: Aronson, 1968).
——, *Perversion: The Erotic Form of Hatred* (New York, 1975).
——, *Sex and Gender: The Transsexual Experiment* (New York, Aronson, 1976).
Storr, A., *Sexual Deviation* (Harmondsworth: Penguin, 1964).

C. OTHER WORKS CONSULTED

Arnold, J. A., and Piriou, J.-P., *Genèse et critique d'une autobiographie: Les Mots de Jean-Paul Sartre* (Minard, 1973).
Aronson, R., *Jean-Paul Sartre: Philosophy in the World* (New Left Books, Verso, 1980).
Bailey, N., 'Le Mythe de la féminité dans le théâtre de Sartre', *French Studies*, xxxi (1977).
Barilier, E., *Les Petits Camarades* (Julliard, 1987).
Barthes, R., *Le Degré zéro de l'écriture* (Seuil, 1953).
——, 'Introduction à l'analyse structurale des récits', *Communications*, 8 (1966).
——, *Critique et vérité* (Seuil, 1966).
Baudelaire, C., *Les Fleurs de mal* (Gallimard, 1972).
Beauvoir, S. de, *Pour une morale de l'ambiguïté* (Gallimard, 1947).
——, *Le Deuxième Sexe* (Gallimard, 1947).
——, *Mémoires d'une jeune fille rangée* (Gallimard, 1958).
——, *La Force de l'âge* (Gallimard, 1960).
——, *La Force des choses* (Gallimard, 1963).
——, *Tout compte fait* (Gallimard, 1972).
——, *La Cérémonie des adieux suivi de Entretiens avec Jean-Paul Sartre* (Gallimard, 1981).

Bowie, M., 'Freud's Dreams of Knowledge', *Paragraph*, 2 (Dec 1983) 53–87.
Breton, A., *Manifestes du Surréalisme* (Gallimard 'Idées', 1967).
Clancier, A., *Psychanalyse et critique littéraire* (Toulouse: Privat, 1973).
Cohen-Solal, A., *Sartre 1905–1980* (Gallimard, 1985).
Collins, D., *Sartre as Biographer* (Cambridge, Mass.: Harvard University Press, 1980).
Contat, M., *Explication des Séquestrés d'Altona de Jean-Paul Sartre* (Lettres Modernes, 1968).
Contat, M., and Astruc, A., *Sartre. Un film réalisé par Alexandre Astruc et Michel Contat* (Gallimard, 1977).
Contat, M., and Rybalka, M., *Les Ecrits de Sartre. Chronologie, bibliographie commentée* (Gallimard, 1970).
Culler, J., *Structuralist Poetics: Structuralism, Linguistics, and the Study of Literature* (Routledge and Kegan Paul, 1975).
——, *The Pursuit of Signs: Semiotics, Literature, Deconstruction* (Routledge and Kegan Paul, 1981).
——, *On Deconstruction. Theory and Criticism after Structuralism* (Routledge and Kegan Paul, 1983).
Deleuze, G., and Guattari, F., *Kafka: Pour une littérature mineure* (Minuit, 1975).
Derrida, J., *L'Ecriture et la différence* (Seuil, 1967).
——, *De la grammatologie* (Minuit, 1967).
——, *Marges de la philosophie* (Minuit, 1972).
——, *La Dissémination* (Seuil, 1972).
Doubrovsky, S., *Pourquoi la Nouvelle Critique: critique et objectivité* (Mercure de France, 1966).
Ducrot, O., and Todorov, T., *Dictionnaire encyclopédique des sciences du langage* (Seuil 1972).
Felman, S., 'Turning the Screw of Interpretation', *Yale French Studies*, 55–6 (1977).
Foucault, M., *L'Ordre du discours* (Gallimard, 1971).
——, *Histoire de la sexualité*, I (Gallimard, 1976).
George, F., *Deux études sur Sartre* (Christian Bourgois, 1976).
Goldthorpe, R., 'The Presentation of Consciousness in Sartre's *La nausée* and its Theoretical Basis', *French Studies*, XXII (1968), XXV (1971).
——, *Sartre: Literature and Theory* (Cambridge: Cambridge University Press, 1984).
Gorz, A., 'Sartre malgré lui?', *Le Nouvel Observateur*, 6 Dec 1976.
Hamon, P., 'Pour un statut sémiologique du personnage', *Poétique du récit* (Seuil, 1972).
Holland, N., *The Dynamics of Literary Response* (New York: Norton, 1975).
Howells, C., 'Sartre and Freud', *French Studies*, XXXIII (1979) 152–74.
Idt, G., *'Le Mur' de Jean-Paul Sartre: techniques et contexte d'une provocation* (Larousse, 1972).
Jameson, F., 'Imaginary and Symbolic in Lacan: Marxism, Psychoanalytic Criticism, and the Problem of the Subject', *Yale French Studies*, 55–6 (1977).
Jeanson, F., *Le Problème moral et la pensée de Sartre* (Myrte, 1947).

——, *Sartre par lui-même* (Seuil, 1955).
——, *Sartre dans sa vie* (Seuil, 1974).
Kafka, F., *Sämtliche Erzählungen* (Frankfurt am Main: Fischer, 1970).
Kristeva, J., *Semeiotike. Recherches pour une sémanalyse* (Seuil, 1979).
——, *Pouvoirs de l'horreur, essai sur l'abjection* (Seuil, 1980).
LaCapra, D., *A Preface to Sartre* (Ithaca, NY: Cornell University Press, 1978).
Lavers, A., 'Sartre and Freud', *French Studies*, XLI (1987) 298–317.
Leiris, M., *L'Afrique fantôme* (Gallimard, 1981).
Lejeune, P., *Le Pacte autobiographique* (Seuil, 1975).
——, *Je est un Autre. L'autobiographie, de la littérature aux médias* (Seuil, 1980).
Lilar, S., *A propos de Sartre et de l'amour* (Grasset, 1967).
Marcuse, H., *Eros and Civilisation: A Philosophical Enquiry into Freud* (Boston, Mass.: Beacon Press, 1974).
Mauron, C., *Des Métaphores obsédantes au mythe personnel. Introduction à la psychocritique* (Corti, 1983).
Mehlman, J., *A Structural Study of Autobiography: Proust, Leiris, Sartre, Lévi-Strauss* (Ithaca, NY: Cornell University Press, 1974).
Merleau-Ponty, M., *Phénoménologie de la perception* (Gallimard, 1945).
——, *L'Oeil et l'esprit* (Gallimard, 1964).
——, *La Structure du comportement* (Presses Universitaires de France, 1978).
Millett, K., *Sexual Politics* (Virago, 1977).
Milner, M., *Freud et l'interprétation de la littérature* (CDU-SEDES, 1980).
Nagel, T., *Mortal Questions* (Cambridge: Cambridge University Press, 1979).
Oulipo, *La Littérature potentielle* (Gallimard, 1973).
Pacaly, J., *Sartre au miroir. Une lecture psychanalytique de ses écrits biographiques* (Klincksieck, 1980).
Perrin, M., *Avec Sartre au Stalag XII D* (Universitaires Ed., 1980).
Ricoeur, P., *De l'interprétation, essai sur Freud* (Seuil, 1965).
Roazen, P., *Freud and his Followers* (Harmondsworth: Penguin, 1979).
Robert, M., *D'Oedipe à Moïse: Freud et la conscience juive* (Calmann-Lévy, 1974).
——, *Roman des origines et origines du roman* (Gallimard, 1976).
Roche, M., *Phenomenology, Language and the Social Sciences* (Routledge and Kegan Paul, 1973).
Saussure, F. de, *Cours de linguistique générale* (Payot, 1983).
Scheler, M., *L'Homme du ressentiment* (Gallimard, 1971).
Scriven, M., *Sartre's Existential Biographies* (Macmillan, 1984).
Sontag, S., *Illness as Metaphor* (New York: Random House, 1979).
Stéphane, R., *Portrait de l'Aventurier* (Le Sagittaire, 1950).
Storr, A., *The Dynamics of Literary Creation* (Harmondsworth: Penguin, 1976).
Sulloway, F., *Freud, Biologist of the Mind* (Fontana, 1980).
Vian, B., *L'Ecume des Jours* (10/18, 1946).
Wollheim, R., *Freud* (Fontana, 1985).
Wright, E., *Psychoanalytic Criticism: Theory in Practice* (Methuen, 1984).

Glossary

This is intended more as an *aide-mémoire* than as a critical guide. I have included only Sartrean terminology. The technical vocabulary of psychoanalysis is by now quite well known and integrated into a wider critical idiom. In compiling this glossary I have consulted the short glossaries provided by Hazel E. Barnes in her translation of *Being and Nothingness* (Methuen, 1972) and Arlette Elkaïm-Sartre in her edition of the *Critique de la raison dialectique*, II (Gallimard, 1985). Small capitals indicate a separate entry for the term in question.

Alienation (*aliénation*). This term has two related senses. (1) Individual HUMAN REALITIES are alienated from each other by virtue of the fact that another FOR-ITSELF is radically unknowable. (2) My being is alienated by the primordial presence of the OTHER in my world: the Other has an objective knowledge of my self (not to be confused with CONSCIOUSNESS), my acts and so on, that is unobtainable for me, and is in this respect the stealer of my being. In later works, Sartre retains this ontological definition of alienation in his adoption of Marxist theories of alienation (alienation from the product of one's labour, etc.).

Anguish (*angoisse*). The uncomfortable awareness that literally nothing relieves me of the constant necessity to choose myself afresh at every instant: the self-awareness of *freedom*. If I feel dizzy as I lean over a cliff, the reason is not fear (of falling), but anguish (before my freedom to throw myself off, should I so choose).

Bad faith (mauvaise foi). A lie told to myself where the liar and the lied-to are one and the same CONSCIOUSNESS. Specifically, 'bad faith' describes the attempt to flee the ANGUISHed apprehension of my own FREEDOM and RESPONSIBILITY. Sartre intended this notion to account for the manifestations of the unconscious, whose existence he strenuously disputed.

Being (*l'être*). A global category that embraces both the being of inert matter (BEING-IN-ITSELF), and the being of consciousness (BEING-FOR-ITSELF).

Coefficient of adversity (*coéfficient d'adversité*). The degree to which the world proves resistant to my PROJECTS. The coefficient of adversity of a mountain will differ depending on whether I plan to climb it or ski down it.

Commitment (*engagement*). At a first level, all human beings are necessarily already committed to the world by the very fact of being 'thrown into' it. At a second level, this term refers to the necessity to commit oneself, through one's acts, to the form of social organisation which guarantees the maximum social and ontological freedom to its members. For the post-war Sartre this means, effectively, socialism.

Consciousness (*conscience*). Virtually synonymous with the FOR-ITSELF. Consciousness is defined as a fundamental lack of being: it comes into being through the NIHILATION or a certain IN-ITSELF, and thus must always strive to 'bring itself to be'. Consciousness is defined as non-coincidence: it is what it is not, and it is not what it is. For Sartre, consciousness is always consciousness *of* something. A further distinction is introduced by (1) **unreflective consciousness** (*la conscience irréfléchie*), a consciousness which does not *know* the object of which it is conscious, but which is accompanied by a 'dumb comprehension' of being consciousness of . . .; (2) **reflective consciousness** (*la conscience réfléchie*), the contemplation by consciousness of its own psychic states. The passage from (1) to (2) could be made clearer by the following example. If I gaze through a keyhole 'I' may become lost in the contemplation of the spectacle: I am still aware that 'I' am engaged in the activity of looking, but this awareness is not accompanied by a *knowledge* of the 'I' that looks. If, however, I suddenly become 'self-conscious' (I might have been disturbed by someone), then the 'I' that is engaged in looking becomes the object of a reflective consciousness. This might take the form of becoming aware of myself as being, objectively, a *voyeur*.

Contingency (*contingence*). Refers to the fact that HUMAN REALITY is not pre-defined: one simply is, before one is anything. In this respect, contingency is the brute fact of being *this particular* FOR-ITSELF rather than another: it is entirely contingent whether I am born crippled, but entirely necessary that I be *that or* something else (see FACTICITY).

Epoche (*epoché*). In Husserl, the 'bracketing-off' of all preconceptions about the world in order to investigate CONSCIOUSNESS independently of the latter's engagement in the world. This is irrelevant to Sartre's purpose, since the FOR-ITSELF is always already engaged in a *world* where there are OTHERS.

Essence (*essence*). Sartre takes this term etymologically as that which has been (*est été*), or that which has been gone past (*le passé*): the past. Since, in human beings, EXISTENCE precedes essence, the essence of any given existent is constantly in the process of creation, in suspense, until the moment of death when that existent ceases to totalise itself.

Glossary

Existence (*existence*). The concrete fact of being there. The defining characteristic of existentialist thought is that existence precedes ESSENCE.

Facticity (*facticité*). The necessary connection of the FOR-ITSELF with the world of inert matter and the past. My body, by past, my birth (in a certain place, at a certain time, into a certain class, etc.) are all aspects of facticity, inasmuch as they were not chosen by the FOR-ITSELF, but the latter cannot choose not to 'exist them' henceforth.

Finitude (*finitude*). Not the same as mortality: the fact that a HUMAN REALITY cannot be everything all at once. If I choose *x*, I impose finitude upon myself by thus automatically excluding the possibilities of *y*, *z*, etc. This term has to be understood in the context of FACTICITY and CONTINGENCY.

For-itself (*être-pour-soi*). Arising in a moment of negation, the for-itself NIHILATES that which it is not (the IN-ITSELF), and 'stands out' from the world by driving a notional wedge of NOTHINGNESS between itself and its past. It temporalises itself by dissociating itself, or taking off from, its past, and projecting itself towards a being which it is not yet, in a vain attempt at self-coincidence. The present of consciousness is therefore always an ANGUISHed moment of leave-taking – a flight in progress.

For-others (*être-pour-autrui*). The mode of being of the FOR-ITSELF as it perceives itself as object for another CONSCIOUSNESS. Sartre writes that the OTHER has a hold on me: the only objective knowledge I can have about myself is that imparted by the Other, but this image will not tally with my 'reality' as it is comprehended by CONSCIOUSNESS. Thus conflict is said to be the fundamental mode of relationship between HUMAN REALITIES. This is clearly no basis for an ethics, so in the *Cahiers pour une morale* Sartre tries to re-establish a version of the Heideggerian *Mitsein* which he had dismissed in *L'Etre et le néant*.

Freedom (*liberté*). The mode of being of the FOR-ITSELF. Human beings are condemned to be free in the sense that they cannot choose not to choose. If I am born a cripple, I am not 'free' to stand up and walk, but I am free to adopt an attitude towards, and thereby assume, this *de facto* situation: hope, despair, resignation, etc. The freedom of CONSCIOUSNESS means that it cannot be *acted upon* by anything outside of itself.

Human reality (*réalité humaine*). Sartre's term for the FOR-ITSELF: used to refer both to individual existents and to humankind as a whole.

Individuation (*personnalisation*). The process whereby the subject SURPASSES and preserves, within the unity of a single totalising PROJECT, that which the world has made of it. After Marx, Sartre writes that I make myself *on the basis of* (*à partir de*) what the world has already made of me.

The italicised words refer to this dual movement of surpassing and preservation. The *personne* (*persona*) that results from this process is never a finished totality, although it does form the basis for any future movement of *personnalisation*. Sartre does, however, admit to the possibility of a sclerosis of the process: in this case, the open-ended TOTALISATION is transformed into a frozen 'character'.

In-itself (*être-en-soi*). The mode of being of non-conscious objects. A rock, for example, is defined tautologically as simply being that which it is: a plenitude of being. A mode of being in which the dichotomy between ESSENCE and EXISTENCE ceases to exist: total self-coincidence.

In-itself-for-itself (*être-en-soi-pour-soi*). A notional mode of being which, were he to exist, would be the mode of existence of God. This mode of being is the futile aim of HUMAN REALITY. Futile because the FOR-ITSELF arises through its very NIHILATION of the IN-ITSELF; any future (re)coincidence is therefore impossible by definition.

Intentionality (*intentionnalité*). A term derived from Husserl (and Brentano) meaning that consciousness is always consciousness (of) something. There is no consciousness that is not consciousness of an object – either THETICALLY or NON-THETICALLY.

Nausea (*nausée*). The physical sensation that accompanies the perpetual revelation of the body to CONSCIOUSNESS (the fact that the body exists without consciousness being the foundation of its existence). The 'taste' of CONTINGENCY.

Nihilate (*néantir*). A Sartrean neologism referring to the way in which CONSCIOUSNESS calls itself into being by inserting a thin lamina of NOTHINGNESS between itself and the object of which it is conscious (see INTENTIONALITY).

Nothingness (*néant*). Nothingness cannot be said to have BEING ('non-being' might be a better translation). The FOR-ITSELF brings nothingness into the world as it surges forth by 'taking its distance' from inert matter.

Other, the (*Autrui/l'Autre*). The existence of others is not, in itself, problematical for Sartre. The presence of the Other is given as original. Thus Sartre can write that sexuality, for example, is nothing but the fundamental attitudes by which a HUMAN REALITY reacts in a world where there are others.

Practico-inert (*pratico-inerte*). Matter worked upon by human PRAXIS in such a way that it is invested with an inertia of its own, which enables it to 'respond' to praxis with a counter-praxis of its own. The invention of aerosol sprays is an instance of praxis; but the sprays destroy the ozone layer and expose human beings to harmful radiation. The original 'end in view' of the praxis (amelioration of the environment) is thus subverted (eventual deterioration of the environment) by the means which praxis had created for its realisation. Similarly, nuclear power stations are created for the provision of cheap energy and, therefore, for the greater well-being of the collectivity; but the noxious by-products of this praxis (toxic waste, nuclear weapons) represent a counter-praxis in that they threaten this projected well-being.

Praxis (*praxis*). Practical action on the world: an organised totality of actions designed to work on matter and transform it in conformity with a desired end. Praxis is distinguished from the PROJECT by two main factors. First, it is *historical* rather than purely local. Second, it is a kind of human project that is not implied by the natural world: if I come to a river, and ford it, this would be the successful realisation of a project; if I deviate the river from its course in order to irrigate arid land, or generate power, this would be praxis. The dam-building of a beaver is not praxis, because the technical means employed by the beaver are not historical: they are instinctual and do not vary in response to varying environmental situations. The human dam-builder will evolve new technology and new materials to achieve his ends.

Project (*projet*). Two interdependent senses: (1) the very mode of being of CONSCIOUSNESS, defined as the flight from one IN ITSELF, towards another which might found it; (2) the concrete actions and plans by which (1) is 'realised' in the world.

Responsibility (*responsabilité*). If I am by definition FREE to 'choose myself', my responsibility consists in my awareness that I alone am answerable for the acts I do choose to commit. By extension, I have a responsibility to all other human beings, in that the acts I commit thereby become universal human possibilities.

Situation (*situation*). Refers to the fact that the FOR-ITSELF is always, already situated: in time, space, in relation to others, etc. A non-situated for-itself is, by definition, unthinkable.

Stress (*stress*). An anglicism imported into the French technical vocabulary of biology and psychology. Used in *L'Idiot* to describe the dangerous tension in the individual as he attempts to ward off unassimilable (or 'unacceptable') elements by throwing up a global defence against them, a defence which can be as dangerous to the organism as the perturbing element itself. Sartre uses, analogically, the biological sense which describes the action of antibodies which damage the organism in their attempt to destroy a foreign body. There is some similarity here with the psychoanalytical notion of dynamic tension between the repressed and the agent of repression. But for Sartre the process occurs within the unity of the *vécu*: any PROJECT is a flight (*fuite*), but by the same token, every flight is a project.

Surpassing/going past (*dépassement*). Neither English term is an adequate translation. *Dépassement* refers to the movement of CONSCIOUSNESS as it NIHILATES the given and goes past it towards the realisation of its own possibilities. The term also implies the preservation, at the heart of the PROJECT, of that which is gone past (*le passé*), in an ongoing, forever open, TOTALISATION.

Thetic and non-thetic (*thétique, non-thétique*). Posited, or not posited, as the object of consciousness. The reflective CONSCIOUSNESS is thus also referred to as a thetic consciousness, and the unreflective consciousness as a non-thetic consciousness.

Totalisation (*totalisation*). At the level of the individual subject, this refers to the process whereby the FOR-ITSELF temporalises itself through its projective movement: each act is like a figure in a column, but the process cannot be stopped and added up (*totalisé*) until the moment of death, when the line is drawn and the sum made. This means that the meaning of an individual's life is constantly deferred, or in suspense. But human existence is always trans-individual for Sartre, and the totalisations that Sartre studies in later works such as the *Critique de la raison dialectique* are those effected by collectivities and groups. In the *Critique* and *L'Idiot* totalisation refers both to a process and to the material products of that process. Inasmuch as *totalisation* is synthetic and integrative, it subsumes the category of PRAXIS.

Transcendence (*transcendance*). Consciousness itself as it goes past (*dépasse*) the given towards its own possibilities.

Value (*valeur*). Values do not exist as pre-established transcendent categories. In inventing themselves, and choosing themselves afresh at every instant, human beings bring value into the world. Ontologically, value is that which it is imagined would make HUMAN REALITY whole: the ultimate, but unattainable, value would be that mode of being described as IN-ITSELF-FOR-ITSELF. A key concept in Sartre's existential psychoanalysis.

Index

Thematic and Technical

Actaeon (and Diana), 17, 25, 77, 87, 122
activity, 3, 6, 10–11, 13, 15, 54, 68, 94
anaclisis, 2
anal stage, 2, 63
archaic mother, 22, 54–5, 92, 94
Autre (the Other), 5–6, 19–21, 32, 61, 65, 66, 69–71, 76, 77, 80, 81, 103, 105, 106, 109–10, 114, 119, 121, 128, 141n., 146n.; defined, 156
autrui (the other), 2, 61, 109–110

cannibalism, 22, 51, 93, 102, 117, 119, 124, 125, 136n., 146n.
castration (complex and anxiety), xi, 15, 17, 19–22, 31, 46–7, 48–9, 54–5, 73, 77, 83, 86, 88, 90, 91–3, 94, 97, 102, 106, 109–10, 112, 114, 115, 122, 129, 131, 137n., 138n., 140n., 142n.
Chef, see the Genitor
cognition, 15–16, 17–18, 21
comprehension, 9, 52, 59, 69, 75, 141n.
consciousness, 5–8, 11, 13, 14–15, 17, 19, 21–2, 23, 27, 32–3, 46, 56–66, 68–9, 71, 75–6, 80–2, 84, 86, 89, 91, 103, 115; defined, 154

desire, 3–7, 15–17, 32–3, 47, 49, 53, 55, 56–78, 79–102, 131, 104n., 141n., poisoned desire, 58, 64, 67, 69–70, 71, 75–6; pure desire, 57–8, 64–5, 67, 70, 76
disavowal (Verleugnung), 77, 126
double-reciprocal incarnation, 6, 66

dream work (Traumarbeit), 59
Dur, see the Genitor

être-en-soi (being-in-itself), 7, 20, 22, 27, 61, 66, 115, 121; defined, 156
être-en-soi-pour-soi (being-in-itself-for-itself), 7, 45, 61, 66; defined, 156
être-pour-autrui (being-for-others), 5, 61; defined, 155
être-pour-soi (being-for-itself), 2, 5, 7, 13, 20, 61, 66, 121; defined, 155

facticité (facticity), 1, 7, 14, 21, 27, 63, 65–6, 69–70, 82, 89; defined, 155
Father, see the Genitor
femininity, 1–22, 27, 30–1, 44, 53, 91, 93, 100, 107
femme–marécage, 23–35, 43–7, 53, 55, 83, 84, 85, 137n.
femme-mirage, 23–35, 43–7, 53, 55, 84

Genitor, 23, 35–43, 45–6, 53–5, 72, 91, 93, 102, 104, 107–28, 138n.
gens de bien, see the Genitor
glissement (sliding), 1, 13, 17–19, 21

holes, 1, 12, 17, 19–22
homosexuality, 11, 40, 51, 90, 100, 103–28

Ichstrahl, 57

159

identification, 4, 10, 38, 42, 54, 76, 91, 96, 102, 111, 117, 120, 125–7, 136n.
imaginary (Lacan), 52–3, 67, 74, 83, 94–5, 97–9, 101, 127, 129
instinct or drive (*Trieb*), 2–3, 61–5, 69, 140n.
intentionnalité (intentionality), 61, 69, 75, 89; defined, 156

jardin public (in *La Nausée*), 85, 88–9, 91
juste, see *the Genitor*

Kronos, 93, 102, 125

liberté (freedom), 6, 56, 69, 105; defined, 155
love, 5–6, 15–16, 61, 67–8, 110

maniement (handling), 9, 52, 94, 100–1, 144n.
masculinity, 1–22, 30, 91–3
masochism, 5–6, 10, 19–20, 67–8, 80–1, 90, 96, 107
mauvaise foi (bad faith), 23, 32, 35, 56, 58, 84, 104, 113–14; defined, 153
mirror phase (Lacan), 74, 98–100, 109, 139n., 142n., 144n.
Moses, 50, 93, 96

Nature, 24–7, 29–30, 33–4, 44, 46, 49–50, 53, 106–8, 113, 143n.
néantisation (nihilation), 7–8; defined, 156
nomination, 106–8, 111, 117–24

odour, 27–8, 45, 113
Oedipus complex, 3–4, 9–10, 21, 40, 47, 50, 67–8, 73–4, 77, 83–4, 95, 106, 108, 119, 126–7, 129, 131, 136n., 138n., 141n.
ontology, 1, 5, 8, 11–12, 14, 21–2, 35, 37, 60–3, 66, 70–1, 72–3, 89, 105
oral stage, 2, 9, 63

passivity, 3, 6, 9–11, 13–14, 17, 52–4, 68, 94

personnalisation (individuation), 72; defined, 155
perversion, 103–4, 110, 111, 114, 128, 140n.
phallic mother, 47, 55, 73–4, 94, 97, 100–2, 110, 129
phallic stage, 2, 63
phallus, 3, 42, 47–8, 55, 73–4, 92–3, 101–2, 110, 115–16, 121–2, 130, 141n., 142n.
phantasy (primal), 83–4, 87, 107, 110, 115, 122, 129, 132, 145n.;
phantasmatic, xii, 1, 11, 22, 23, 36, 43, 47, 49, 55, 77, 89, 97, 112, 125–6, 129–34, 138n.
phenomenology, 1, 33, 57, 63, 65
possession, 13–14, 17–19, 40, 51, 54–5, 71, 91, 93–4, 97, 103–9, 109–28, 145n., 146n.
psychoanalysis (and literary criticism), ix–xii, 55, 78, 85, 105–6, 112–13, 126, 129–34, 135n.

réalité humaine, 2, 7, 62, 104, 144n.; defined, 155
regard, 5–6, 15–17, 40, 48–9, 71, 106–7, 113–14, 115–16, 117–18, 122, 124–5, 146n.

sadism, 5–6, 10, 15, 18–20, 67–8, 79–80, 90, 107, 122, 136n.
salaud, see *the Genitor*
sevrage (weaning), 95, 137n., 144n.; contre sevrage, 95, 144n.
statue, 17, 36–8, 41–3, 47–8
stress, 72; defined, 157
symbolic order (Lacan), 9, 67, 74–6, 97, 99–100, 102, 117, 127

totalisation, 9, 73; defined, 158
trouble (clouding/desire), 6, 19, 65–6, 80–1
transference, ix, 77, 133, 146n.

vécu, 7–8
viscous, 1, 12–18, 21–2, 24, 29–31, 44, 46, 52, 60, 92

zar, 70–1, 109, 111, 116, 118, 120, 125, 141n., 145n.

Proper Names, Sartre's Works and Characters

Achille, Monsieur (*La Nausée*), 38, 48
Anny (*La Nausée*), 34, 43–4, 137n.
Anne-Marie (Sartre/Mancy), 9, 93–8, 100–2, 126
Arnold, J. A., 150
Aronson, Ronald, 150
Astruc, Alexandre, 151
Aupick, Général (*Baudelaire*), 39–40, 53–4

Bailey, Ninette, 150
Balint, M., 134
Barilier, Etienne, 141n., 150
Barnes, Hazel, 153
Barrès, Maurice, 111
Barthes, Roland, 150
Basaglia, F., 134
Baudelaire, 8, 39–40, 51–4, 93, 138n., 139n., 141n., 143n., 147
Baudelaire, Charles, 8, 39–40, 52–4, 105, 143n.
Beauvoir, Simone de, 31, 56–7, 106, 137n., 150
Bergère ('L'Enfance d'un chef'), 118, 143n., 144n.
Blévigne, Olivier (*La Nausée*), 37, 48–50
Boris (*Les Chemins de la liberté*), 26, 45, 82–3
Bowie, Malcolm, vi, 151
Brentano, 156
Breton, André, 120, 151
Brunet (*Les Chemins de la liberté*), 26, 46, 130

Cahiers pour une morale, les, 8, 69–72, 103, 141n., 142n., 144n., 148n., 155
Carnets de la drôle de guerre, les, 19–21, 96, 136n., 144n., 148
'La Chambre', 29, 34, 39, 138n.
Chasseguet-Smirgel, Janine, 148
Chemins de la liberté, les, 25–9, 31–2, 39, 42, 44–6, 49–51, 79, 80–3, 88, 113–16, 118, 122–5, 130–1, 136n., 137n., 138n., 142n., 143n., 145n.
Clancier, Anne, 151
Clytemnestre (*Les Mouches*), 26–7, 46
Cohen-Solal, Annie, 151
Collins, Douglas, 151
Contat, Michel, 51, 85, 138n., 139n., 151
Cooper, David, 134, 150
Cranston, Maurice, 142n.
Critique de la raison dialectique, la, 72, 127, 131, 148, 158
Culler, Jonathan, 141n., 151

Dali, Salvador, 39
Daniel (*Les Chemins de la liberté*), 28–9, 31, 49, 113–16, 118, 124, 136n.
Darbédat, Madame ('La Chambre'), 29–30, 39
Darbédat, Monsieur ('La Chambre'), 39
De Gaulle, Charles, 131, 133
Deleuze, Gilles, 148, 151
Derrida, Jacques, 151
Descartes, René, 57
Diable et le bon Dieu, le, 34, 127, 147
Dickens, Charles, 101
Doubrovski, Serge, 151
Ducrot, Oswald, 151

Egisthe (*Les Mouches*), 41
Electre (*Les Mouches*), 33, 46–7
Eléna (*Kean*), 127
Elkaïm-Sartre, Arlette, 153
'L'Enfance d'un chef', 25, 39, 42, 80–1, 83–4, 94, 117–19, 125, 138n., 142n., 143n., 144n., 146n.
'Erostrate', 50, 114, 120–2, 136n.
Esquisse d'une théorie des émotions, 56, 58–60, 65, 139n., 147
Estelle (*Huis Clos*), 14, 31, 33, 46
Etre et le néant, l', 1–2, 4–8, 10–22, 30, 49, 59, 61–70, 76–7, 79–80, 81, 103–5, 108–9, 113, 122, 136n., 140n., 141n., 147, 153, 155

Eve ('La Chambre'), 34
Eve (*Les Jeux sont faits*), 25, 46
Existentialisme est un humanisme, l', 35, 147

Fasquelle, Monsieur (*La Nausée*), 92
Felman, Shoshana, 151
Flaubert, Achille (*L'Idiot de la famille*), 9–11, 91, 145n.
Flaubert, Achille-Cléophas (*L'Idiot de la famille*), 9–10, 38, 40, 54, 76–7, 91, 112, 127, 136n., 144n., 145n.
Flaubert, Caroline (*L'Idiot de la famille*), 9–10, 52, 95, 136n.
Flaubert, Gustave (*L'Idiot de la famille*), 8–11, 52, 54, 58, 74–5, 77, 83, 95, 107, 110, 112–13, 127–8, 144n., 145n.
Fleurier, Lucien ('L'Enfance d'un chef'), 25, 80, 83–4, 94, 117–19, 125, 143n., 144n.
Fleurier, Madame ('L'Enfance d'un chef'), 25
Fleurier, Monsieur ('L'Enfance d'un chef'), 39, 42, 83, 117–19, 125, 138n.
Fliess, Wilhelm (*Le Scénario Freud*), 77
Foucault, Michel, 51
Françoise (*La Nausée*), 24, 84–5
Frantz (*Les Séquestrés d'Altona*), 34, 42, 123–4, 145n., 146n.
Freud (*Le Scénario Freud*), 55, 76–7, 127, 139n.
Freud, Sigmund, 1, 2–4, 6, 9, 11, 15, 16, 19, 21, 52, 55, 56–64, 67–77, 84–5, 105–6, 112, 127, 129–30, 131–3, 135n., 136n., 137n., 138n., 139n., 140n., 142n., 148–9

Garcin (*Huis Clos*), 14, 31, 46
Genet, Jean, 8, 11, 100, 103, 104–12, 115–17, 145n.
George, François, 128, 135n., 143n., 146n., 151
Gide, André, 139n.

Goetz (*Le Diable et le bon Dieu*), 34, 130
Goldthorpe, Rhiannon, 143n., 151
Gomez (*Les Chemins de la liberté*), 130
Gorz, André, 143n.
Guattari, Félix, 148, 151

Hamon, Philippe, 151
Hegel, 140
Heidegger, Martin, 243
Hilbert ('Erostrate'), 50, 113, 120–2, 125, 136n.
Hilda (*Le Diable et le bon Dieu*), 34
Hoederer (*Les Mains sales*), 28, 33, 130
Holland, Norman, 151
Horney, Karen, 149
Howells, Christina, 141n., 144n., 151
Hugo (*Les Mains sales*), 40, 145n.
Hugo, Victor, 42
Huis Clos, 14, 31, 33, 46, 110, 136n., 147
Husserl, Edmund, 17–8, 52, 57–8, 60, 154, 156

Idée fondamentale de la phénoménologie de Husserl: L'Intentionnalité, une, 17–18, 139n., 140n.
Idiot de la famille, l', 1, 8–11, 32, 38, 40, 47, 51–5, 56, 58, 72–7, 83, 87, 91, 93, 95, 102, 105–7, 109, 112, 114, 124, 127–8, 132, 136n., 138n., 140n., 141n., 142n., 143n., 144n., 145n., 146n., 148, 157, 158
Idt, Geneviève, 151
Impétraz, Gustave (*La Nausée*), 36, 39, 41, 47
Imaginaire, L', 32–3, 60, 82, 147
Imagination, L', 147
Inès (*Huis Clos*), 31, 33
'Intimité', 30, 31–2, 137n.
Irène (*Les Chemins de la liberté*), 26
Ivich (*Les Chemins de la liberté*), 28, 32–3, 34, 45–7, 88, 137n.

Jacques (*Les Chemins de la liberté*), 39, 42, 47, 50

Index

James, William, 68
Jameson, Fredric, 151
Jean-Baptiste (Sartre), 91, 93, 101–2, 145n.
Jeanson, Francis, 151
Jessica (*Les Mains sales*), 28, 33
Jeux sont faits, les, 25, 46, 71, 147
Johanna (*Les Séquestrés d'Altona*), 34, 47, 123
Jones, Ernest, 129, 149
Jung, C. G., 106
Jupiter (*Les Mouches*), 41, 46, 50

Kafka, Franz, 102, 120, 152
Karl (Schweitzer), 35, 41–2, 47, 93, 95–7, 101–2, 118, 125–6, 138n.
Karsky (*Les Mains sales*), 40
Kean, 108, 127, 143n., 146n., 147
Kean (*Kean*), 108, 127, 143n., 146n.
Kelly, Mike, vi
Klein, Melanie, 149
Kristeva, Julia, 152

Lacan, Jacques, 3, 9, 56, 67, 72, 73–6, 97, 99–100, 129, 139n., 140n., 142n., 144n., 149
LaCapra, Dominick, 152
Lacaze, Général (*Les Chemins de la liberté*), 39, 50, 116
Laplanche, J., 43, 137n., 138n., 141n., 146n., 150
La Rochefoucauld, 57, 60
Leiris, Michel, 71, 125, 152
Le Lionnais, 142n.
Laing, R. D., 134, 150
Lavers, Annette, vi, 142n., 144n., 146n., 152
Leclaire, Serge, 150
Lejeune, Philippe, 152
Lettres au Castor, les, 31, 148
Lilar, Suzanne, 24, 137n., 142n., 152
Lola (*Les Chemins de la liberté*), 26–7, 32, 50, 82–3
Louise (Schweitzer), 101, 138n.
Lucienne (*La Nausée*), 89–92
Ludwig, Emil, 96
Lulu ('Intimité'), 31–2, 137n.

Mains sales, les, 28, 34, 40, 130, 147
Mallarmé: la lucidité et sa face d'ombre, 139n., 148
Mannoni, Octave, 73
Marcelle (*Les Chemins de la liberté*), 25–9, 31–2, 34, 44–5, 50, 81, 143n.
Marcuse, Herbert, 73, 152
Marx, Karl, 8, 11, 35, 72, 133, 155
Mathieu (*Les Chemins de la liberté*), 26, 27–9, 31–2, 34, 42, 44, 47, 49–51, 81–3, 88, 114, 122–5
Maud (*Les Chemins de la liberté*), 81
Maud ('L'Enfance d'un chef'), 80–1, 84
Maurice (*Les Chemins de la liberté*), 46, 131
Mauron, Charles, 152
Mehlman, H., 152
Merleau-Ponty, Maurice, 152
Millett, Kate, 152
Milner, Max, 152
Morts sans sépulture, 147
Mots, les, 9, 41–2, 47, 52, 91, 93–102, 111, 114, 116, 118, 125–6, 130, 138n., 139n., 143n., 145n., 148
Mouches, les, 26, 33, 40–1, 46, 50, 123–4, 138n., 147

Nagel, Thomas, 140n., 144n., 152
Nausée, la, xi, 23, 24, 27–30, 34, 35–9, 41, 43, 46–9, 79, 84–93, 97, 133, 138n., 143n., 145n.
Nekrassov, 147
Nietzsche, Friedrich, 50

Odette (*Les Chemins de la liberté*), 47, 50
Oreste (*Les Mouches*), 33, 42, 46, 50, 123–5, 138n
Ovid, 17

Pacaly, Josette, xi, 129, 132–3, 135n., 138n., 139n., 146n., 152
Pacôme (*La Nausée*), 37
Parrotin (*La Nausée*), 37, 38, 48–50
Père, le (*Les Séquestrés d'Altona*), 34–5, 40, 42–3, 47, 119–20, 123–4

Perrin, M., 152
Philippe (*Les Chemins de la liberté*), 39, 42, 50, 116, 118, 122
Pierre ('La Chambre'), 34
Pierre (*Les Chemins de la liberté*), 80–1
Pierre (*Les Jeux sont faits*), 46
Pinette (*Les Chemins de la liberté*), 46, 83–4, 138n.
Pingaud, B., 134, 146n.
Piriou, J.-P., 150
Pontalis, J.-B., 43, 56, 60, 129, 134, 137n., 138n., 141n., 146n., 150
Postière, la (*Les Chemins de la liberté*), 46, 82–3
Poulou (*Les Mots*), 41–2, 47, 91, 93–102, 116, 118, 125, 131, 138n.
Prince de Galles, le (*Kean*), 127
Putain respectueuse, la, 40, 147

Qu'est-ce que la littérature?, 76, 87, 147
Questions de Méthode, 72, 147

Réflexions sur la question juive, 147
Reich, Wilhelm, 143n., 150
Ricoeur, Paul, 152
Rirette ('Intimité'), 30
Roazen, Paul, 152
Robert, Marthe, 152
Roche, M., 152
Rogé (*La Nausée*), 37–8, 48
Rollebon (*La Nausée*), 89–92, 139n.
Roquentin (*La Nausée*), xi, 24, 34, 36–8, 40, 42, 43, 46–9, 84–94, 102, 111, 138n., 139n.
Rybalka, Michel, 151
Rycroft, Charles, 150

Safouan, M., 150
Saint Genet, Comédien et martyr, 8, 40, 51, 75, 94, 104–17, 119, 121, 124, 132, 138n., 139n., 141n., 144n., 145n., 147
Sarah (*Les Chemins de la liberté*), 26, 34
Saussure, Ferdinand de, 152
Scénario Freud, le, 55, 56, 76–7, 83, 127, 129, 139n., 142n., 146., 148
Scheler, M., 152
Schneider (*Les Chemins de la liberté*), 130
Scriven, Michael, 51, 139n., 152
Segal, H., 150
Séquestrés d'Altona, les, 34, 40, 42, 47, 83, 119–20, 123–4, 127, 138n., 146n., 148
serveuse, la (Brasserie Vézélize; *La Nausée*), 24
serveuse, la (Café Mably; *La Nausée*), 27, 28
Simonnot, Monsieur (*Les Mots*), 42, 47, 101
Sontag, Susan, 152
Stendhal, 92
Stéphane, Roger, 152
Sterba, Richard, 140n., 150
Stoller, Robert J., 136n., 150
Storr, A., 150, 152
Sulloway, Frank, 152

Théâtre de situations, un, 148
Todorov, T., 151
Transcendance de l'ego, la, 56–9, 60, 65, 75, 139n., 147

Vian, Boris, 152

Werner (*Les Séquestrés d'Altona*), 42, 47, 120, 125
Wilhelm, Kaiser, 96
Wollheim, Richard, 152
Wright, Elizabeth, 135n., 152

Zézette (*Les Chemins de la liberté*), 46